VOLUME EDITOR

SCOTT C. LOWE is Professor of Philosophy and Chair of the Department of Philosophy at Bloomsburg University of Pennsylvania. His current interest is in the political philosophy of Richard Rorty. He is the editor, along with Steven Hales, of *Delight in Thinking: An Introduction to Philosophy Reader* (2006).

SERIES EDITOR

FRITZ ALLHOFF is an Assistant Professor in the Philosophy Department at Western Michigan University, as well as a Senior Research Fellow at the Australian National University's Centre for Applied Philosophy and Public Ethics. In addition to editing the *Philosophy for Everyone* series, Allhoff is the volume editor or co-editor for several titles, including *Wine & Philosophy* (Wiley-Blackwell, 2007), *Whiskey & Philosophy* (with Marcus P. Adams, Wiley, 2009), and *Food & Philosophy* (with Dave Monroe, Wiley-Blackwell, 2007).

PHILOSOPHY FOR EVERYONE

Series editor: Fritz Allhoff

Not so much a subject matter, philosophy is a way of thinking. Thinking not just about the Big Questions, but about little ones too. This series invites everyone to ponder things they care about, big or small, significant, serious … or just curious.

Edited by Scott C. Lowe

CHRISTMAS
PHILOSOPHY FOR EVERYONE
Better Than a Lump of Coal

Foreword by Stephen Nissenbaum

A John Wiley & Sons, Ltd., Publication

This edition first published 2010

© 2010 Blackwell Publishing Ltd except for editorial material and organization
© 2010 Scott C. Lowe

Blackwell Publishing was acquired by John Wiley & Sons in February 2007. Blackwell's publishing program has been merged with Wiley's global Scientific, Technical, and Medical business to form Wiley-Blackwell.

Registered Office
John Wiley & Sons Ltd, The Atrium, Southern Gate, Chichester, West Sussex, PO19 8SQ, United Kingdom

Editorial Offices
350 Main Street, Malden, MA 02148–5020, USA
9600 Garsington Road, Oxford, OX4 2DQ, UK
The Atrium, Southern Gate, Chichester, West Sussex, PO19 8SQ, UK

For details of our global editorial offices, for customer services, and for information about how to apply for permission to reuse the copyright material in this book please see our website at www.wiley.com/wiley-blackwell.

The right of Scott C. Lowe to be identified as the author of the editorial material in this work has been asserted in accordance with the UK Copyright, Designs and Patents Act 1988.

Library of Congress Cataloging-in-Publication Data

Christmas – philosophy for everyone: better than a lump of coal / edited by Scott C. Lowe.
    p. cm.—(Philosophy for everyone)
  Includes bibliographical references.
    ISBN 978-1-4443-3090-8 (pbk.: alk. paper) 1. Christmas. I. Lowe, Scott C.
II. Title: Christmas – philosophy for everyone.
  BV45.C548 2010
  263′.915—dc22

                             2010006824

A catalogue record for this book is available from the British Library.

Set in 10/12.5pt Plantin by SPi Publisher Services, Pondicherry, India
Printed in Singapore

01   2010

To John Hirschi
"... it was always said of him, that he knew how to keep Christmas well ..."

CONTENTS

FOREWORD

Joining the Manger to the Sleigh?

Here's a philosophical exercise of sorts. Imagine, first, the manger scene, set in Bethlehem. You will of course visualize the newborn infant Jesus, the Virgin Mary and her husband Joseph, and perhaps several shepherds, angels and animals; possibly also the three wise men. All right, now place into that same scene, just in front of the holy infant, the kneeling figure of … Santa Claus.

Something wrong with this picture? Does Santa not quite belong in this scene? And why not? If you find this exercise puzzling, then you have entered into a Christmas problem that may be deemed philosophical. The nineteenth-century American poet Emily Dickinson once recalled that as a child in the 1830s she secretly "loved Santa Claus" more than "the Lord Jesus Christ." And in that preference (though perhaps not in the acknowledgment of it) Emily Dickinson was – and remains – far from alone. In their hearts, many people today probably love Santa Claus more than Jesus Christ. As certain Christians point out, the mere reversal of two letters turns *Santa* into *Satan*.

The contest between Santa and Jesus is not the only philosophical dispute that Christmas has ignited over the years. In the seventeenth century the Puritans actually *banned* the celebration of Christmas (it was illegal for a time both in Oliver Cromwell's England and in the colony of Massachusetts). In Puritan eyes, Christmas was a pagan holiday, not a Christian one. They argued, quite accurately, that there is no scriptural basis for celebrating the birth of Jesus; indeed, there is no evidence at all that he was born in December. (The nativity scene so vividly described in the Gospel of Luke – the shepherds abiding in their fields, keeping watch over their flocks by night, when an angel appeared to announce the birth "this day, in the city of David" of Christ the Lord – offers no clue about *when* "this day" happened to fall.) The Puritans were fond of saying that that if God had intended for the birthday of his only begotten son to be observed, he would surely have provided some indication of when it occurred.

Actually, that dispute leads back to an earlier one, the very dispute that provoked the Church Fathers to decree the celebration of Christmas in the first place. This decree was levied as late as the year 395 CE, fully 400 years after Jesus' birth. Why only then, and not before? The answer has to do with a certain philosophical idea that was winning many adherents in the fourth century; this was the idea that Jesus had *never been a physical being at all*, that he was instead a pure spirit who had only *appeared* to take on human form. (At the risk of committing sacrilege, you might imagine a parallel question about the identity of Santa Claus.) In the fourth century, when the nature of Christian "orthodoxy" was still being hotly debated, such an idea posed a real philosophical threat: it challenged the reality of Christ's incarnation, even of his crucifixion. In order to suppress that dangerous idea (it was called *Docetism*, after the Greek word meaning "to seem"), the Church Fathers realized that nothing would make Jesus more physically human than having a *birthday*.

Of course, by that time nobody had any memory of when Jesus was born, so a date had to be devised. And it had to be a date that Christians would be likely to celebrate. It was for this reason that the Church Fathers settled on late December, for this was a time of general celebration that long preceded Christianity. Late December was the winter solstice (thus the ritual of seasonal lights, practiced by Jews at Chanukah). Late December was also a season of extended leisure time and culinary bounty (the harvest work was finally completed, and there was plenty of fresh food and alcohol to be consumed). In Rome itself, at the center of Christianity, these very days of late December had traditionally been celebrated as the boisterous *Saturnalia*. So the Church Fathers in the year 395 CE chose to place the nativity of Jesus on December 25. But doing so involved a serious trade-off: on the one hand, the Church Fathers could be confident that the new holiday would be widely celebrated (and that Christians would come to accept the idea that Jesus was a real human being). On the other hand, it would be difficult to insure that the new holiday would be celebrated in a spirit of pious Christian devotion. There were simply too many powerful associations of this particular date, associations that had more to do with eating, drinking and being merry than with praying.

And so Christmas began with a kind of philosophical dilemma. I would argue that this dilemma has never been resolved (its modern form involving the battle between piety and presents, between Jesus and Santa Claus). I might even say, perhaps a bit provocatively, that Christmas has always proven extremely difficult to *Christianize*. That, at any rate, was precisely what the Puritans came to conclude, and so they decided to simply suppress it. And when Christmas finally did enter mainstream American culture, beginning in the 1820s, it was courtesy of the ever-bulging pack that Santa carried on his back. As one of the essays in this book points out, "The Night before Christmas" (first published in 1823) is a wholly secular poem. By the 1830s Santa Claus had already become established as a commercial icon, appropriated by shopkeepers in urban America. By the end of that decade it was already possible for a New England girl like Emily Dickinson to love Santa – and the presents he left – more than Jesus. It's all too easy to conclude that Santa has won the battle for Christmas.

And yet. And yet if we moderns find it so difficult to imagine Santa kneeling down before the infant Jesus – so tough to join the manger to the sleigh – perhaps our very difficulty suggests that the sleigh has not completely won the battle after all. Early in the twentieth century some American merchants actually *did* insert the figure of Santa Claus into the elaborate manger scenes they installed to drum up business. It didn't work and their efforts were ridiculed. Today, too, as I write this I have located an Internet website advertising 231 different products that show Santa kneeling before Jesus; these include figurines and Christmas tree ornaments. You wouldn't buy any of these … would you?

Keep reading.

STEPHEN NISSENBAUM

INTRODUCTION

Behold! The virgin will be with child and shall
bear a son,
And they will name him Immanuel.
(Matthew 1:23)

The stockings were hung by the chimney
with care,
In hopes that St. Nicholas soon would be there.
(Clement Clarke Moore,
" 'Twas the Night Before Christmas")

The new fallen snow blankets the moonlit hills as sleigh bells jingle in the distance. Inside, the lights shine, the tinsel sparkles, all the ornaments are hung with care and presents are piled high under the tree. It's Christmas and there's magic in the air. Cousins and aunts and uncles and grandparents gather together from far and near for feast and fellowship, and maybe a little football, too. There will be delicious food, sweet treats, and a few spirits (of the alcoholic variety) as well. And presents, yes, lots of presents. It's the stuff of fond memories. It's Christmas just like Norman Rockwell or Charles Dickens pictured it.

That's what the holiday's all about, isn't it? Family, togetherness and, well, presents. Maybe, maybe not. For what's supposed to be a holly, jolly holiday, Christmas sure stirs up a lot of controversy. There's not much agreement about the origins, history, practices, point or purpose of this holiday. *Wait a minute*, you say, *everybody knows that Christmas is about the virgin birth of baby Jesus, right?* Everybody? Guess again. *Well, at least it's about the birth of some baby on a cold December night in a drafty manger.* Hardly, that one's pretty clearly *not* true. *Well, then, it's about that time honored Christian practice of decorating pine trees.* Oh, come on now, what have you been smoking? *It's about Santa?* Please, don't get the fundamentalists started! *Nativities on the courthouse lawn?* Don't get Bill O'Reilly started! You see what I mean?

What does seem clear is that Christ's mass has been part of the church calendar since about the fourth century, that the early Christian church moved the celebration to December to coincide with existing pagan (or maybe Roman) solstice celebrations, that we picked up decorating pine trees from existing pagan practices, and that it wasn't until fairly recently that Christmas was accepted as the day of festive celebration that we recognize. (Did you ever notice that Bob Cratchit had to *ask* Mr. Scrooge for Christmas day off?) An interesting aspect of the history of Christmas is the degree to which this celebration of Christ's birth was associated with existing non-Christian holidays as a way of winning and keeping converts. Presumably, early Christians weren't willing to throw out everything old in adopting their new religion, so adapted existing holidays to new, Christian, purposes. The modern Christmas celebration has ancient connections with a number of winter solstice feasts, including the Roman festival dedicated to Sol Invictus (the unconquered sun) and Germanic and Scandinavian Yule festivals. Similarly, later Christmas celebrations picked up elements from non-Christian sources, such as the decorating of Christmas trees and the burning of Yule logs which also come from Germany and Scandinavia. In fact, the practice of decorating a Christmas tree is only about a century and a half old in the English speaking world. It was not until the 1840s that the practice became widespread in England, in part due to Queen Victoria's adopting a custom from Prince Albert's native Germany, and not until the latter half of the nineteenth century that Christmas trees caught on in the United States.

And then there's that other part of our modern Christmas, the big man, that right jolly old elf: Santa. Where he came from and how he's supposed to fit in has a long, uncertain and decidedly non-Christian history, too. There was (probably) a St. Nicholas, but even the little bit we know of him bears scant resemblance to our modern Santa. Rather, Santa Claus seems to be descended from a hodge podge of figures, none of whom have any connection to Christmas or Jesus of Nazareth. The Santa who brings gifts to good little boys and girls owes more to

SCOTT C. LOWE

Poseidon and Neptune, Odin and Thor, and a rather disreputable fellow named Krampus, than to any Christian saint. There's a lot more to be said about Jesus, virgin birth, Santa Claus and celebrating Christmas. The essays that follow will shed some light on all of this and more.

In the first part of the book, "Christmas: In the Beginning," we look at the origins of Christmas. And in the beginning, there was the birth of Christ. Of course, Jesus was a man; Jesus, the Christ, Immanuel, "God with us," was human and walked the earth. But humans are conceived in the familiar way and then "born of a woman" about nine months later. And these familiar events are exactly what happened according to Zachary Jurgensen and Jason Southworth in their essay "Jesus, Mary, and Hume: On the Possibility of the Virgin Birth." A virgin birth would be a miracle, so would be completely outside what our experience tells us is possible. Following the works of the great eighteenth-century Scottish philosopher, David Hume, Jurgensen and Southworth argue for the impossibility of miracles and so the impossibility of the virgin birth of Christ. Obviously, their view holds important implications for what we are celebrating at Christmas time. In response, theologian Victor Lyons defends the miraculous conception of Jesus in "The Virgin Birth: Authentic Christmas Magic." Contrary to Jurgensen and Southworth, as well as contemporary skeptics like Richard Dawkins and Sam Harris, Lyons points to the coherence of New Testament accounts of the conception and birth of Christ in Matthew and Luke. Further, reality as we know it does not have to be observable and repeatable as demanded by science. Perhaps there is room in our reality for extraordinary events, and perhaps the virgin birth is one of them. Medievalist Todd Preston rounds out this part arguing that those who want to put "Christ back into Christmas" may not understand what they're asking for. In "Putting the 'Yule' Back in 'Yuletide'" he shows us how the earliest Christians in the English speaking world won converts precisely by incorporating pagan practices and beliefs into the new Christianity. This early paganized Christmas was full of feasting and merriment, every bit as much as it was of religious ceremony. It turns out that Christmas has been a largely secular holiday even from its beginning.

In the next part, "Is Celebrating Christmas Really a Good Idea?," we look at some of the problems and controversies that surround our contemporary celebration of Christmas. Philosopher Scott Aiken takes the bull by the horns in his essay, "Armed for the War on Christmas." Christmas has been caught up in the ongoing culture wars. Conservative commentators like Bill O'Reilly and John Gibson claim that the liberal media are promoting the secularization of Christmas and liberal judges are suppressing the rights of the Christian majority. Aiken argues that the conservatives are confused on both counts and that there really has been no war on Christmas. But given how poor the Christmas message is both theologically and culturally, Aiken suggests that maybe there *should* be.

Guy Bennett-Hunter comes next with his take on the theological controversies surrounding the holiday. In "Christmas Mythologies: Sacred and Secular" he reminds us that there are two myths that are part of Christmas. On the one hand, there is the myth of Santa Claus, a myth which parents treat as myth, yet accept because of the message of generosity and giving which belief in Santa encourages in children. On the other hand, there are the religious myths of the stories from the Bible. These myths we are often reluctant to give up as we mature, remaining, as Bennett-Hunter puts it, "agnostic" about their literal truth. In his essay Bennett-Hunter pushes us to get off the fence about our religious myths. Appealing to the work of theologian Paul Tillich, he argues that the lessons of the Bible are to be found in its myths, and worrying about whether they're literally true or not will just distract us from seeing those lessons. Just as we grow out of believing in Santa Claus, so we ought to grow out of regarding the Christmas story as literally true. Only then can we understand its true message.

An important part of the "War on Christmas" is the push to remove Christian Christmas displays from public places. One argument for restricting Christmas displays comes from the perspective of multiculturalism, the view that societies should encourage different cultures and communities to live together in the same neighborhoods, towns and cities. Multiculturalists are often against the public display of explicitly Christian symbols like crosses and crèches because they "privilege" the dominant Christian culture. Mark Mercer, a philosopher at Saint Mary's University in Nova Scotia, argues that such displays are not a threat to multiculturalism. In his essay, "The Significance of Christmas for Liberal Multiculturalism," he defends a version of "liberal multiculturalism" that focuses on promoting the wellbeing of each individual in part through promoting their cultural identity. For such liberal multiculturalists, Christmas, especially in its contemporary more secular form, can play a positive part in bringing different cultural groups together in a well ordered multicultural society.

And speaking of the Christmas story, we close this section with a very popular part of our Christmas memories. In "Crummy Commercials and BB Guns: Son-of-a-Bitch Consumerism in a Christmas Classic,"

Erin Haire and Dustin Nelson show us the lessons of the much loved movie *A Christmas Story*. The Parker family is an absolutely typical American family in the 1940s Midwest who want to have the perfect Christmas. But for them the perfect Christmas has nothing to do with any Christian holy day. Haire and Nelson argue that consumerism was their religion. Sadly, between the Bumpus hounds and the fact that Ralphie really did shoot his eye out, that consumerism let them down on Christmas day. But after all that could go wrong goes wrong, they discover the value of Christmas in the togetherness they share as a family.

In the third part, "Santa: A Deeper Look," the dark and mysterious side of the Man in Red is revealed. In "The Mind of Santa Claus and the Metaphors He Lives By" William Deal and S. Waller start us off discussing how we mere mortals can grasp how the mind of Santa works. He has great powers like the ability to read our intentions and know all of our actions. Not only that, he has inerrant moral knowledge, so he knows precisely what we deserve as reward or punishment for what we have done in the previous year. Drawing on current work in cognitive science, they show how we understand Santa and his powers in terms of metaphors such as the Moral Accounting metaphor or the Moral Authority is Parental Authority metaphor. Only by seeing Santa's God-like powers through these very human metaphors can we grasp how Santa operates.

Richard Hancuff and Noreen O'Connor continue this theme of Santa as moral arbiter. In "Making a List, Checking It Twice: The Santa Claus Surveillance System" they examine Santa's role as disciplinarian helping to keep kids in line, especially as Christmas approaches. How does he do this? By watching, all the time. We know he knows, even though we can't see him. Hancuff and O'Connor argue that Santa's power is an example of what the French philosopher Michel Foucault called "panopticism," forcing compliance through the *possibility* that I'm always being watched by an unseen observer. If little Johnnie really wants that special toy truck for Christmas, well he'd better behave, just in case Santa's watching.

Will Williams explains that we should probably watch out for the real St. Nick as well. His essay "You'd Better Watch Out ..." takes us back to events in the life of St. Nicholas of Myra, a fourth-century bishop from what is now Turkey. In the year 325 Nicholas is reputed to have attended the Council of Nicaea, a gathering of early church leaders who were to decide on the divinity of Christ. One member of the council, Arius, argued that, having been created by God, Jesus could not be as fully divine as God. This claim so infuriated Nicholas that he did what any true defender of the faith would do – he punched Arius in the face! Given how far our modern Christmas has strayed from its religious message, Williams wonders what St. Nicholas would do to *us* if given a fighting chance.

Finally, Matthew Brophy, a kind and caring soul, shows his concern for those little beings who work so hard to make Christmas possible for all of us. In his exposé "Santa's Sweatshop: Elf Exploitation for Christmas" he takes us into the miserable world of the average toymaking elf. Hard work, low pay, dangerous conditions, no benefits – these poor elfs give their all for our enjoyment. What could justify their exploitation? Brophy, not afraid of the coal that is surely coming to him, considers several familiar arguments in support of treating elfs this way. But, of course, in the end we must just recognize that each of us is complicit in the evil of elf exploitation.

In the fourth part of the book, "The Morality of Christmas," we examine important ethical issues raised by the way we celebrate Christmas. For most of us, Christmas started with a lie: "Look what Santa brought you!" A pair of philosophers from colleges named Kings debate the acceptability of this lie. In "Against the Santa Claus Lie: The Truth We Should Tell Our Children" David Kyle Johnson of King's College in Pennsylvania argues that any good that comes from the Santa lie is more than outweighed by the ills it promotes. Encouraging children to believe in Santa will only contribute to poor moral decision-making, such as being good only to get a reward, and intellectual laziness and poor critical thinking skills from believing in something without sufficient evidence, indeed in the face of significant counter-evidence. Era Gavrielides from King's College London takes a different approach in her essay, "Lying to Children about Santa: Why It's Just Not Wrong." She agrees that the way we talk to kids about Santa is a lie. Unlike what we tell them about fictions like unicorns or Snow White, talking about Santa includes encouraging children to believe that he's *real*; in other words, we lie to them. Yet, some lies are not wrong. Not because the evil of the lie is outweighed by its benefits, but because some types of lies are not wrong, they are actually good and noble. Gavrielides argues that the Santa lie is such a falsehood. Appealing to Plato in the *Republic*, she argues the lies that are part of our cultural storytelling and mythmaking aren't wrong and may be part of *developing* good character in children.

Santa gets a further boost from philosopher Steven Hales. In "Putting Claus Back into Christmas" Hales maintains that celebrating Santa is exactly what Christmas should be all about. Santa is generous and selfless, and, at least for adults, a way to practice these virtues and more. In this way Santa is a *myth*, valuable and useful without any pretense that he's real. This is where believing in Jesus has gone wrong. The nineteenth-century philosopher Friedrich Nietzsche criticized Christianity for losing sight of the value of gods as part of mythmaking, of cultural definition; we go off track when we start thinking of the gods as real. Belief in Santa avoids this problem; he's a myth that keeps on giving. Hales concludes that it's Santa, not Jesus, who is the better role model for generosity and giving at Christmas time.

We close this part with a visit to another Christmas classic. Ethicist Dane Scott helps us see the virtue in generosity through the life of Ebenezer Scrooge. A central theme in Dickens' *A Christmas Carol* is the need for us to be generous to one another. But generosity is a quality of character that takes nourishing and practice, which has long been lacking in Scrooge's solitary life. In "Scrooge Learns it All in One Night: Happiness and the Virtues of Christmas" Scott explains how Scrooge's magical Christmas eve transformation not only changes the lives of those around him, such as his impoverished clerk Bob Cratchit, but serves to save Scrooge from a sad and morally bankrupt end. In surrendering his greed, he gains those virtues that make him a good man.

In the closing part of the book, "Christmas Through Others' Eyes," we look at Christmas from some very untraditional perspectives. Ruth Tallman defends a view that at first glance might seem paradoxical. In her essay, "Holly Jolly Atheists: A Naturalistic Justification for Christmas," she explains why the rejection of Christianity doesn't demand the rejection of Christmas. Christmas themes of peace and love of humanity don't depend on religion, and the traditions of "cultural Christmas" are valuable to us from generation to generation. Following the work of George Santayana, Tallman explains how an atheist Christmas is coherent and valuable. Marion Mason approaches the holiday from the perspective of the psychology of religion. In "Heaven, Hecate, and Hallmark: Christmas in Hindsight" she offers her own spiritual journey as an example of the Stages of Faith model of religious development advanced by James Fowler. Moving from agnosticism to fundamentalism to Unitarianism to paganism, patterns of spiritual development reappear, each with its own approach to celebrating Christmas.

Yet, some people really would give up on celebrating Christmas. For some, the consumerism and hassle and stress are just too much. Surely there's a better way. Caleb Holt thinks he's found a superior December holiday. In "Festivus and the Need for Seasonal Absurdity" he explains the odd attraction of a holiday devoted to an unadorned metal pole, the airing of grievances and wrestling. Rather than making the season too hectic, a time when we do too much, Festivus offers us catharsis, release from all the holiday craziness. OK, sitting around the living room explaining how your loved ones have wronged you or pinning the head of household to the floor may seem a little odd. But, as Holt points out, at least that way we reduce the guilt in our lives, not just pile on another year's worth.

And then there are those who celebrate Christmas, but not in ways familiar to many of us. In closing this part of the book, Cindy Scheopner explains how the Hawaii Santa with bare feet and a shaka wave welcomes holiday visitors to downtown Honolulu. The crowd that this Santa greets is as ethnically and religiously diverse as any in the country. Many Islanders are not Christians, so what does Santa have to offer them? In her essay, "Common Claus: Santa as Cross-Cultural Connection," Scheopner argues for the usefulness of Santa as a cultural icon who can unite a diverse society around common values. Santa's generosity, and his ability to keep children from misbehaving, can be worthwhile for everyone. At a time of year when our religious differences seem so sharp, Santa welcomes all of us, Christian and non-Christian alike.

The afterword to this collection comes from a very special contributor. Santa found out that this book was in the works (you *were* paying attention during the discussion of panopticism above, right?) and wanted a chance to respond. How could I refuse? Well, in his afterword Santa makes it clear that he's not altogether pleased with what he's read here. Sure, there are bright spots praising his generosity, extolling him as a role model and even placing him above a lot of ancient gods. But he's more than a little miffed that despite all this praise, there seems to be broad agreement among the other contributors that he doesn't actually *exist*. (One of the few authors who takes his existence seriously accuses him of elf abuse, so that's no help.) Using his ability to accurately assess who has been naughty and who has been nice, and then dole out presents or coal in perfectly just proportions, Santa is prepared to stick it to us this Christmas. So, despite our sincere efforts to only speak the truth as we know it and offer insights as we see them, your authors and editor are going to suffer for their love of wisdom. (Pretty virtuous, don't you think? Kind of like Socrates and the hemlock.) I suppose I've had worse Christmases before, but, really, this one's not looking very promising. Lumps of coal all around!

SCOTT C. LOWE

PART I

CHRISTMAS: IN THE BEGINNING

CHAPTER I

JESUS, MARY, AND HUME

On the Possibility of the Virgin Birth

Some wise men, a stable, sheep, and a young virgin giving birth to the mortal son of a perfect God. Ask anyone, and they will tell you Jesus' virgin birth is an essential part of the Christmas story. We talk about it so often there is even a shorthand way of referring to it – the Christmas miracle. Given how important this extraordinary claim is to people around the world, and how often we hear it made (almost every day for no less than a month every year), it is surprising how little attention and reflection is paid to establishing the truth of the claim. In this essay we set aside our yuletide spirit in order to evaluate the truth of the Christmas miracle.

Miracle on Definition Street

Before we get too far, we need to be clear on what we mean by a miracle and how exactly the virgin birth of Jesus is supposed to be a miracle. When we use the term "miracle" we are using the definition given by the Scottish philosopher David Hume (1711–76). Hume defines a miracle as "a transgression of a law of nature by a particular volition of the Deity, or by the interposition of some invisible agent."[1] This definition seems to capture the commonsense meaning of the word. To put it in terms of an often used example, if God interceded and cured Grandma's terminal cancer, that would be a miracle. If, on the other hand, Grandma gets better without God's intervention, no miracle occurred – she was just lucky.

Essential to Hume's account of miracles is his understanding of laws of nature. A law of nature, as Hume understands it, is formed by consistently observing a regularity in a series of experienced events. It is the goal of the sciences to discover and explain these laws of nature. Hume's paradigm example of a law of nature is that "all men must die."[2] As evidenced throughout humanity, we experience with uniform regularity that if you are mortal, then you will die at some point. Although it may be very surprising to see a young person of good health suddenly die, it is by no means a miracle, as Hume notes, because it has been observed to happen in the past. Such an event would not constitute a violation of a law of nature because it conforms to past regularities. However, Hume agrees that it would be a miracle if a mortal person were to die and then come back to life. There is uniform regularity in our experience that points to the fact that death is irreversible. So, if a person were to come back to life after being dead, this event would violate a law of nature that has been firmly established from past, uniform experience. Notice this is perfectly in keeping with how the term is normally used. Christians say that it is a miracle that Jesus rose from the dead because such events are outside regularly established natural laws.

What the Bible Says

If you ask believers why they think Jesus was born to a virgin mother, they will tell you, "It's in the Bible." So it seems like the Bible is a reasonable place to start our search for truth about the virgin birth. While most readers no doubt know the basics regarding the structure and organization of the Bible, let's do a quick review. The Bible is divided into two parts: the Old and New Testaments. The dividing line is the life of Jesus. Everything about Jesus is in the New Testament. The New Testament itself is divided into four gospels, each written by a different person. The names traditionally ascribed to the gospel writers are Matthew, Mark, Luke, and John, although authorship was not assigned until considerably after the texts themselves were written.[3] All four of the gospel writers offer what they see as the important highlights of Jesus' life. Just like with

ZACHARY JURGENSEN AND JASON SOUTHWORTH

a biography, the gospels are not complete histories, but all significant events are supposed to be covered. For example, all four gospels discuss Jesus' death by crucifixion and his resurrection. Since all the gospels covered the miraculous rebirth of Jesus, you would think they would all also cover his birth, if it was equally miraculous. This is not the case, however. Mark and John say nothing about Jesus' birth at all. This leaves us with only Matthew and Luke. Both of whom, we will see, say very little about the virgin birth.

Matthew's story starts with a lineage tracing Jesus' ancestry back to Abraham. The narrative proper begins with Mary learning from an angel that she is going to have a baby through the Holy Spirit. From there, the account moves to Joseph, a part of the story often ignored in retellings found in books and films. When Joseph finds out about Mary's pregnancy he tells her that he is going to set aside their marriage contract. But then Joseph also gets visited by an angel. Joseph's angelic visitor tells him that he should marry Mary because she conceived through the Holy Spirit and, like most people who are told to do something by a supernatural being, he does so. Most importantly, Joseph is told that the baby's birth will fulfill the Old Testament prophecy that "'a virgin will conceive and bear a son, and his name will be Emmanuel,' a name which means 'God is with us.'"[4] This quote is a reference to a passage in Isaiah (from the Old Testament).[5] Never again in the rest of the gospel is the virgin birth mentioned.

Luke also offers an account of an angel visiting Mary. This time, the angel is given the name Gabriel, but the content of his message is the same, although more detailed. Mary asks Gabriel how it is she is going to have a baby, since she is a virgin. The angel explains that the Holy Spirit will be the cause of her pregnancy. Luke does not give Joseph's side of things like Matthew does, but he does note that Joseph and Mary were *not* married (they were betrothed) when she gave birth.[6] Just like with Matthew, after this brief account of Mary's conversation with the angel, the miracle of Jesus' virgin birth was not mentioned in the rest of the gospel.

Now Testify

Now that we know what the Bible says, we can evaluate how we should understand it. As rational agents, we don't just believe everything we are told. Instead, we look for reasons to think certain things are true before we take them as fact. When we only have some reason, or our reasons aren't great, we reserve judgment or we hold weaker claims, like something probably is true, or might be true. Consider the following example: if your little sister tells you she saw mommy kissing Santa Claus underneath the mistletoe last night, that isn't going to be enough reason to take it to be true. But, given what you know about your mom, you might think, "That sure sounds like mom, it probably happened."

This intuitive way of understanding the way rational people come to beliefs was put a little more concretely by David Hume when he claimed that a wise person will form and hold beliefs in proportion to the supporting evidence of the claim. It helps to think of how evidence influences belief in terms of a sliding scale, with all the available hypotheses piled on it. Every time there is a new piece of evidence to consider we will move certain theories up on the scale and others down, based on which theories the evidence supports. Sometimes, like in the case of mommy kissing Santa Claus, there are only two hypotheses – either she kissed or she didn't. With others, like an account of quantum mechanics, there can be hundreds of hypotheses. Whichever theory is at the top is the one that we ought to believe, but we should only believe it to the extent to which it beats out the other theories.[7]

But how do we weigh evidence? With scientific data this is easy, since for the most part things are easily quantifiable, and experiments are designed specifically to test individual hypotheses. With testimony, however, whether it is from your sister or the authors of the Bible, things are a little more complicated. In these cases, the evidence needs to be evaluated on two standards: how credible is the person giving the testimony and how plausible is the purported event. So, say that you hear from your cousin in Florida that it snowed in Orlando on Christmas morning. In this case, the credibility of your cousin's testimony is important, given that the likelihood of it actually snowing in Orlando is pretty low. If your cousin is honest, finds practical joking distasteful, has keen senses, and isn't prone to hallucinations, then he is fairly credible, and you would have strong, but not absolute, reason to trust him. If your cousin has a deficiency in any of these areas, then you will have less of a reason to trust him. Now, consider a similar case where your cousin calls and tells you that not only is it snowing in Orlando, but that talking snowmen are falling from the sky. At this point, the credibility of your cousin's testimony doesn't play much of a role, no matter how trustworthy he is. This is because what he is telling you (at least the snowmen are falling from the sky part) is, though not logically impossible, so highly improbable

ZACHARY JURGENSEN AND JASON SOUTHWORTH

given everything you know about the world that you can't give it credence. In some cases, "the incredibility of a fact" is enough to invalidate even the most accredited testimony.[8]

It is also important to note that you can have multiple people giving testimony about something. When this happens you have to evaluate the testimony of all parties in the way we have just laid out. It will often be the case that some witnesses will be more credible than others. The addition of testimony of a more credible witness will bolster the claims of a less credible individual when they agree, but several meritless witnesses will not make the testimony much more believable. So, if your cousin who tells you about the snow in Orlando is a liar, but his story is confirmed by his honest mother, then it is more likely to be true. If that whole side of the family tends to be loose with the truth, then you still shouldn't believe them, even if everyone in the house tells you about the snow. Given this, you can always look for more credible witnesses to confirm or deny what you have been told through testimony. You can also search for first hand or scientific evidence. So, if you're skeptical about your cousin's testimony that it's snowing in Orlando, you could try to confirm it by watching a meteorologist's weather report of Orlando, as well as seeking out visual confirmation of the snowfall. Comparatively, if you sought verification in the case where your cousin tells you talking snowmen are falling from the sky, you would most likely end up disconfirming the testimony in light of the scientific evidence. In cases where testimony by itself is not convincing, attempting to verify the testimony by scientific authority can be very helpful.

Everything You Ever Wanted to Know About the Gospels But Were Afraid to Ask

So, are Matthew and Luke credible sources of testimony regarding the virgin birth? To answer this question, we need to know a little more about these gospel writers, and unfortunately, we don't have a lot to go on. Tradition has it that Luke the gospel writer is the Luke mentioned in two of Paul's letters as his physician traveling companion. Historians and biblical scholars have reason to doubt the accuracy of this tradition, however. First, there is no extra-textual evidence of this claim – no other document of historical record says that this is true. In fact, Luke himself does not make this claim, either in his gospel or in the Book of Acts, which is believed to be a continuation of the narrative by the same author. The second reason is that Luke's writings do not demonstrate much knowledge about Paul, which is strange if they were companions. Although Paul's letters were written much earlier than Luke or Acts, the author does not seem to have access to the information contained in them. That is strange if you consider how much you know about people in your life that you don't even like, let alone your friends. Those problems aside, Paul didn't know Jesus, so the absolute best case is that Luke is getting his information third hand (from the disciples and others who knew Jesus, to Paul, to Luke). Luke also claims to have conducted interviews and that he used these interviews to write his gospel. While Luke sees these interviews as making his account more scholarly, he doesn't tell us who he interviewed. We can assume, however, that none of the interviews gave him anything closer than third hand information, or he probably would have told us about it. Another reason to think Luke's information could not have been better than third hand is that his gospel wasn't written until about 90 CE. By this time Jesus had been dead for about sixty years. Most of his contemporaries would have been dead, or extremely old.[9]

In addition to interviews, scholars believe Luke relied on three sources when writing his gospel. The first is the Gospel of Mark, the earliest of the gospels. The second source is lost to us now, but is referred to as "Q." This source is believed to predate the gospels, taking the form not of a narrative, but of a collection of sayings or quotations from Jesus. Matthew and Luke contain many of the same quotations (not included in Mark), and the only way this could have happened is if these two gospel writers had access to a shared source unavailable to Mark. The likelihood that there was a common source is what leads to the belief that there was a text (of which no copies are extant) that Matthew and Luke were both drawing from. There is also additional material, unique to Luke (dubbed "L"), which is believed to stem from either a written or an oral source available only to Luke, probably coming from the church community where he lived. Again, none of these sources are very close to the events discussed in the gospel. Mark, being written earlier, is a more reliable source, but Luke apparently found Mark's gospel to be lacking, as he chose to rewrite it. We can't say very much about the credibility of Q or L, since we don't know anything about them (nor can we be certain that they existed).[10]

We know even less about Matthew than we do about Luke. Since he tells us nothing about himself or his sources, we are left reconstructing

ZACHARY JURGENSEN AND JASON SOUTHWORTH

things as best we can. Just as in Luke, it is clear that Matthew relied on Mark and Q, and he also had a third source, "M," which was not available to the other gospel writers. We can be pretty sure about these things, given the similarities between the synoptic gospels (i.e., those written by Matthew, Mark, and Luke). Given the lack of information about Matthew, however, we can't treat him as a very credible source of testimony.[11]

In addition to the problems with the credibility of Matthew and Luke, there is also a language issue. If you have ever paused and reflected on how old the Bible is, you probably realized that it was not written in English. The Old Testament was written in Hebrew and the New Testament in Greek. As you might expect, different languages do not translate word for word, and this is especially true for ancient languages. The variable ways to translate words and phrases result in the astonishing number of translations of the Bible, and as you might expect, different translations will end with the same passage meaning different things. Given these translation difficulties, it makes sense to go to the original Greek and Hebrew when you want to know what the authors of the Bible were literally saying. The passage from Isaiah which Matthew quotes is one of these cases where there seems to be a translation problem. Recall the passage is, "a virgin will conceive and bear a son, and his name will be Emmanuel."[12] Well, Hebrew has two words that can mean "virgin." One, *bethulah*, only means virgin, while the other, *almah*, is much more ambiguous. It can mean virgin, maiden, young woman of marriageable age, or newly married woman. Which do you think is used in the quote? If you guessed the second, you're correct. So, there is some ambiguity regarding what was meant by the prophecy in Isaiah. When Matthew translated this passage into Greek he eliminated the ambiguity by translating it into the Greek word *parthenos*, which means a literal virgin. However, there is good reason to think that this was a serious mistake (or deliberate alteration) since the writer of Isaiah chose to use the word with ambiguous meanings, rather than the word with a single clear meaning.[13]

One additional reason to call into question the credibility of both Matthew and Luke is that they contradict each other on a pretty major point – the marital status of Mary and Joseph at the time of Jesus' birth. Matthew says they're married; Luke says they're yet to be married. If one of them can get such an important fact wrong, it seems likely that they could have gotten other facts wrong, especially when the other two gospel authors did not find anything of importance to tell us about Jesus until much later in his life.

Oh Come On, All Ye Faithful

Setting aside problems with the specific testimony about the virgin birth, David Hume identifies four general problems with all testimony concerning miracles. First, Hume points out that most (if not all) of the miracles that are used to justify religious belief (including the virgin birth) have only been testified to by a handful of individuals, and then passed on through several secondary sources. If you heard about the virgin birth from a relative or a preacher, you got the story *at best* fourth hand. The further along the chain of retelling a story, the more likely it is that the story gets twisted or elaborated (like the children's game of telephone).[14] As such, a wise person would be cautious in lending full credibility to the testimony of so few people, especially when they are of unproven character.

Second, Hume casts doubt over what motivates a person to testify in favor of a miracle. Specifically, he contends that there are certain "agreeable emotions," namely wonder and surprise, which come with believing that a miracle has occurred.[15] People take pleasure in hearing about, and believing in, the incredible and miraculous. Hume argues that even those who may not derive personal pleasure out of believing in miracles may testify to others in order to make them excited or happy. Couple this appetite for wonder and awe with a story that is meant to help spread the presumably noble teachings of a religion (remember the gospels were intended as a tool for religious conversion), and it may be the case that even a person who does not believe that the miracle actually occurred would testify in its favor, simply to spread what they believe is a good-natured message. Nonetheless, the idea that there may be an ulterior pleasure derived from testifying in favor of a miracle speaks to the credulity of people in general, and gives reason for pause when evaluating the credibility of testimony for a miracle, especially when we have very little evidence in favor of the individual being credible.[16]

The third point Hume discusses is closely related to the first. He points to the fact that most miraculous events have been observed primarily by nations and people who were underdeveloped and uneducated.[17] Essentially, Hume is concerned that the people who were witnesses to alleged miracles and spread the testimony of such events were not in a position to provide rational explanations of what they saw. If you don't understand the concept of a law of nature or the fundamentals about

ZACHARY JURGENSEN AND JASON SOUTHWORTH

how the natural world works, then you might think that something is a miracle that isn't. As evidence of this claim Hume directs our attention to the fact that, as nations develop and the common people become more enlightened, the reports and testimonies of miracles occurring begin to fade and are less frequent. The more you know, the less you find inexplicable. Seemingly miraculous events become understandable and the need to evoke a supernatural explanation fades away.[18]

The final point Hume discusses concerns the wide range of miracles that have been testified to by different religious groups. Essentially, Hume points out that rival religions use alleged miracles as support for their specific teachings. As such, the supposed miracle of one religion can be taken as an attempt not only to justify its teachings, but also to discredit the miracles and teachings of other, competing religions. With so many competitors, there is no justifiable reason to claim that one religion's miracles are any more believable than the other. Remember the sliding scale of hypotheses we talked about earlier. If every miracle story is supposed to push up a particular religion on the scale of truth, while pushing all others down, everything ends up a wash when you count every religion's stories.[19]

One More Kink for the Christmas Miracle

At this point you might think that we have exhausted every argument against the possibility of Jesus' virgin birth, but you'd be wrong. Hume gives one more argument against the possibility of miracles, and it's a doozy. Remember Hume's definition of a miracle: it must be a violation of a natural law. Well, given this fact, it must be the case that there will "be a uniform experience against every miraculous event, otherwise the event would not merit that appellation."[20] But here is the kicker: if that is the case, there is a lot of evidence (all the rest of human experience) that the so-called miracle never happened. Given the very nature of a miracle, a rational person would need extraordinarily strong evidence to support the idea that a miracle has in fact occurred, since we are essentially being asked to believe in something that is contrary to all prior experiences. It seems impossible that any testimony could be of that strength, given all the problems with establishing the credibility of testimony regarding unlikely events. The way Hume puts it, "no testimony is sufficient to establish a miracle, unless the testimony be of such a kind, that its falsehood would be more miraculous, than the fact, which it endeavours to establish."[21] This might sound like there is an out for the believer of miracles, allowing for them in exceptionally rare cases. Not so. If it turned out that the falsehood of the claim would be more miraculous than the fact it is being used to prove, you would not have a miracle; you would have evidence that you were wrong about what you thought was a natural law. Recall the talking snowmen case. If it turned out that the falsehood of your cousin's testimony would be more miraculous than the possibility of talking snowmen, it would mean that talking snowmen don't violate the laws of nature after all. It would mean that we were wrong in our belief about the law of nature which previously caused us to doubt the existence of the talking snowmen.

So let's bring it all back home and apply what we have learned to the virgin birth. Clearly, if Jesus was in fact born of a virgin mother, then the event should be deemed a miracle. There is an obvious violation of a law of nature, as past experience has taught us with uniform regularity that virgins do not give birth to children. The question is, what evidence do we have to believe that Mary gave birth to her son while she was still a virgin? Absent a time machine and directions to the nativity, the only evidence we can look to in support of Jesus' virgin birth are the written testimonials from the Bible. So, we must compare the likelihood of the allegation that a child was born of a virgin mother with the credibility of the source of testimony. As we have seen above, we have little to no evidence in support of Matthew and Luke's credibility and some pretty serious reason to call it into question. However, even if we assume that the testimony of Jesus' virgin birth came from the most reliable sources, Hume has still made the case that this is not enough to believe that the miracle has actually occurred, and the uniformity of our experience of the laws of nature (that do not allow for virgin births) gives us exceedingly good reason to believe those laws to be true rather than new ones that allow for virgin births.

Countin' on a Miracle (Objection) to Come Through

Before concluding, it will be helpful to discuss a common objection that has been raised against Hume's attack on miracles. First, it has been argued that Hume is too quick to dismiss as unbelievable testimony

ZACHARY JURGENSEN AND JASON SOUTHWORTH

against uniform regularities. Philosopher C. D. Broad points out that sometimes testimony against supposed laws of nature has turned out to be correct, and that if we follow Hume's lead and are unfairly skeptical towards such testimony in all cases, scientific progress will be severely limited.[22] What Broad has in mind here is that, according to Hume, we ought to reject the testimony which supports the idea that a purported law of nature has been violated, and continue to believe in the so-called law. However, over the course of history, science has found laws of nature to be amendable. Yet, it seems Hume's account would not allow for second guessing *any* law of nature. Broad writes:

> So that it would seem on Hume's theory, that if, up to a certain time, I and everyone else have always observed A to be followed by B, then no amount of testimony from the most trustworthy persons that they have observed A not followed by B ought to have the least effect on my belief in the law. ... If scientists had actually proceeded in this way, some of the most important natural laws would never have been discovered.[23]

Essentially, Broad is arguing that Hume's position on the testimony of miracles does not allow for scientific inquiry to progress naturally. Anytime we might hear of a law of nature being violated, instead of questioning whether or not the law actually is a law, we should assume that the person's testimony is mistaken.

Unfortunately, Broad's critique depends on a misunderstanding of how scientific progress works. When a researcher claims to have made a new discovery, the scientific community does not just accept it – no matter how reputable the source of the information. Instead, the methods used in the study are repeated by many other researchers. It is only when there is independent confirmation by other researchers that the new discovery comes to be accepted as truth. This happens in accordance with how Hume argued rational men come to form beliefs – they accept the belief only in proportion to the supporting evidence for the claim. The more studies you have that say the same thing, the more the scientific community will come to hold the belief as true. It is also of note that the credibility of scientific testimony works just as Hume said it should. When improbable claims like the theory of relativity and cold fusion are proposed, scientists are dubious at first. As Einstein's calculations are repeated and not refuted, his claims gain credibility, as the repeated confirmation of the results make the claims more and more probable. Conversely, the lack of result confirmation makes the improbable claims about cold fusion made by Fleischmann and Pons even more improbable, and their claims even less credible.

Hume, Joyful and Triumphant

So where does this leave the possibility of the virgin birth? Not good at all. We have shown that a little investigation into Matthew and Luke reveals that there is little evidence of their credibility and plenty of reason to suppose that they are not credible. These reasons range from a lack of personal information about the men, to their conflicting testimony, to a dubious chain of testimony telephone, to questions about their translating practices, to simple facts about human nature. Even if these men were the most credible witnesses, however, the claims would seem extremely implausible given the uniformity of human experience concerning reproduction. We don't know many virgins, and the ones we know don't have kids. There doesn't seem to be any option for the rational person other than to deny the virgin birth and all other miracles. For anyone upset by this conclusion, feel free to call us Scrooges. You can even call us Grinches – just don't call us wrong or late for Christmas dinner.

NOTES

1 David Hume, *An Inquiry Concerning Human Understanding*, 3rd edn., ed. L. A. Selby-Bigge (New York: Oxford University Press, 1975), p. 115.
2 Ibid., p. 114.
3 The order they were actually written in is Mark, Matthew, Luke, and John.
4 Matthew 1:22. All biblical quotations are from the Revised English translation.
5 Matthew 1:18–25.
6 Luke 1:26–2:7.
7 Hume, *An Inquiry Concerning Human Understanding*, p. 111.
8 Ibid., p. 113.
9 Information about the gospel writers is available in any introductory work on the Bible. A good source is Stephen L. Harris, *Understanding the Bible* (Mountain View: Mayfield Publishing, 2000).
10 Ibid., pp. 355–61.
11 Ibid.

12 Isaiah 7:14.

13 Non-Hebrew and non-Greek speakers can engage in biblical word study through the use of a concordance, which offers a word-by-word index of the Bible, giving each instance of the word, in the original language, as it appears in the Bible. The best source is *Strong's Exhaustive Concordance of the Bible*, which is keyed to several English translations. A concordance alone is not enough, however, as it does not offer detailed translations or information about possible ambiguities and debates. Pair up your concordance with a good lexicon for each language, and a detailed word study source, and you're all set. The best biblical Hebrew lexicon is the *Brown-Driver-Briggs Hebrew Lexicon*. The best biblical Greek lexicon is the *Liddell and Scott Greek-English Lexicon*. *Vine's Bible Dictionary* is a good detailed word study.

14 Hume, *An Inquiry Concerning Human Understanding*, p. 117.

15 Ibid.

16 Ibid., p. 119.

17 Ibid., pp. 119–20.

18 Ibid., p. 119.

19 Ibid., p. 121.

20 Ibid., p. 115.

21 Ibid., pp. 115–16.

22 C. D. Broad, "Hume's Theory of the Credibility of Miracles," in Alexander Sesonske and Noel Fleming (eds.) *Human Understanding: Studies in the Philosophy of David Hume* (Belmont: Wadsworth, 1965), p. 91.

23 Ibid.

CHAPTER 2

THE VIRGIN BIRTH

Authentic Christmas Magic

A good example of the coloring by religious agendas is the whole heart-warming legend of Jesus' birth in Bethlehem, followed by Herod's massacre of the innocents.[1]

But the case of the Virgin Birth is the easiest possible proof that humans were involved in the manufacture of a legend.[2]

When in the process of reclaiming our humanity will it be important to know that Jesus was born of a Virgin?[3]

Believe it or not, 61 percent of Americans, including myself, believe in the virgin birth.[4] Why is that important? The Christmas story is the essential means by which Immanuel – "God with us" – becomes reality. That represents the real message of Christmas. The nativity scene with Mary, Joseph, and the baby Jesus is a symbol of the first Christmas in Bethlehem. Shepherds and wise men, angels and the star of Bethlehem – all make up the magic of the season. The wise men's camels are sometimes exchanged for a burro or a llama for multicultural applicability. We can rediscover the evidence that led to the belief in the virgin birth. Our Christmas faith can then be renewed and inspired by the simple but multilayered story of God's action and Mary and Joseph's obedience.

Two thousand years ago, Mary, a very young girl of twelve or thirteen years, is engaged to Joseph, himself perhaps no more than fourteen or fifteen years old, when the angel Gabriel visits her bringing a message from God.[5] During the visit she protests, then accepts, that though a virgin, she will bear a child, who will be the Messiah named Jesus. This rather odd story is at the heart of the doctrine of the virgin birth. How mainstream is this article of faith in the Christian churches today? Often neglected, sometimes ridiculed, and certainly underappreciated, *discovering and understanding the virgin birth of Christ can be a special gift this Christmas season.*

What Our Churches Confess

The doctrines and creeds of most Christian churches continue to affirm overwhelmingly the English equivalent of the old Latin phrase *conceptus de Spiritu sancto, natus ex Maria virgine,* "conceived by the Holy Spirit, Born of the Virgin Mary." The earliest use of this formula is found in the early second century baptismal creeds in Rome, which developed into the Apostolic Creed by the fourth century.[6] As early as 215 CE the Roman presbyter and martyr Hippolytus asked those who were to be baptized the following question: "Do you believe in Jesus Christ the Son of God, who was born of the Holy Spirit and the Virgin Mary?"[7] New Christians were expected to answer affirmatively and regard this doctrine as an essential part of their new-found faith in Christ. This was not a secondary article of faith. New Testament theologian J. Gresham Machen goes farther: "Belief in the virgin birth was probably universal in the Roman Church and was probably required of every candidate for baptism long before it was given stereotyped expression in a definite baptismal confession."[8] The phrase withstands the test of time in very diverse Christian congregations. A few examples include the belief systems of Southern Baptists, Presbyterians, and Methodists. The statement of faith of the Southern Baptist Convention states, "conceived of the Holy Spirit and born of the virgin Mary." The Westminster Confession, one of the official doctrinal statements of the United Presbyterian Church-USA underscores "conceived by the power of the Holy Ghost, in the womb of the Virgin Mary, of her substance." The Articles of Religion of the Methodist Church instruct, "took man's nature in the womb of the blessed Virgin." The Roman Catholic Church affirms the Virgin Birth in the strongest of language. The church also affirms additional dogmas from church tradition, dogmas that go beyond the teachings of the New Testament: the dogmas of the perpetual virginity of Mary; the Immaculate Conception, the belief that Mary did not have the taint of original sin and was therefore always sinless; the Mother of God, and the Assumption into Heaven; Mother of the Church; Mary, co-redeemer, mediator, advocate ... Queen of Heaven.

Early Christian Communities

Did the early church believe in the virgin birth and if so, how widespread was this belief? The writings of many Church Fathers acknowledge and defend the doctrine of the virgin birth. Ignatius of Antioch, a disciple of the Apostle John, defends the virgin birth in his writings *To The Ephesians, To the Smyrneans, To the Magnesians,* and *To the Trallians.* Ignatius affirms the origin of Christ: "born of the Virgin Mary without any intercourse with man."[9] Justin Martyr, philosopher and second-century apologist, addresses his *Apology* to the Emperor Antonius Pius and his adopted son Marcus Aurelius, future emperor under whom he would become a martyr in Rome in 165 CE:

> And when we say also that the Word, who is the first-birth of God, was produced without sexual union, and that He, Jesus Christ, our Preacher, was crucified and died, and rose again, and ascended into heaven, we propound nothing different from what you believe regarding those whom you esteem sons of Jupiter. For you know how many sons your esteemed writers ascribed to Jupiter.[10]

Another early Church Father who defends the virgin birth is Irenaeus of Lyons, a disciple of Polycarp who, in turn, was a disciple of John the Apostle. Irenaeus wrote *Against Heresies* around 175 CE and affirms the virgin birth.[11] Other Church Fathers defend the doctrine of the virgin birth from diverse Christian communities in the ancient world.[12]

Church father and philosopher Origen of Alexandria, the church's first systematic theologian, replies to the attacks on Christianity in *The True Word* written by noted philosopher Celsus. In 248 CE, as the city of Rome is celebrating a thousand years since its founding, Origen responds to Celsus' attack on Christianity with his work *Contra Celsus.*[13] Celsus was familiar with a scandalous Jewish account of the birth of Jesus. Origen includes this account of Celsus, writing, "when she was pregnant she was turned out of doors by the carpenter to whom she had been betrothed; as having been guilty of adultery, and that she bore a child to a certain soldier named Panthera."[14] Origen defends the use of the word "virgin" in Matthew's gospel as the fulfillment of the Messianic prophecy found in the Book of Isaiah.[15] Moreover, Celsus attacks Christianity with a theme echoed by contemporary Christian critics Sam Harris and Christopher Hitchens, stating that Christianity does not use reason, but repeats admonitions that call for a blind faith: "Do not examine, but believe" and "Your faith will save you."[16] For Celsus, Greek philosophy is reasonable and everything is to be judged against that worldview.

The Heart of the Evidence: Matthew and Luke

For conservative Christians, the Reformation phrase *sola scriptura*, "by scripture alone," underscores the authoritative nature of the canonical scriptures of the Old and New Testaments. According to this worldview, the evidence found for the virgin birth within those sacred pages reveals the Truth. In the New Testament, Paul's Second Letter to Timothy admonishes: "All Scripture is God-breathed and is useful for teaching, rebuking, correcting and training in righteousness."

The crucial passages in which the virgin birth unfolds are in the gospels of Matthew and Luke. Both narratives place emphasis on Mary as a *virgin*. In Matthew, Mary's pregnancy is seen as a fulfillment of the passage in Isaiah that she will have a son, Immanuel. The angel's words in Joseph's dream proclaim that the child within Mary has been "conceived by the Holy Spirit." The interpretation of these passages by modern scholars is controversial. There is disagreement about the translation between the Greek of the gospels and the Hebrew of Isaiah. Do the passages indicate specifically a "virgin" or, more generally, "a young maiden"? However, there is reason, in keeping with Jewish scholarship (the "midrashic haggadah"), to maintain that Mary was a virgin, thus fulfilling the Isaiah prophecy.[17] As in many passages of the Old Testament, it was rabbinic thought that there is a simple significance and also a deeper hidden significance. Christians see this deeper hidden significance in the person of Jesus. Here in Matthew's gospel, Jesus is in the richest sense *Immanuel, God with us.*

On the other hand, Luke underscores Mary's virginity through a personal encounter between Mary and the angel Gabriel. In the narrative of Luke, the word "virgin" is mentioned twice in reference to Mary. After Mary is told that she will become pregnant, she asks, "How can this be, since I am a virgin?" The answer to Mary's question links the two narratives together. Gabriel responds that the Holy Spirit will come upon you and "overshadow" you. The phrase "conceived by the Holy Spirit and born of the Virgin Mary" comes into being in these scriptural passages. Both passages reveal the concept of a virginal conception, not that of a virgin birth. The miracle does not occur at birth but at the conception. These passages provide the biblical basis of the doctrinal statements found throughout Christendom.

Despite similarities in the major themes of Matthew and Luke, the uniqueness of each underscores their independence. Raymond E. Brown, New Testament scholar, states: "Since it is almost unanimously agreed by scholars that the Matthean and Lucan infancy narratives are independent of each other, and since so many similarities can scarcely have arisen by accident, we are led to the probability of a basic pre-Gospel annunciation tradition that each evangelist used in his own way."[18] The story of the virgin birth, or virginal conception, then predates the writing of both Luke and Matthew. The Gospel of Luke is the work of a Gentile addressed to Theophilus around 65–80 CE. The Gospel of Luke and the Acts of the Apostles comprise two volumes by the same author.

While Luke is focused on a Gentile audience, Matthew's gospel is written for a Jewish audience. Moreover, Matthew sees the nature of the virginal conception of Jesus as a probable scandal. To counter this, Matthew highlights four other women from Christ's genealogy: Tamar, Rahab, Ruth, and Bathsheba, "the wife of Uriah." What do these women have in common? Baptist theologian E. Frank Tupper underscores two common threads: "(1) each of these women had a well-known story of marriage that contained varying elements of sexual scandal – unions, however, 'irregular,' which continued the lineage of the Messiah. Second, each woman actively participated in the events that became part of God's purpose in the fulfillment of the messianic heritage, identifying them as the instruments of the providence of God."[19] Joseph's near rejection of Mary suggests how real the scandalous nature of Mary's predicament might be. His fears were only calmed by the words of the angel in his dream, which foretells the virginal conception. If the virginal conception is indeed a matter of established faith in two very different communities, those of Matthew and Luke, then it predates the work of both gospel writers.

VICTOR LYONS

The Objection of Empiricism

The major objection to the claim of virgin birth comes from empiricism, the belief that knowledge is derived from experience, observation, and experimentation. Thomas Jefferson highlights this objection in a letter written on April 11, 1823 to John Adams:

> And the day will come when the mystical generation of Jesus, by the supreme being as his father in the womb of a virgin will be classed with the fable of the generation of Minerva in the brain of Jupiter. But we may hope that the dawn of reason and freedom of thought in these United States will do away with all this artificial scaffolding, and restore to us the primitive and genuine doctrines of this most venerated reformer of human errors.[20]

In other words, human experience and reason do not allow for such a thing as a virgin birth.

David Hume, the eighteenth-century British philosopher of empiricism, states: "Though experience be our guide in reasoning concerning matters of fact; it must be acknowledged, that this guide is not altogether infallible, but in some cases apt to lead us into errors ... a wise man proportions his belief to the evidence."[21] Writing about miracles, Hume affirms: "A miracle is a violation of the laws of nature; and as a firm and unalterable experience has established these laws, the proof against a miracle, from the very nature of the fact, is as entirely as any argument from experience can possibly be imagined."[22] At first glance, Hume's arguments seem to obligate us to reject the doctrine of the virgin birth. But let us examine the evidence of the experience presented to us in the gospels of Matthew and Luke concerning Mary and Joseph.

The first skeptic of the virgin birth – or better, virginal conception – was Mary herself. This event was not within her framework of natural experience. As noted above, she responds to the angel's declaration with the words, "How can this be, since I am a virgin?" Mary's alarm signals the awkwardness and unnaturalness of this process for her. She was not seeking, imagining, desiring, or preparing for such a moment. Yet, she accepts the unnatural, the supernatural, with the words "may it be done according to your word." Her faith in God overrides her life experience up to that point. Her past experiences give her no guidance as she deals with this new experience, this new reality. She will be pregnant even while remaining a virgin. Mary's only relief seems to be the news that the elderly Elizabeth is also pregnant. She immediately goes to her home and remains with her for three months. This extraordinary experience was almost more than Mary could bear.

Would Hume have Mary deny this experience? Would Hume try to have Mary explain away her experience with the old reality?

The second skeptic of the virginal conception of Mary was her betrothed, Joseph. How he receives the news and what Mary, perhaps through an intermediary, shares with him is not recorded. The account states only that "she was found to be with child," adding, "through the Holy Spirit." Robert Bratcher, biblical translator and scholar, points out that this passage is written in the passive voice and so can be translated: "it was discovered that she was pregnant."[23] And New Testament scholar A. T. Robertson adds:

> The discovery that Mary was pregnant was inevitable and it is plain that she had not told Joseph. She was "found with child." This way of putting it, the usual Greek idiom, plainly shows that it was the discovery that shocked Joseph.[24]

Joseph must now react to this reality. Experience has taught him that pregnancies come from sexual relations between a man and a woman. If he isn't the father of the child, then who is? How could she break her commitment to him and their engagement? As Bratcher points out, the Jewish betrothal "was a binding relationship, not a tentative one, as in many modern societies, and could be broken only by death or a formal act of divorce."[25] So binding was the marriage arrangement during this period that New Testament scholar Donald Hagner states: "If one of the partners died before the marriage, the other was a widow or widower."[26]

Further, at this time being pregnant outside of wedlock was a very serious matter. The Book of Deuteronomy calls for death by stoning for an unmarried pregnant woman. In the greater Hellenistic world, Emperor Augustus "expressed concern over various social problems in Rome. Adultery was widespread and divorce common ... he was dismayed by the relaxed moral standards of his time and ... wanted to return Rome to the standards of the 'good old days.' He therefore passed laws (18 BC, the Julian Laws regulating adultery and marriage ...) meant to encourage marriage and to discourage adultery."[27]

A milder way of dealing with the situation would have been for Joseph to "break the engagement publicly and denounce Mary as an adultress."[28] In the midst of the hurt and sense of disillusionment, Joseph decides that he will not expose her to public disgrace and ridicule. Instead, he will divorce her privately without announcing a cause. Joseph decides to act in an honorable and merciful way toward Mary. However, that is not the end of the story. In a dream an angel appears to him, and he is told that the child in Mary is conceived by the Holy Spirit, that the child has a divine purpose, and moreover, that all these events fulfill prophecy. Joseph's response is obedience: he takes Mary as his wife and (according to some interpretations) lives with her but without having normal sexual relations; he names the child Jesus.

Empiricists are correct when they readily admit that experience is not an infallible guide, as Hume does. Experience does not stop where the skeptic draws a line, declaring everything on the other side to be unnatural or miraculous. Thinking and living life outside the empiricist's box is part of many disciplines, including science. The outright rejection of the mysterious and miraculous *a priori* limits the integrity of empirical research and creates a circular *a priori* conclusion. One must build upon experience, but not limit oneself to a category or a few categories and say that everything must fall into one of these categories. There must be a desire to be open to all experiences.

The Objection of the Absurd

Sam Harris dismisses the doctrine of the virgin birth as the foundation for a twisted and negative view of human sexuality:

> Mary's virginity has always been suggestive of God's attitude toward sex: it is intrinsically sinful, being the mechanism through which original sin was bequeathed to the generations after Adam. It would appear that Western civilization has endured two millennia of consecrated sexual neurosis simply because the authors of Matthew and Luke could not read Hebrew. For the Jews, the true descendants of Jesus and the apostles, the dogma of the virgin birth has served as a perennial justification for their persecution, because it has been one of the principal pieces of "evidence" demonstrating the divinity of Jesus.[29]

No doubt there are those within Christianity who have exaggerated the positive nature and the positive effects of celibacy. Nevertheless, quite literally from the beginning, early in the Book of Genesis, human sexuality is understood as a gift from God and is divinely blessed.

More often than not, God's involvement in our lives is through the natural flow of his creation. Nevertheless, scripture shows that there are moments when God wants others to know that it is he who is at work. In the battle of Jericho, as recounted in the Book of Joshua, God has the children of Israel march around the wall for seven days, and on the seventh day, horns were blown and the people all "shouted," and the wall fell. It was a moment in which God's presence was felt and the ordinary means of battle were replaced by unorthodox and extraordinary means. Similarly, in the story of the virgin conception of Mary, God acts in an extraordinary manner so that Mary and Joseph may know that it is God at work, and not they themselves. They would never have chosen this way of acting. The event is awkward, even scandalous. No doubt during their lifetimes some would have understood this as God's will, as was the case of Elizabeth and her encouragement to Mary, while others may never have accepted the fact of a virginal conception. Nevertheless, it is an article of Christian faith that the God who has created the natural, also acts in the extraordinary, the awkward, the absurd. God can't be easily placed in any one philosophical box.

Authentic Christmas Magic

The oral and literary histories of the virgin birth of Jesus go back to within twenty or thirty years after the death of Jesus. Jewish-Christians were still a significant part of the early church, and Matthew and Luke record their narratives of the virgin birth from communities that believed strongly in it. One may assume that the silence of those twenty or thirty years is due to the modesty of Jesus' inner family circle. Nevertheless, soon the belief spread throughout the ancient world and congregations across a wide ethnic population readily accepted this article of faith, even incorporating it into the baptismal confession of the new Christians.

The preexistent *logos* or Word found in John's Gospel and proclaimed by the Apostle Paul in both the Gospel of John and in the Letter to the Philippians came into this world by means of the virgin Mary, becoming Immanuel, God-with-us, fulfilling prophecy, revealing the true nature of God in the present, and preparing a future for those brought together by the good news of God's impending kingdom. The virgin birth is authentic Christmas magic. With the shepherds, we can hear the angels proclaim, "Glory to God in the highest, and on earth peace among men."

The Consequences of the Virginal Conception

First, affirming the virginal conception affirms the fulfillment of God's promises in the scriptures. The promises given to Abraham and to David of eternal blessing and an eternal kingdom are being realized. The Jewish Messiah has come. God's kingdom is at hand, a new day is dawning. This child can only come as a result of God's action and not the intervention through natural processes of a man and woman. God is sovereign over all history.

Second, this coming of God means the revelation of the invisible God. Indeed, God himself has come in flesh as stated in the Gospel of John. The incarnation takes place. "The Shekinah glory where the cloud of glory represents the presence and power of God"[30] is suggested in the phrase "the power of the Most High will overshadow you." This is the message of Christmas: Jesus says, "I and the Father are one." With Thomas, we can see the risen Christ and say, "My Lord and My God."

Third, affirming the virginal conception means that Jesus has the divine nature, is sinless, and can redeem fallen humanity. He has the divine nature of God through the Holy Spirit and the nature of fallen humanity through Mary. Moreover, his absolute obedience to the will of God and his absolute dependence on the Holy Spirit reconfirm his sinlessness and his ability to be the sacrifice for the sins of others. This sinless nature is necessary for the new creation.[31]

In closing, I turn to the words of the theologian Karl Barth. In "The Miracle of Christmas" Barth gives an overview of the beauty of the virginal conception of Christ with the following words:

> God has acted solely through God and in which God can likewise be known solely through God … this is a real event accomplished in time and space as history within history. In it God's revelation comes to us, in it our reconciliation takes place…. The dogma of the Virgin Birth is thus the confession of the boundless hiddenness of the *vere Deus vere homo* – very God and very man – and of the boundless amazement of awe and thankfulness called forth in us.[32]

NOTES

1   Richard Dawkins, *The God Delusion* (Boston: Houghton Mifflin, 2006), p. 118.
2   Christopher Hitchens, *God is Not Great: How Religion Poisons Everything* (New York: Grand Central Publishing, 2007), p. 116.
3   Sam Harris, *The End of Faith: Religion, Terror, and the Future of Reason* (New York: W. W. Norton, 2004), p. 23.
4   "More Americans Believe in the Devil, Hell and Angels than in Darwin's Theory of Evolution," The Harris Poll, December 10, 2008; available online at www.harrisinteractive.com.
5   I. Howard Marshall, *The Gospel of Luke: A Commentary on the Greek Text* (Grand Rapids: Eerdmans, 1978), p. 64; Bruce W. Frier and Thomas A. J. McGinn, *A Casebook on Roman Family Law* (Oxford: Oxford University Press, 2004), p. 27; Joel B. Green, *The Gospel of Luke* (Grand Rapids: Eerdmans, 1997), p. 86.
6   Philip Schaff and David S. Schaff (eds.) *The Creeds of Christendom, Vol. 1: The History of Creeds*, 6th edn. (Grand Rapids: Baker Book House, 1983), pp. 16–23.
7   Kirsopp Lake (ed.) "Apostolic Tradition by Hippolytus," in *The Apostolic Fathers*, 2 vols. (New York: Loeb Classical Library, 1925–30), 21:12ff.
8   J. Gresham Machen, *The Virgin Birth of Christ* (Grand Rapids: Baker Book House, 1974), p. 4.
9   Alexander Roberts and James Donaldson (eds.) *The Ante-Nicene Fathers*, Vol. 1 (Grand Rapids: Eerdmans, 1979), pp. 52, 64, 71, 87.
10 Ibid., p. 170.
11 Ibid., pp. 454–5, 547.
12 Robert Gromachki, *The Virgin Birth: A Biblical Study of the Deity of Jesus Christ*, 2nd edn. (Grand Rapids: Kregel Publications, 2002), pp. 97–9; Gresham Machen, *The Virgin Birth of Christ*, pp. 2–43.
13 Alexander Roberts and James Donaldson (eds.) *The Ante-Nicene Fathers*, Vol. 4 (Grand Rapids: Eerdmans, 1979), pp. 395–669.
14 Ibid., p. 410.
15 Ibid., p. 411.
16 Ibid., pp. 399–400.
17 Donald A. Hagner, *Matthew 1–13, Word Biblical Commentary*, Vol. 33A (Columbia: Word, 1993), p. 16.
18 Raymond E. Brown, *The Birth of the Messiah* (Garden City: Doubleday, 1977), p. 159.
19 E. Frank Tupper, *A Scandalous Providence: The Jesus Story of the Compassion of God* (Macon: Mercer University Press, 1995), p. 95.
20 Lester J. Cappon (ed.) *The Adams-Jefferson Letters* (Chapel Hill: University of North Carolina Press, 1987), p. 594.

21 David Hume, *An Enquiry Concerning Human Understanding* (Online: Filiquarian, 2007), p. 100.

22 Ibid., pp. 103–4.

23 Robert G. Bratcher, *A Translator's Guide to the Gospel of Matthew* (London: United Bible Societies, 1981), p. 7.

24 Archibald Thomas Robertson, *Word Pictures in the New Testament*, Vol. 1 (Nashville: Broadman Press, 1930), p. 6.

25 Bratcher, *A Translator's Guide to the Gospel of Matthew*, p. 7.

26 Hagner, *Matthew 1–13*, p. 17.

27 Jo-Ann Shelton, *As the Romans Did: A Sourcebook in Roman Social History* (New York: Oxford University Press, 1988), p. 54.

28 Bratcher, *A Translator's Guide to the Gospel of Matthew*, p. 7.

29 Harris, *The End of Faith*, p. 95.

30 Archibald Thomas Robertson, *Word Pictures in the New Testament*, Vol. 2 (Nashville: Broadman Press, 1930), p. 14.

31 E. Schuyler English, *Things Surely To Be Believed: A Primer of Bible Doctrine*, Vol. 1 (Lancaster: Rudisill, 1956), pp. 61–2.

32 Karl Barth, *Church Dogmatics*, Vol. 1.2, trans. G. T. Thomson and Harold Knight (Edinburgh: T. & T. Clark, 1986), p. 177.

CHAPTER 3

PUTTING THE "YULE" BACK IN "YULETIDE"

 It's a familiar Christmas scene. The day: December 24. The time: 7:43 p.m. The place: any shopping center parking lot in America. We are the sad, desperate mass of humanity that has put off Christmas shopping until the very last of minutes. Having been force-fed holiday cheer since before Halloween, we grudgingly fold to the commercial demands of the season, frantically searching for gifts that will most likely find their way back to the returns desk in a week or two. At best, maybe that all-in-one electric olive pitter/peeler/presser will eventually turn up in a distant relative's Easter basket.

Of course, the mercantile madness is just half the picture. First, you have to get to and from the store. Gridlocked at the mall exit, knuckles whitened as I convulsively grip the steering wheel, Jose Feliciano fruitlessly tries to convince me, yet again, to have a "Feliz Navidad." If only I had the sense to bring along a CD, an iPod, or anything else to spare me from Christmas season radio. After months of being told to have a "Holly, Jolly Christmas" and "A Merry Little Christmas" and to "Deck the Halls," I've taken just about as much direction as I can handle. Then, on the rear bumper of the car in front of me, is a sticker with yet one more command: "Put Christ Back in Christmas."

Now, I'm all for Christians showing pride in their faith, but as a medievalist, this is where I have to draw the line. First, given the sheer number of plastic nativity scenes, religious Christmas carols, and rebroadcasts of

Mel Gibson's *Passion of the Christ* over the past three months, Christ seems to be very much in evidence this time of year. More to the point, if this directive signals a desire to return to a more "authentic" celebration of Christmas, the key should not be in *promoting* the Christian aspect of the season, but in *balancing* the Christian and non-Christian elements of the holiday. In the English tradition, and subsequently the American one, this balance was solidified in the medieval period, and has cultural, linguistic, philosophical, and literary components that explain it.

Christmas's Cultural Context

In medieval England the balance between Christian and non-Christian was an integral part of the culture. Two of the most influential thinkers who set the philosophical stage for this blending of traditions were St. Augustine of Hippo (354–430) and Ancius Manlius Severinus Boethius (ca. 480–525). Augustine, one of the most important figures in the development of Western Christianity, had personal experience with negotiating his faith in the face of the temptations of the material world. My favorite Augustinian quote on this struggle comes from his aptly titled *Confessions*, in which he asks God to "grant me chastity and continence, but not yet." Here was a man who had a very practical take on the intersection of Christian ideals and life in the "real world." When it came to reconciling Christian thought with non-Christian philosophy, Augustine was unprepared to throw the proverbial baby out with the bathwater. In his *On Christian Doctrine* Augustine stumps for the (admittedly conditional) acceptance of non-Christian thought. According to Augustine, if those "philosophers happen to have said anything that is true, and agreeable to our faith, the Platonists above all, not only should we not be afraid of them, but we should even claim back for our own use what they have said." In the Augustinian view, proper Christianity *embraces* the non-Christian in order to further its own reach.

Boethius does just that in his wildly popular *Consolation of Philosophy*, a veritable medieval bestseller. Written while unjustly imprisoned and facing execution, Boethius creates a fictionalized account of his imprisonment, addressing the question of why bad things happen to good people (namely him!). Guided by Lady Philosophy, an allegorical embodiment of philosophy who is partial to Plato, the Boethius of the story is led to a better understanding of humanity's relationship to God through instructional dialogue. For the Boethius of the text (and, one imagines, the author as well), it is only through the ministrations of Philosophy that Christian theology can be properly understood. For both Augustine and Boethius, philosophy (as represented by the non-Christian ancients) was a necessary corollary to Christian doctrine. The medieval church, stereotypical visions of the Spanish Inquisition aside, was not necessarily about squelching other ways of interpreting the world, but about incorporating those elements of non-Christian thought that were useful, so long as they were not in direct opposition to the faith.

This strategy of adoption and adaptation was bred in the medieval bone, as it were, due to the very nature of the settlement of the British Isles. The early inhabitants of Britain, the Celtic Britons, were conquered by the Romans in 43 CE. While the Britons may not have been happy about being conquered, running water, paved roads, and hot baths seemed to have gone some way to assuage their wounded pride. For almost four centuries the Britons were slowly Romanized (as the conquering Romans were surely Britonized as well). Unfortunately, this pleasant arrangement was not to last forever. Trouble on the home front, in the form of invading Visigoths at Rome's door, led to a relatively hasty Roman decampment from Britain in 410.

After the Romans left, the Britons, grown complacent and soft under Roman rule, were now on their own against those scary, hairy, kilt-wearing folks to the north and across the Irish Sea. In a bid to stave off a Celtic invasion, the Britons, too weak to defend themselves but rich in resources, hired people even hairier and scarier than the Celts: Germanic warriors. These Germanic Angles, Saxons, and Jutes were more than happy to serve as mercenaries for the Britons. However, one obvious problem with hiring stronger people to fight your battles for you is that they may decide not to leave once the job is done. "Why go back to the freezing weather and raw fish of Northern Europe," these Germanic warriors might well have thought, "when you have perfectly cozy sheep country right here in Britain?" Needless to say, the Germanic peoples stayed and the Britons had little they could do about it.

The resulting cultural mixing of the native Britons and the Germanic invaders formed what became known as the Anglo-Saxon people. Starting in the late sixth century with the arrival of St. Augustine, the Anglo-Saxons were slowly but steadily converted to Christianity by Irish missionaries, only to have that conversion tested and threatened repeatedly by the Viking invasions of the ninth through the eleventh centuries. The martial and cultural power struggles between Anglo-Saxon, Roman, and Viking influences resulted in a markedly mixed culture for a people cut off from the rest of Europe by the North Sea. It's not beyond reason to imagine an ethnically Celtic Briton who practiced some meager form of Roman Christianity while living in a Nordic settlement. It comes as no surprise, then, that the religious holidays of the people living in these circumstances could be as mixed in character as their culture.

Christmas: What's Yule Got to Do With It?

The diversity of early medieval culture and religion in Britain is clearly shown in the treatment of Christmas terminology by the competing medieval words *Christmas* and *Yuletide*. The Old English word *Cristesmæsse* (literally, "Christ's mass") can be traced back to the *Anglo-Saxon Chronicle*, a set of historical records kept at various locales throughout England from the ninth through the twelfth centuries. The earliest record of the word appears in the record for the year 1021 in the *Worcester Chronicle*. The chronicle entry for this year simply states that Bishop Ælfgar died "on Cristesmæssan uhtan" (on Christmas morning). There is no mention of Christ's birth, religious connotation, or even a single sugarplum. In fact, each of the 38 times *Christmas* turns up in the *Old English Corpus* (a collection of all extant Old English texts), *Christmas* simply marks a date, not unlike the feast day of any other important religious figure such as St. Michael, whose feast day of September 29 is known as Michaelmas. For the Anglo-Saxons, the term *Christmas* was simply another liturgical signpost on the calendar.

The lack of holiday hoopla surrounding the early medieval Christmas may have been an effect of understanding the date as symbolic, rather than actual. Saints' days were peppered throughout the calendar as a way to manage time among illiterate Christians in early medieval Europe. Lacking free calendars from their banks or insurance agents, medieval agriculturalists had to rely on the progression of saints' days throughout the year to help mark time. Livestock, for example, were killed at what was known as the "Martinmas slaughter" on St. Martin's feast day, November 11. This early winter butchering was as much a functional time for the curing and laying in of preserved meat for the long winter ahead as it was a religious observance.

As opposed to the rather generic use of the word *Christmas, yule* has a more specifically religious connotation in Old English. The *Old English Martyrology*, a list of saints' feast days, composed around the year 900, begins reckoning the calendar with December 25:

> On þone forman dæig on geare, þæt is on þone ærestan geoheldæig, eall cristen folc worþiað Cristes acennednesse.
>
> (On the first day of the year, that is the first yule-day, all Christian folk praise Christ's nativity.)

Like *Christmas, geoheldæig* (yule-day)[1] marks a certain date (December 25, the religious beginning of the year), but is here specifically connected to the celebration of Christ's birth in a way that Christmas is not in the Old English texts. But just what is a *yule* and how did it become connected to Christmas?

Part of the answer to this question lies with the Venerable Bede (ca. 672–735), a Northumbrian cleric and scholar of the eighth century. Bede is a wealth of information about early medieval England. In his *Historia ecclesiastica gentis Anglorum (Ecclesiastical History of the English People)*, for example, he not only traces the origin of the Christian church in England, but also the region's political and natural histories. In his *De temporum ratione (On The Reckoning of Time)* he focuses on the *computus*, the mathematical mechanism for calculating the proper date of Easter, but also provides an overview of the early English calendar. According to Bede, the ancient Britons called December and January *Giuli*, or Yule. Specifically, he claims that these early, non-Christian Britons

> began the year with December 25th, the day we now celebrate as the birth of our Lord; and the very night to which we attach special sanctity they designated by the heathen term *modraniht*, that is, the mother's night – a name bestowed, I suspect, on account of the ceremonies which they performed while watching this night through. (*De temporum ratione*, XV)

Does anyone else hear the *Twilight Zone* theme music at this point? Christians *just happen* to celebrate Christmas on the exact same night as a non-Christian celebration? Let's look at *Modraniht* (Mother's Night) and see what, if any, relationship it has to Christmas.

Descriptions of Mother's Night, as practiced in Orkney and the Shetland Islands of Scotland as recently as the nineteenth century, portray the night as one during which mothers would watch over their

TODD PRESTON

children to save them from being swapped for changelings by trolls or fairies. Eventually, the holiday would evolve into a request for the Virgin Mary to watch over the souls of one's children in a more general sense. Both Christmas and *Modraniht*, then, focus on children and mothers. The holidays seem to complement each other, showing two sides of the same natal coin: for Christians, it is a night when one child comes to save us all; for non-Christians, it is a night to save all children.

This overlapping of Christian and non-Christian tradition has a long history. One of these non-Christian midwinter celebrations was the Old Norse *Jól* (roughly pronounced as "yole"), a term parallel to, or perhaps the source of, the Old English *Geol* (Yule). *Jól* appears in the Scandinavian sagas as a protracted midwinter festival, usually running until the food and booze gave out, celebrating the return of lengthening days and shortening nights. Extending before and after the solstice (usually December 21 or 22), this celebration could easily straddle both Christmas and New Year's, which might explain Bede's confusing identification of both the English December and January as *Giuli*, or Yule. The reason for the Old English two-month-long month named Yule, according to the *Old English Martyrology*, is "that one of them [December] precedes the sun, before it turns to lengthen the day, the other [January] follows it." Ultimately, Yule corresponds with the winter solstice, when the days begin to lengthen again, signaling the (distant) hope of the coming spring. Christmas, then, was coincident with non-Christian seasonal celebrations of birth and nativity. While this is not necessarily news to any of you, what is curious is that the medieval church did not simply eradicate what it most likely saw as those pesky pagan practices.

Christmas and Christian Apologetics

So did the medieval church not only allow vestiges of non-Christian celebrations to survive, but actually incorporated them into *their* most important holiday? How does that even happen? First of all, we need to come to terms with the fact that Christmas was not the most important date on the medieval Christian calendar. While Easter serves as a distant also-ran to Christmas in the US today, and is handily overshadowed by New Year's, Halloween, and even Super Bowl Sunday, the celebration of Christ's resurrection was the paramount holiday of medieval Christendom. For example, when King Alfred the Great, who reigned from 871 to 899, established a holiday schedule for freeborn men in his law code, he allowed vacation days for the 12 days of Yule (not surprisingly, these days off were for freeborn men only; hired men, slaves, and Wal-Mart clerks got no such leeway). This seems like a pretty generous allotment, until you compare it to Easter. For the celebration of the resurrection, free men could look forward to the "7 days at Easter and the 7 days after" to relax and contemplate just what Christ's sacrifice has to do with an anthropomorphic rabbit circulating colored chicken eggs (the topic, I'm sure, of another volume in the *Philosophy for Everyone* collection). On the medieval vacation calendar, at least, Easter beats out Christmas by two days!

In addition to providing a concrete example of the relative importance of Easter and Christmas, King Alfred provides a window into the kind of cultural accommodation early medieval Christianity allowed; devotion to Christianity wasn't going to get in the way of getting the king's work done. Faced with seemingly endless incursions of Scandinavian raiders, Alfred continually fought off the invaders, making treaties with them confirming that they would leave and not come back. As Alfred's contemporary biographer Asser describes the situation for the year 876:

> With this [Viking] army Alfred made a solemn treaty, to the effect that they should depart out of the kingdom, and for this they made no hesitation to give as many hostages as he named; also they swore an oath over the Christian relics, which with king Alfred were next in veneration after the Deity himself, that they would depart speedily from the kingdom.

Alfred chooses what he thinks are the most sacred objects for this pact: Christian relics. However, those sneaky Scandinavians would not hold to their word. Asser recounts how the invaders repeatedly broke the oaths made over Christian relics and stole away to plunder some more. Alfred, confounded by these pagans' lack of regard for Christian relics, makes the only logical choice. The next time he defeated a raiding party, Alfred made sure the Vikings "swore with oaths on the holy ring, which they would not before to any nation, that they would readily go out of his kingdom" (*Anglo-Saxon Chronicle*). This "holy ring" has been associated with the Norse god Thor and seems a strange choice of an oath-object for a Christian king. However, Alfred was nothing if not a realist. If Christian relics wouldn't hold the Vikings to their word, he was perfectly willing to use a non-Christian relic to get the job done.

TODD PRESTON

What allowed Alfred the flexibility of mind to invoke the non-Christian when necessary was the intellectual heritage of Christian apologetics. Put simply, Christian apologetics explores the rational arguments supporting the Christian faith. A significant strain of these arguments was adapted from classical philosophy. Just as Alfred felt justified in using Thor's ring to ensure the safety of his Christian subjects, early medieval Christian apologists felt justified using the themes and techniques of secular philosophy to understand their religion.

Although not a philosopher himself, Alfred was obviously deeply influenced by the works of two founding Western Christian apologists, Boethius and Augustine. The king was responsible for translations into Old English of both Boethius' *Consolation of Philosophy* and Augustine's *Soliloquies*. Augustine and Boethius both tried to justify and promote their faith through philosophical argument. For them, their belief system had to be more than just a matter of faith, but a supportable reality. In the *Consolation*, as previously noted, Boethius attempts to do this by co-opting the technique of Socratic dialogue to explore the question of God's role in humanity's expression of free will and its consequences. Similarly, Augustine's *Soliloquies* is a philosophical dialogue between a personified Reason and a fictionalized Augustine. The purpose of the dialogue, according to the Augustine of the text, is to better know God and the nature of the soul through rational discourse. Both Augustine and Boethius were willing to use the tools of the non-Christian ancients in order to make a case for Christianity.

This open-mindedness to non-Christian practices was part and parcel of the conversion process in early medieval England. When Pope Gregory I (ca. 540–604) counseled his missionaries in Britain, he encouraged them to make allowances for the folk beliefs and practices of the native Britons. As reported in Bede's *Historia*, Gregory explains his *modus operandi* of conversion: "there is no doubt that it is impossible to efface everything at once from their [i.e., non-Christians'] obdurate minds; because he who endeavors to ascend to the highest place, rises by degrees or steps, and not by leaps." Thus, Gregory recommends that the missionaries do not try to stop non-Christian practices, but repurpose them. If the non-Christians slaughtered cattle as sacrifices to their gods, let the sacrificing continue, but "no more offer beasts to the Devil, but kill cattle to the praise of God in their eating." The philosophical accommodation of the non-Christian in the Christian apologetics of Augustine and Boethius finds practical application in Gregory's admonitions to his missionaries.

It then comes as no surprise that King Alfred begins his law code with a translation of the Ten Commandments, but then follows them with a translation from the Acts of the Apostles. After laying down the Old Testament law, Alfred is sure to include a letter to the apostles proselytizing in Antioch. In Alfred's translation of the letter, the apostles are instructed to "not set any burden on you [the people of Antioch] beyond that which was a necessary thing for you to hold." In other words, we want you to convert and follow God's laws, but we don't want to scare you off either. So, if you need to slaughter the occasional ox, that's okay with us, just dedicate it to the Christian God instead of Thor or Baal or L. Ron Hubbard.

Of course, not every accommodation of the non-Christian was as genteel as a paper letter or a regal law code. The English St. Boniface (ca. 634–709), known locally by his birth name of Wilfrid, practiced what could most diplomatically be described as "cultural accommodation with extreme prejudice." His biographer, Eddius Stephanus, relates that while Boniface was serving as a missionary near Geismar, Germany, he had had enough of the locals' reverence for the old gods. Taking an axe to an oak tree dedicated to Norse god Thor, Boniface chopped the tree down and dared Thor to zap him for it. When nothing happened, Boniface pointed out a young fir tree amid the roots of the oak and explained how this tree was a more fitting object of reverence as it pointed towards the Christian heaven and its triangular shape was reminiscent of the Christian trinity.

The important aspect of this interchange is not Boniface's destruction of the non-Christian oak, but of the swapping of the oak for the fir. The same method of devotion – tree worship – is preserved, even if the aim of that worship is different. Despite the saint's obvious disdain for the non-Christian religion, he allowed the cultural practice to continue, albeit with a different object of veneration. The spirit of Christian apologetics can be seen behind Boniface's actions. Instead of trying to wipe out the non-Christian beliefs, he incorporated them into the Christian faith. Of course, this new object of veneration, the fir tree, has become the Christmas tree of today.

The Medieval Christmas: Christ and Kissing Games

After the conversion period, when Christianity was well established in medieval England, one would expect Christ's presence to be foremost in the celebration of Christmas. However, a quick overview of English

TODD PRESTON

medieval literature paints a different picture. The ideal of the medieval court is personified in King Arthur's Camelot. However, despite the Arthurian devotion to Christianity, as seen in the court's quest for the Holy Grail, Christmas appears to be a rather secular affair.

In *Sir Gawain and the Green Knight* (ca. 1375), King Arthur's court gathers for a Christmas feast. Rather than being a time of pious reflection, the court is occupied with "merriment unmatched and mirth without care / ... the feast was unfailing full fifteen days, / with all the meats and all the mirth that men could devise, / such gladness and gaiety as was glorious to hear, / din of voices by day, and dancing by night." As the feasts stretch toward the New Year, the partying continued with only a brief aside that things really got going once "chapel came to an end." Christ seems to be far from the revelers' minds as they call for New Year's gifts and handsels (small presents). A knight, holding a present behind his back, asks a lady to guess which hand it is in. If she guesses wrong, the knight wins a kiss! The days are marked by food, drink, and song with hardly a word as to the "reason for the season."

We might be able to brush off this image of holiday merriment as the trappings of romantic fiction. King Arthur and his court are *supposed* to be engaged in all of these courtly diversions by their very nature as chivalric fictions, right? This might be true, but the wild, secular fun of the Christmas season was such a fundamental part of the holiday that the stewards of the faith have been complaining about its excesses for centuries.

John Wyclif (ca. 1324–84) was a theologian who was particularly upset by the immoderation of Christmas celebrations. Being the first translator of the Bible into English, he certainly had a pro-Christian agenda, but Wyclif's list of abuses sheds some light on what a "traditional" Christmas was really like. In a tract explicating the "Ave Maria," Wyclif calls holiday merrymakers on the carpet:

> But now he that can best play a pageant of the devil, singing songs of lechery, of battles and lies, and cry as a crazy man, and despise God's majesty, and swear by the heart, bones, and all the limbs of Christ, is held to be a most merry man and shall have the thanks of the rich and the poor; and this is called the worship of the great solemnity of Christmas.

Even though Wyclif was at odds with the church on the acceptability of a vernacular Bible, he is orthodox enough to be horrified by what he sees as the perversion of the point of the holiday.

Ultimately, it seems that Christmas, in actual practice, was never strictly about Christ. It was the grafting of a Christian holiday onto an existing non-Christian season of festivity. From the earliest incarnation of the holiday, the celebration was a balance of the Christian and non-Christian. One was never eliminated completely in favor of the other. Just as the early Church Fathers and secular rulers realized that Christianity would go down with their new converts much easier with a spoonful of familiar non-Christian tradition, so the holiday itself became a mixture of the sacred and the secular. If we want to be true to the original spirit of the holiday, we should be much more concerned with balancing the Christian and the pagan elements of the holiday.

So, sitting in traffic, taking in the bumper sticker command before me to "Put Christ Back in Christmas," I'm happy to give those observant Christians their due and recognize Christ's role in the holiday. That said, I'd only ask that they, in turn, practice the flexibility of spirit of their theological forebears. Follow the examples of St. Augustine, Pope Gregory, and King Alfred. Embrace the Yule log, the party games, and the smooching under the mistletoe ... just keep your mitts off of my eggnog.

NOTE

1   The Old English *g* is pronounced as a *y* in front of certain vowels. Thus, *geoheldæig* would be pronounced something like "yay-ogh-el-day," with the first two syllables combined into one. Its root word, *geol*, would be pronounced "yayol," as one syllable, and not too differently from the Modern English *Yule*.

PART II

IS CELEBRATING CHRISTMAS
REALLY A GOOD IDEA?

CHAPTER 4

ARMED FOR THE WAR ON CHRISTMAS

 Over the past few years a number of conservative figures and self-proclaimed culture warriors have made the case that there is a War on Christmas. The war, they say, is on two fronts. One is that Christmas stories and imagery not explicitly depicting Jesus' birth constitute a program of "taking the Christ out of Christmas." These objections range from the reasonable complaint that the season has become a consumerist holiday to the insipid furor over the replacement of "Christ" with "X" in the abbreviation "Xmas." (The "X," of course, is not a Latin letter at all, but a Greek *chi*, which stands for Christ, or *Christos*.) The second form of the War on Christmas is a purported secular ban on Christmas in all its forms in public life. Here, the stories of Christmas under fire range from the incredible (a prohibition on red and green decorations for a school party in Plano, Texas) to the questionably relevant (Wal-Mart's short-lived switch to the non-sectarian greeting "Happy Holidays"). These reports have moved Pat Buchanan to say that we are witnessing a rash of "hate crimes against Christianity."[1]

The reports of Christmas under siege culminated in the winters of 2004 and 2005, when Fox News put the story in millions of living rooms. Fox News anchor John Gibson penned *The War on Christmas: How the Liberal Plot to Ban the Sacred Christian Holiday Is Worse Than You Thought*, and he frequently was a guest on a number of other programs on the network talking about his research. Additionally, Bill O'Reilly regularly reported and fumed over sightings of "holiday" or "friendship" trees, uses of "Happy Holidays," and any other secular sanitizing of the sacred days in December.

The two fronts of the War on Christmas are really illusions. The first is simply a misunderstanding of the phenomenon of cultural Christianity – everyone, even avowed non-Christians, know a laundry list of details about Christ's life, teachings, and his purported place in heaven. But it is either so obvious or goes without saying that most people at least are aware of or acknowledge these points. Everybody knows. The protectors of the tradition seem not to recognize and be able to appreciate their own success – the Good News is Old News now. Christmas is a picture of an effective cultural marketing campaign for a religion, and the thing about booming month-long events is that they have a tendency to have all sorts of elements that the guardians of the tradition did not anticipate. The fact that Christmas has so many parts to it beyond repeating the story of Jesus' birth doesn't mean that it's no longer about Jesus. It means that the season is all the more culturally relevant to its practitioners. Cultural Christianity's Christmas still has many moments about Jesus, and the only people who are confused about Christmas's Christian significance are gift-crazy children (they'll grow up) and genealogy-drunk amateur historians claiming that it is really a pagan holiday (they won't). Hardly anybody disputes that Christmas is a Christian holiday.

The second front of the War on Christmas is also an illusion. The reason why the public schools don't have nativity scenes and "Jesus is THE Reason for the Season" banners is that it is simply not the government's job to be in the business of religious education. And this is something that Christians should acknowledge is in their interest. Imagine a Christmas pageant with a fifth grader playing Mary looking up from the manger and announcing *she* was born of a virgin, too. Catholic parents may smile, but the Protestant ones probably won't. And if this is a matter of religious expression, perhaps imagine further that the Jewish boy playing a shepherd jumps in to correct her – according to the Babylonian Talmud, Mary actually had an affair with a Roman by the name of Pandera.[2]

Theology is a choppy sea and it seems reasonable we shouldn't trust public schools to wade even a little into these waters. Witness the difficulty the schools have teaching something as clear as grammar and arithmetic. An educator's job is difficult enough in subject areas with little or no dispute, but overt defenses of theological stances invite such wide-ranging disputation that effective teaching may be impossible. Or if some core curriculum can be taught, given the disputation about theology, very few will have any agreement with it. Having public schools refrain from Jesus-emphatic celebrations is not a War on Christmas, it's an attempt to save Christmas for those who care about it most.

There is the additional consideration of the non-establishment clause of the First Amendment: "Congress shall make no law respecting an establishment of religion." For most people, this closes the case. But not for all. In response, John Gibson insists that enforcing this first clause often tramples the following clause: "or prohibiting the free exercise thereof ..." Gibson then invokes majoritarian democratic ideals as evidence of the travesty:

> The secularists, the humanists, the religionists other than Christian do not want to hear the reality that they are a very small minority of non-Christians in a sea of Christians that stretches to the horizons in all directions.[3]

Gibson then proffers some numbers – a Pew Research Poll in 2002 reveals that 84 percent of the United States population is Christian, and a Fox News Poll in 2004 had it that a whopping 96 percent celebrate Christmas (surely no sampling issues with those who respond to a Fox News poll). The question he poses is why such a small minority (4 percent!) should be allowed to hold everyone else hostage to their oversensitive tendencies to get offended by stories of Jesus. An institution pursuing non-establishment stands in the way of free expression, which amounts to "secularists ... suppress(ing) the religion of the supermajority." It is a simple point, Gibson insists, about *majority rights*.[4]

The problem is that the constitutional amendments are not there for the purpose of protecting *majority* rights, but instead to protect *minority* rights. And there is good empirical evidence that most Christians fail to understand the point of minority rights precisely because they identify with or see themselves as the majority. Bruce Hunsberger and Bob Altenmeyer of the University of Manitoba asked a group of fundamentalist Christians whether they approved of a law requiring public schools to teach that Christianity was true. A solid 84 percent of the fundamentalists thought it would be a good law. However, when a similar group was asked further questions about whether or not an Islamic democracy should have compulsory public education that Islam is true or that in Israel that Judaism is true, only 20 percent said they would allow it for their children in Israel and a meager 5 percent would abide it in Islamic countries.[5] It is very easy, it seems, to be for majority rights when one is in the majority, but change the situation and minority rights look more reasonable. But this point seems lost on the culture warriors. It is a shame, Gibson reasons, that *even when Christianity is right and in the majority*, they may still be held in contempt. In fact, the very notion that a minority needs protection in these matters is testament, he thinks, to the vice of the society:

> A growing number of Christians feel that it is wrong for their religion to be treated as something people should be protected from.[6]

The fact that people are being protected from Christianity is a cause for concern not only about the morality of the protecting government but more importantly the people being protected. It's as if to say: the worries of a "tyranny of the majority" with Christians are tantamount to religious bigotry. Gibson thinks that people feel the need to be protected from the state mandating Christian love and the grace of God is testament to just how much they need it. This thought, of course, can be turned right back around by any dogmatic view: for the communists, people's resistance to communism was testament to how much they needed reprogramming; for fundamentalist Muslims, the West's failure to take the Prophet's teaching seriously is evidence of how much they need it. If you see the latter two dogmatic attitudes as wrong not because the views they hold are wrong but because they do not treat others as free and equal human beings (many communists and Muslims have thought the same thing), you can see what is wrong with Gibson's take on the matter. Gibson, in expressing his moral contempt for those who don't want to be Christians and who want the state to protect them from and refrain from proselytizing, just crossed the line between free expression and state establishment of religion.

Gibson and O'Reilly had a meeting of the minds regarding the War on Christmas on O'Reilly's show, *The Factor*, and O'Reilly made the case that Christmas is a good way to instill virtue in children, because it is a means of introducing them to Jesus. Gibson agreed wholeheartedly:

O'Reilly: See, I think it's all part of the secular progressive agenda –
Gibson: Absolutely.
O'Reilly: – to get Christianity and spirituality and Judaism out of the public square. Because if you look at what happened in Western Europe and Canada, if you can get religion out, then you can pass secular progressive programs like legalization of narcotics, euthanasia,

SCOTT F. AIKEN

	abortion at will, gay marriage, because the objection to those things is religious-based, usually.
Gibson:	You have France or you have – or you have Holland, you have legalized prostitution, you have drugs. All those things come in which religious organizations tend to oppose. Once you start taking out even the secular symbols of religious holidays – Christmas trees, Santas, so forth – refuse to use the word "Christmas," you can shove this religious stuff indoors, out of sight.
O'Reilly:	Yeah, because no kid is going to come home and ask Mom what winter break is.
Gibson:	No.
O'Reilly:	But a kid might come home and say, "Hey, what's this Christmas thing all about? Who is this baby Jesus guy?" You know?
Gibson:	Right.[7]

O'Reilly thinks that Christmas is a very good way for children who do not know Jesus to come to know him. He is right: Christmas is a tool for promoting Christianity. Christmas is a religious recruiting tool. And it is a powerful one. Christmas-envy is a serious problem for non-Christians, especially the young ones who are impressed with the prospects of a holiday that promises a load of presents rivaling or surpassing a birthday. Witness Adam Sandler's "Hanukkah Song," dripping with resentment: "If you're the only kid in town without a Christmas tree, here's a list of people who are Jewish, just like you and me …" But if Christmas is a gateway holiday for Christianity, then public schools embracing it would clearly be running afoul of the non-establishment clause. That really should seal it.

But I think that a case against publicly subsidized and promoted Christmas can be made along an entirely different line. Christmas, regardless of its religious ties, should be evaluated on its own cultural merits both in terms of being stories worth telling and celebrations that make us better. The real problem with Christmas is that as a cultural phenomenon, its myths are insipid and, contrary to the O'Reilly-Gibson theory of them promoting virtues, actually make us worse.

Christmas mythology has two forms: one is the Jesus nativity myth, the other is the Santa myth. Both are bad myths. I'll start with Jesus and the nativity. The first problem is that the story doesn't make a lick of sense. The gospels make plenty of room for Thomas to doubt the resurrection, but nobody gets to play that role in the opening story. Joseph has his doubts at the beginning, in that he considered having the marriage contract put aside when he found she was with child because, according to

Matthew, "he was a man of principle." An angel had to set things straight with Joseph, telling him that the baby was conceived by the Holy Spirit, and so he should follow through with the marriage. Beyond this, there is no evidence to put matters to rest with regard to the virgin birth independent of Mary's say-so (which is never introduced, by the way). At least an acknowledgment of the fact that the birth is a miracle and it was a surprise to *someone* (Mary, anyone?) would be better than the matter-of-fact prose of ho-hum miracle cataloguing. Regardless, nary an eyebrow is raised, and it does not even seem to be a matter of *faith*, since at least acknowledging that right-minded folk would take the story as silly is a requirement for faith. Instead, it seems simple *credulity* is the only requirement – one doesn't need to appreciate miracles as miracles, one just needs to believe. Surely this does not make us better, especially if one thinks faith is a virtue. On this story, the faith isn't even tested or even presented as faith.

The second problem is that the Gospel of Matthew opens and the Gospel of Luke closes the nativity story with Joseph's genealogy. *Joseph's.* Why is Joseph's lineage important? He's not the father. Literary genealogizing was clearly a way of displaying the gospel story's connection with the prior Jewish tradition (despite the fact the two genealogies don't match very well), but such a trope should be used for some real purpose. But Joseph's genealogy doesn't matter because he's been cuckolded by the Holy Spirit.

The third problem is with the wise men from the East. They were purportedly led by a star. How can that happen? Stars don't lead anyone anywhere, especially East to West, because stars don't sit still in the sky. *They all* rise in the East and go down in the West (excepting the ones at the poles). And how one star led them to a particular part of Judea is really a mystery. The official story, in Matthew at least, is that the wise men, after having met with Herod, saw the star, and it "went ahead of them until it stopped above the place where the child lay." So did it stay there, did it blink out, did it continue on its way in the movements of the heavens? No word. Moreover, it is still unclear how a star can pick out any one manger in Bethlehem once it is overhead. Was it *right over* the manger? (Imagine giving directions to your house: "I am directly under the really bright star right ... now.") Moreover, if the star were to have this sort of specificity, it is certainly strange that nobody else in Bethlehem, except for some shepherds (who, in fact, needed an angel to direct them), even noticed. Wouldn't the neighbors at least be curious about what's happening in the stable with the star sitting on top of it?

A fourth problem is that the nativity story doesn't fit with the rest of the gospels. Mary and Joseph had to flee Judea because of Herod's reign of terror. If there had been wise men from far away with them recently, it seems much more reasonable for the family Christ to go try to stay with *them* instead of going to Egypt. Surely one of the wise men, on departing, would say, "If you need anything ..." They clearly recognize the danger Herod poses, because, Matthew tells us, they even go out of their way to avoid Herod on their return home. This seems, really, perfectly negligent on their part. They don't offer any help to the family in the short term, not even a warning, and they make no effort later, either. In fact, the wise men *never* make a return appearance. Shouldn't they try to find Jesus, Mary, and Joseph when Herod orders the murder of innocents? Maybe they could come to Jesus' Bar-Mitzvah. Or later teach him some astronomy. Why would the wise men be interested in coming to see Jesus when he's just a baby, but they have no more interest in him once he can talk? They surely would have appreciated the miracles or the Sermon on the Mount. Wouldn't it be poignant for them to arrive at Golgatha for the crucifixion? Or for them at least to show up with a bribe for Pilate? It's almost as though the wise men went to all that trouble to see a baby whom they recognized as very very special, but once they dropped off their gold, frankincense, and myrrh they just weren't interested anymore. The point, of course, is that the nativity myth is simply shoddy storytelling. By narrative standards it is third rate, and bad myths aren't worth our time.

Cultural Christianity also has the myth of Santa, so what's wrong with him? For starters, it's clear he's a slave-owner. The elves and reindeer all seem either his chattel or at least his perpetual servants. The story of Rudolph is a tale of one such slave who comes to adore his bonds. Rudolph is ill-suited for the tasks of a reindeer, which makes him an object of scorn. Santa must certainly be aware of him, but does not step in to protect him or find a better role for him. Surely not a charitable community, the North Pole. However, when he *does* need Rudolph, Santa has no qualms about approaching him and requesting help. No apologies or even acknowledgments of mistreatment are necessary. Santa simply offers a bridle and Rudolph is redeemed by submitting to Santa's whip. This is not a myth for children who are to grow up to be free. It is certainly not a story that provides any role model for those who should question authority.

But Santa's cause is good, yes? He distributes gifts to children on the basis of their good behavior. This, perhaps, is what O'Reilly sees as

Christmas instilling virtue. Surely it is a good thing to reward those who are good, but we must be aware of how rewards influence the psychology of those receiving them. Such a repeated and advertised reward (and punishment) system makes doing good no longer intrinsically motivating, but a means to the end of appeasing a bearded saint or sadist who knows when you deserve presents or paddlings. "Be good, for goodness sake!" in the Christmas carol should be loosely rendered, "Be good, or else!"

Santa mythology, then, promotes a psychology wherein slaves who can be bought off for their submission are the ideal. And the mythology of Jesus' birth is simply poor writing promoting credulity (not even faith). We would not want to teach these myths to children as stories that edify or improve their character, as it is clear that they do not do so on their own merits. The only reason anyone would think either story should be taught at all is that they are true. And I believe they have about equal evidence, and this is a significant point, especially for people who are serious Christians. The two Christmas myths are often told alongside each other and children are encouraged to believe both. The problem is that at least one of them, the manger myth, is clearly false, and even Christians, the very people telling the stories, recognize it. I believe that Christians should have two serious qualms about the Santa myth simply on the basis of their religious commitments.

First, Santa myths verge on blasphemy, if not outright idolatry. Santa is morally omniscient – he knows all ethically relevant facts about all agents. He also knows about your sleep habits.

> He knows if you are sleeping, he knows if you're awake.
> He knows if you've been bad or good, so be good
>   for goodness sake!

These are god-like powers. He performs miracles: he can fly (or controls flying reindeer), provides a bounty of presents that rivals (and bests, in my opinion) Jesus' miracle of the loaves and the fishes, and seems to have the capacity to travel at amazing speed to deliver the bounty. Being a saint is one thing, but these are the works of a demi-god. Now, remember that the first commandments deal with the exclusivity of worshipping and recognizing only one god, that is God:

> You shall have no other god to set against me. You shall not make a carved image for yourself nor the likeness of anything in the heavens above or on the earth below or in the waters under the earth.[8]

SCOTT F. AIKEN

Santa myth-making sounds like crafting a god, and teaching it to children as the truth about another god-like being certainly sounds like teaching them to recognize and worship a second god. If exclusive recognition and worship of God is the demand of the commandments, then promoting Santa mythology as anything true is the promotion of idolatry. Santa mythology makes idolators of children, and Christian parents should worry about that.

A second reason why Christian parents should worry about Santa mythology is that they know it is a false story of miracles. They teach their children to believe it, and when the children grow old enough to figure out the deception, parents often laugh it off. And we positively worry about children who continue to believe in Santa into adolescence. Imagine a thirteen year old really believing all the stuff about Rudolph or asking questions about what Santa does with the rest of the year. Santa is for young, gullible children. But Christians have another story of miracles to tell, and that story is supposed to be true. Christian parents, then, have two similarly unbelievable stories, and one they expect their children to grow out of (and are disappointed if they don't) and another they expect their children never to grow out of (and are disappointed if they do). On the one hand, telling the Santa story undercuts the necessary requirements of testimonial authority to confirm the truth about miracles. If you were to hear that some miracle occurred, but know that your source of information also gave you information about bogus miracles, then you would be unjustified in relying on his testimony. Santa mythology, the knowledge that it is false, and the expectation that children will grow out of it actually undercut parents' authority to teach the gospel as true. From a theological perspective, Santa mythology is a really bad idea.

In the end, I reject the Christian theological perspective. The incarnation and trinity seem to me category errors, and Jesus himself is a shoddy exemplar. He heals the sick, but does not provide cures for sickness. He raised the dead, but does not give us any means for preventing premature death. He could have at least also brought the good news of soap, personal hygiene, and the value of ensuring that water is clean. When given a chance to do some philosophy with Pilate, who asks him "What is truth?," he seems to just clam up. Not so good for someone who purports to have the wisdom of God. And worst of all, he has absolutely no sense of proportion when it comes to punishment. He promises eternal damnation for those who fail to live up to his teachings. And, according to Mark, eternal damnation is to be put into a "fire that never goes out," by an *unquenchable* fire. Why must it be an "eternal fire," as Matthew has it? No matter how bad a person has been, that person has only done *finite evil*. Why punish someone with *infinite punishment*? No matter how much someone deserves severe punishment – perhaps a really good spanking, a large fine, and community service – that punishment, if proportioned to the offense, will end. But divine punishment never ends. Never. The punishment should fit the crime, and Jesus promises punishment that infinitely exceeds it. And he is thereby spiteful and clearly unjust. I wouldn't celebrate his birthday any more than I would Hitler's, Pol Pot's, or Stalin's.

This has not been an argument that Christmas should be banned. People may participate however they want in whatever religious festivals they want, so long as they do not desire that the government subsidize it or that it be used as a tool for proselytizing children. This has been an argument that Christmas neither needs a defense nor does it deserve one.

NOTES

1 Patrick Buchanan, "Christianophobia," WorldNetDaily Commentary, December 13, 2004. Available online at www.worldnetdaily.com/news/article.asp?ARTICLE_ID=41900.
2 Peter Schafer, *Jesus in the Talmud* (Princeton: Princeton University Press, 2007).
3 John Gibson, *The War on Christmas* (New York: Sentinel, 2005), p. 15.
4 Ibid., p. 20.
5 Bruce E. Hunsberger and Bob Altenmeyer, *Atheists: A Groundbreaking Study of America's Nonbelievers* (Amherst: Prometheus Books, 2006), pp. 73–4.
6 Gibson, *The War on Christmas*, p. 184.
7 Transcript from *The Factor*, November 18, 2005. Available online at www.mediamatters.org/items/200511210003.
8 Exodus 20:3–4.

CHAPTER 5

CHRISTMAS MYTHOLOGIES
Sacred and Secular

 On December 24th and 25th every year two very different stories are told: one in people's homes, by the fireplace or Christmas tree, to pyjamaed but excited and sleepless children; the other to people of all ages in the more imposing setting of candlelit churches and cathedrals. Does the telling of these two stories have anything in common? What can we learn by comparing them? The first one, the one I call the "secular" mythology, is the story of Father Christmas. The second, "sacred" mythology is the religious reason why Christmas was ever celebrated *as* Christmas at all. Although the figure of Santa partly originated in an early Christian bishop (and partly in pagan figures), he has these days become rather more secularized – even, for some, a symbol of secular commercialism. I want to compare these two mythologies as they might effect the way in which we think about Christmas today. Philosophical reflection along these lines will allow us to draw some interesting conclusions relevant to theology and religious belief.

Do Christmas Mythologies Even Exist?

First of all, I'm assuming that the stories I'm dealing with here *are* "mythologies." What exactly do I mean by that? And can this assumption be defended? Isn't it possible to compare our sacred and secular stories without bringing in the idea of mythology at all? For instance, some people would suggest that the Christian story of the birth of Jesus Christ and the story told to children about Santa are similar in that they both involve equally unbelievable claims. You can imagine an atheist dismissing the "childishness" of religious people by likening their beliefs to a child's belief in the man who comes down her chimney on Christmas Eve delivering presents. The belief that Jesus was conceived by a virgin and born to her in a Bethlehem stable is no more credible than the belief in a quasi-omniscient, quasi-omnipotent man with a white beard and a sack who manages to get round every good child's house in one night. The only difference between them is that we (usually) stop believing in Santa when we've grown up. By this time the weight of evidence against his existence has become too great to allow us to carry on believing in him. Religious people, on the other hand, often carry on believing in the virginal conception of Jesus into adulthood, old age, even until death, despite the lack of evidence in favor of these beliefs (or even positive evidence to the contrary). In the child's case, there may be a traumatic realization when, in pretended sleep on Christmas Eve, she sees her parents creeping into her room with armfuls of presents instead of Santa with his trademark sack. There may be a painful shift in her worldview as something that she may have suspected for some time is confirmed – Santa doesn't exist! Perhaps, in the atheist's best-case scenario, a few of the more enlightened religious people will experience something similar in relation to their own beliefs, as did the English writer Edmund Gosse (1849–1928).

In his autobiography, Gosse recalls his father telling him as a child about the sin of idolatry, of worshipping anything other than God. Gosse Senior tells the young Edmund that "God would be very angry, and would signify His anger, if any one, in a Christian country, bowed down to wood and stone."[1] Edmund decides to test the matter out for himself. He hoists a small chair onto a table, kneels down in front of it and loudly says his daily prayer, "substituting the address 'O Chair!' for the habitual one."[2] He anxiously awaits the result of his heresy:

> God would certainly exhibit his anger in some terrible form, and would chastise my impious and wilful action. I was very much alarmed, but still more excited; I breathed the high, sharp air of defiance. But nothing happened; there was not a cloud in the sky, not an unusual sound in the street. Presently I was quite sure that nothing would happen. I had committed idolatry, flagrantly and deliberately, and God did not care.[3]

For the atheist, an experience like this should prepare the way for us to "grow up" and realize that religious belief, like the story of Santa, is a collection childish fictions, inappropriate to adult life. There is just not enough evidence to justify either belief. But, if this is so, why do parents still persist in telling their children about Santa if belief in him is nothing more than an irrationality that they'll just have to abandon in later life? Clearly, the parents themselves can't believe that Santa exists, since they're the ones who buy the presents. And if it were as simple as a choice between the truth and falsity of the story, the parents would opt for the "false" option every time and the story of Santa would have died out long ago. Why hasn't it died out?

The Secular Christmas Mythology: The Santa Story

One popular answer to this question suggests that it might be helpful to think of our Christmas stories, sacred and secular, as *mythologies*. Some parents recognize that, although the story of Santa isn't factually or liter-ally true, it's a "nice story" which communicates something deeper than just information about where the presents come from. Perhaps the figure of Santa embodies "the spirit of Christmas," the altruistic sentiments which motivate parents to buy presents for their children. The French thinker Roland Barthes (1915–80) claimed that the proper way to respond to myths is to disregard the facts "except inasmuch as they are endowed with significance."[4] And this is precisely what parents do when they tell their children about Santa without believing in him themselves. The story isn't a just a way of explaining who put the presents under the tree (wouldn't it be less misleading, and simpler, if the parents just admit-ted to this themselves?). It's a way of bringing out the significance or meaning that Christmas has in family life. It's about altruism, selfless-ness, love, and so on. The mythological figure of Santa embodies the selfless kindness that Christmas is supposed to be all about. Whether he actually exists or not is beside the point.

With the German philosopher Hans-Georg Gadamer (1900–2002), we can go further than this. If the secular Christmas story *is* a mytho-logy, then proof that Santa exists would destroy the point of telling it. The answer to the question "Why do you tell your Children the story of Santa?" would then simply be "Because he exists, of course." The story would then be told not because it communicates something of the meaning of Christmas but because it communicates facts about what happens on Christmas Eve. On the other hand, a myth, for Gadamer, is made true by nothing other than the act of telling it. If the story of Santa could be proven to be true by pointing to evidence, to states of affairs outside the story (Santa actually coming down the chimney, for example), it would not really be a myth. In Gadamer's view, "the only good definition of myth is that *myth neither requires nor includes any possible verification outside of itself*."[5]

On this view, the fact that Santa most probably doesn't exist adds weight to the case that his story is a myth. But this argument doesn't involve the claim that it's logically impossible for Santa to exist. It's always possible, if rather unlikely, that he might come down my own chimney *next* year. What I want to suggest is that, as a mythology, it wouldn't be this evidence for Santa's existence that would make the story worth telling, but the significance that the story embodies simply by being told. When we are dealing in mythologies, we should heed the journalists' dictum and "never let the facts get in the way of a good story." Whether or not Santa exists, and whatever the strength of the evidence in either direction, this question is irrelevant to the meaning that Santa has for the children who are told the story year in, year out. And this might be one reason why parents continue to tell the story every year, even though they don't believe in its literal or factual truth. They do so in order to communicate this meaning, internal to the story itself. This is what makes it a Christmas mythology, on Gadamer's view.

A Sacred Christmas Mythology: The Virginal Conception

Theologians have long thought about aspects of the sacred Christmas mythology, the story of the virginal conception of Christ, for example, along similar lines. In the Jewish tradition, miraculous conceptions sometimes took place when angels impregnated human beings.[6] The Christian story follows this tradition, but with some differences. When Gabriel appears to Mary and tells her that she will conceive a son, the author of Luke's Gospel is keen to make it clear that he keeps his distance and that it's not him but the Holy Spirit that will cause Mary to conceive. Just to hammer the point home, the name "Gabriel" even means "strong man of God." So the story of the virginal conception has a point or meaning which can be considered quite separately from the question of its factual accuracy. The story is also intimately bound up with the history of our culture. This point was made some years ago by the Archbishop of Canterbury, Rowan Williams, when he pointed out that there was no biblical basis for the image of the three kings. He said that anything other than the idea that an unspecified number of wise men or priests came from somewhere outside the Roman Empire was "legend," but that "It works quite well as legend."[7] In medieval art, these people became kings to emphasize the importance of Jesus, his "royalty." There were three of them: one European, one Asian, and one African, each representing one of the three continents of the Old World. One was young, one middle-aged, and one elderly, each representing one of the stages of human life. It's very unlikely that this is what actually happened, and it's not reported in the Bible, but the story is told in this way to make the point that Jesus is significant or meaningful to all humanity regardless of race or age. The story is presented in works of art and it takes on a cultural significance that forces us to think outside the confines of literal fact. T. S. Eliot described culture as "the incarnation (so to speak) of the religion of a people."[8] It's when we think not in terms of facts but of meanings and of significance that religion takes flesh, as it were, and its abstract ideas are clothed in concrete forms and symbols in texts, paintings and sculptures.

The Problem of Literal Truth

Despite this similarity between our two mythologies, that they both *are* mythologies, it seems that there is a very major difference which was anticipated by our atheist critic of both of them. In the case of the Santa mythology, belief in its literal truth is something that we typically grow out of in adulthood. But this doesn't seem to be the case with the sacred mythology. I've been arguing that, as a mythology, the significance of the story of Christ's birth can be considered separately from the question of its literal truth. Typically, however, religious people are committed to both. It's *because* Jesus was God incarnate, they think, that he was born of a virgin. If Jesus *was* God, it shouldn't be surprising that the circumstances surrounding his birth were peculiar. The peculiarity of these circumstances doesn't just convey a deeper mythological message about the significance that Jesus has for Christians. It may also, for the theologian, constitute evidence that Jesus was, in fact, divine.

But the philosopher will ask at this point whether the weight of evidence is convincing. David Hume (1711–76) argued that when it comes to any miracle which breaks a law of nature (the virginal conception being a good example) the evidence will, by definition, never be persuasive.[9] This is because the weight of evidence will always be greater in favor of the natural law than against it. An observation about the world (even one that's made regularly) is only ever formulated into a natural law when the weight of evidence is in favor of it. We know from experience that children generally aren't conceived by virgins, just as we know from experience that the sun rises every morning. But as with any general rule formulated from experience, it's not logically impossible that there might be exceptions. A virgin might possibly have conceived two thousand years ago. It's possible that one might do so tomorrow, in just the way that it's possible that, tomorrow, the sun should fail to rise or that it failed to rise two thousand years ago. (Incidentally, one book of the Bible reports that the sun stood still in the sky for a whole day.)[10] But what we do have to go on here is the balance of probability. Every time we wake up with the sun streaming through our bedroom window, and on every new day that virgins don't suffer from morning sickness, the weight of evidence increases in favor of the general rules that the sun rises every morning and that virgins don't have babies. As this happens, the probability of there being nights that last for 48 hours or virginal conceptions steadily diminishes, though it never reaches the state of being logically impossible.

The philosopher's aim is to discover what's rational to believe, what can be justified by evidence or argument and to think as clearly as possible about the ideas which she's dealing with. Clearly, on Hume's view, it's irrational to believe in the literal truth of religious claims like the virginal conception on the basis of the weight of evidence. And here is a similarity between the sacred and secular mythologies. We admitted earlier that it's always possible that Santa might exist and that, *next* year, he might come down the chimney. But, in the face of the evidence, it is so unlikely that, for practical purposes, it's not rational to believe it. And, for practical purposes, most adults behave as though Santa does not exist. If they behaved as though he did, they would most likely have some very disappointed children on Christmas morning, *sans* presents! I would argue that it is no more rational to believe in the literal truth of the sacred mythology than it is to believe in the secular one. It's more rational to trust our repeated observation that virgins don't have children than the reports of only two of the four gospel writers (50 percent of them) that

GUY BENNETT-HUNTER

there was at least one exception to this law two thousand years ago. Just because we can never be absolutely certain that Santa doesn't exist or that virginal conceptions are impossible doesn't make it any more rational to believe in it, or to behave as if it were true.

The Philosophical Case Against Literal Truth: Russell's Teapot

The Cambridge philosopher Bertrand Russell (1872–1970) gives us a famous illustration of this thought, dubbed "Russell's Teapot." In his quintessentially English tone, he writes:

> If I were to suggest that between the Earth and Mars there is a china teapot revolving about the sun in an elliptical orbit, nobody would be able to disprove my assertion provided I were careful to add that the teapot is too small to be revealed even by our most powerful telescopes. But if I were to go on to say that, since my assertion cannot be disproved, it is an intolerable presupposition on the part of human reason to doubt it, I should rightly be thought to be talking nonsense.[11]

Russell draws an analogy with religious beliefs, illustrating that, in the absence of evidence, the burden of proof is not upon the skeptic or doubter but on the believer. It's the absence of evidence that causes the believer to rely on the (sound) argument that these beliefs can't be entirely disproved because new evidence might always turn up. The teapot is too small to be observed with the current technology, but it's always possible that, one day, we might invent a telescope powerful enough to detect it. But for every new, more powerful, telescope that's invented, and whose gaze the teapot still eludes, the believer can always argue that the teapot is still too small and the telescope still not powerful enough. But the probability that the teapot exists at all and will be revealed by our next telescope, that Santa will come down my chimney next year, and that there will one day be evidence to support the idea of a virginal conception, are all on the same level. They are all extremely improbable and the fact that they can't be disproved doesn't make it any more rational to believe.

Russell called himself an agnostic rather than an atheist because he recognized that it was not impossible for God to exist and that it would be equally irrational flatly to rule out his existence, since good evidence for it might turn up at any time. However, the improbability of God's existence led him to a point not far removed from atheism:

> An agnostic may hold that the existence of God, though not impossible, is very improbable; he may even hold it so improbable that it is not worth considering in practice. In that case, he is not far removed from atheism ... he is, for practical purposes, at one with the atheists.[12]

Interestingly, it was this agnosticism about God's existence which made Russell skeptical about our sacred Christmas mythology. He thought that, since the virginal conception depended on the idea of a God who brought it about, his practical atheism also entailed an attitude of skepticism towards that mythology.[13]

The Religious Case Against Literal Truth: Tillich's Broken Myths

So much for philosophy! It turns out that, from a philosophical perspective, it's no more rational to believe in the literal truth of the sacred mythology than it is to believe in the literal truth of the Santa story. But I want to suggest that there are other, religious reasons *not* to believe in the literal truth of religious mythologies such as the virginal conception of Jesus. As we saw earlier, their status as mythologies implies that questions about their religious significance and about their literal truth can be considered quite independently. So it follows that it's possible to reject the literal truth of the mythology, without also rejecting its religious significance, and not contradict oneself.

The theologian Paul Tillich (1886–1965) argued that there are very powerful religious reasons to disbelieve the literal truth of sacred mythologies, including our Christmas one.[14] For Tillich, myths are present in every act of faith and they use material from ordinary experience to make a point about divine things which are beyond the scope of ordinary experience. If God is truly ultimate, then he is beyond time and space. But any story about God, about him intervening in human history or interfering with the laws of nature, draws him into the human framework of time and space which, as God, he is infinitely beyond. Tillich even thinks that to speak of God at all is to draw him into time and space so that any expression of faith inevitably misrepresents God, depriving him of his ultimacy

GUY BENNETT-HUNTER

or majesty. He argues that Christian mythologies (including the Christmas one, "the virgin birth of the Messiah") require what theologians clumsily call "demythologization."[15] This doesn't mean getting rid of the mythology altogether. Mythologies, as Barthes saw, are always part of the human consciousness. One mythology can be replaced with another, but mythology *per se* can't be totally removed from humanity's spiritual life.

Instead, demythologization means the recognition that the sacred mythology *is* a mythology (not verifiable by anything external to itself, like evidence) but without removing or replacing it. It then becomes what Tillich (rather oddly) calls a "broken myth," a myth which is recognized as a myth. It's important to note that he sees a broken myth as a *good* thing so, contrary to what we might at first think, the phrase isn't meant simply to describe a myth that doesn't work properly. The religious reason for "breaking" the myth, explicitly revealing its mythological status, is the first of the Ten Commandments against idolatry. If the myth were thought to be literally true (or "unbroken") God would be thought of as a highest being who is still a part of the human world (albeit a very big, or the supreme, part of that world). It's only as part of the worldly chain of cause and effect that we can explain God's intervention with our Christmas miracle, for example. But since God, for Tillich, is infinitely beyond the chain of cause and effect, it would be idolatrous to worship a part of the world instead of him. As Tillich writes, "Faith, if it takes its symbols literally, becomes idolatrous! It calls something ultimate which is less than ultimate" by drawing God into the human world of time and space.[16] Therefore, it's not the rational philosophical criticism of the mythology, like Hume's and Russell's, which carries most weight, but the "inner religious criticism."[17] Both criticisms put together are devastating for the idea that we should believe in the factual accuracy or literal truth of the sacred Christmas mythology.

Tillich describes the potential religious resistance to this criticism at both individual and institutional levels:

> Those who live in an unbroken mythological world feel safe and certain. They resist, often fanatically, any attempt to introduce an element of uncertainty by "breaking the myth".... [S]uch resistance is supported by authoritarian systems, religious or political, in order to give security to the people under their control and unchallenged power to those who exercise the control.[18]

This resistance is often expressed as an attitude of literalism to the mythology. In the case of our Christmas example, "the virgin birth of the

Messiah is understood in biological terms" and the creation of the world is taken for a "magic act."[19] Not only does this kind of interpretation make God just another part of the human world (for whose existence there is no convincing evidence), but it also gets in the way of the symbolic and non-literal character of the mythology which is their real "truth and power."[20] It detracts from the way in which these stories help to make sense of the lives of religious believers by turning the world into a place which was visited at Christmas by the Son of God. If the truth of this idea doesn't lie in anything outside of the story, then it can't be expressed in any other way than through the story itself. The sacred mythology actually inaugurates or creates the religious significance of Christ as the incarnation of a mysterious God in the human world. And this significance is not necessarily dependent on the factual circumstances surrounding the birth of Jesus of Nazareth. In fact, if the story is a mythology, then it can't be dependent on these circumstances. Although the balance of probability might suggest that these circumstances weren't miraculous, we can never be totally certain of this. We must always be open to the theoretical possibility that they were.

Sacred mythologies are not trying to explain why the world is as it is any more than the point of the secular mythology of Santa is to explain how the presents appear under the tree or in a Christmas stocking. And once we have realized that neither of the mythologies is an especially good explanation of the facts, it's sometimes hard to see how they could have any value at all. But once the child realizes that Santa doesn't exist, and perhaps after a period of entirely dismissing the story as nonsense, they may begin to see a very different kind of value in it. They may begin to see the secular mythology as "broken"; not factually accurate but no less valuable for that. And they may one day tell the story to their own children for just this reason. If Tillich is right about the sacred mythology, the analogous experience of the young Edmund Gosse is not the end of the story, but the beginning. It's the realization of the "broken" nature of the myth; a realization that its literal and factual accuracy must be sacrificed for a kind of truth that's far more valuable because it can't be communicated in any other way. That is why the mythology can't simply be abandoned. My suggestion is that we should look at the sacred Christmas mythology in the same way as we look at the secular one: we don't need to believe in some rather outlandish claims to justify telling it to our children. The belief that the sacred mythology is any more literally true than the secular one has some serious criticism to contend with, both philosophical and religious, and that belief actually gets in the way

GUY BENNETT-HUNTER

of its more profound meaning and significance. This is so in just the way that literal belief in Santa gets in the way of the true significance of Christmas which he embodies. But literal belief is, in both cases, a necessary stage on the journey towards seeing the sacred and secular Christmas mythologies for the "broken myths" that they are. It's a ladder that, once we have climbed, we must kick away.

NOTES

1 E. Gosse, *Father and Son* (Oxford: Oxford University Press, 2004), p. 31.
2 Ibid.
3 Ibid.
4 R. Barthes, *Mythologies*, ed. and trans. A. Lavers (London: Paladin, 1973), p. 110.
5 H.-G. Gadamer, "Religious and Poetical Speaking," in A. M. Olson (ed.) *Myth, Symbol and Reality* (Notre Dame: University of Notre Dame Press, 1980), pp. 86–98.
6 See, for example, Genesis 6:4.
7 R. Gledhill, "It's All a Christmas Tall Story," *The Times*, December 20, 2006.
8 T. S. Eliot, *Notes Towards the Definition of Culture* (London: Faber and Faber, 1948), p. 28.
9 D. Hume, "Of Miracles," in *Enquiries Concerning the Human Understanding and Concerning the Principles of Morals* [1777], ed. L. A. Selby-Bigge (Oxford: Clarendon Press, 1966), pp. 109–31.
10 Joshua 10:12–14.
11 B. Russell, "Is there a God?" [1952], in J. G. Slater (ed.) *The Collected Papers of Bertrand Russell, Vol. 11: Last Philosophical Testament 1943–68* (London: Routledge, 1997), pp. 542–8.
12 B. Russell, "What is an Agnostic?" [1953], in J. G. Slater (ed.) *The Collected Papers of Bertrand Russell, Vol. 11: Last Philosophical Testament 1943–68* (London: Routledge, 1997), pp. 549–57.
13 Ibid., p. 552.
14 P. Tillich, *Dynamics of Faith* (London: George Allen and Unwin, 1957), pp. 48ff.
15 Ibid., p. 50.
16 Ibid., p. 52.
17 Ibid.
18 Ibid., p. 51.
19 Ibid., pp. 52, 51.
20 Ibid., p. 53.

CHAPTER 6

THE SIGNIFICANCE OF CHRISTMAS FOR LIBERAL MULTICULTURALISM

Christmas worries some multiculturalists. It shouldn't worry those who are also liberals. Indeed, Christmas can play a small, but significant, role in creating and maintaining a well-ordered, secular, liberal, multicultural society. A multiculturalist is a person who would like to see her society become or remain a multicultural society, a society, that is, that gathers together different cultures and communities within a continuous geographical area and a single political state. Some multiculturalists, in advocating multiculturalism for their societies, would ban Christmas decorations and celebrations from public places. That is, they would ban Christmas from spaces under government control, such as government offices, court houses, and public parks. And they would strongly discourage owners of shopping malls, gas stations, stores, and the like from putting up displays or playing Christmas music. They would do so because they think that to honor Christmas publicly is to privilege a particular tradition, and the constellation of values associated with that tradition, over all the other traditions and constellations of values current in their multicultural society. Privileging that one tradition, they add, disparages other holidays or traditions of celebration, and that, in turn, marginalizes or excludes everyone for whom Christmas is alien. Those who celebrate Christmas should certainly be free to do so, these multiculturalists insist, but they should do so in their own houses or meeting places and on their own time.

Multiculturalists who would ban Christmas from public life might not apply the same reasoning to Chanukah, Muharram, Kwanzaa, or other celebrations or observances that often occur during the Christmas season. Christmas is a mainstream or majority celebration in their societies, while these others belong to minority cultural, ethnic, or religious groups, and that makes a difference. In contemporary multicultural societies, Christmas overshadows these other celebrations or observances. Because these other celebrations and observances exist within minority traditions, shopkeepers, libraries, and municipalities would do well to honor them with displays or greetings. People from minority cultural, ethnic, or religious groups will feel valued and at home were they to note that people in the wider society recognize their celebrations and observances. Perhaps, in time, as people in a society become more aware of other holidays and celebrations, holidays and celebrations outside their own traditions, we could begin again to acknowledge Christmas publicly, for then it would take its place as one among many special times to acknowledge and appreciate in public life. It would no longer dominate other traditions and marginalize their adherents.

Those who propose that Christmas take its place as just one among many sectarian celebrations have overlooked something important, though. They have overlooked the fact that Christmas is not an exclusively Christian holiday any more. For at least three or four generations now, even before the recent waves of immigration and the advent of multiculturalism, Christmas has been evolving into a secular holiday. Nowadays, Christmas is, for many of us, a holiday that has no religious significance at all. In Canada, the United States, Great Britain – in any contemporary multicultural society – millions of people celebrate and enjoy Christmas with nary a religious thought. Christmas, for both the Christians and non-Christians who honor it, is a celebration of good will, generosity, and peace among nations. It is a time to appreciate and enjoy the company of family and friends. Children, of course, are central to Christmas – a great lot of Christmas traditions are devoted to creating fun and excitement for children, and adults get a kick out of seeing the kids enjoying themselves. None of this need have any connection to religion, and for many people none of it does.

Now, for the Christians among us, Christmas marks the birth of Jesus, so it is also an occasion for worship. But it isn't any such occasion for the rest of us. And while the activities and symbols through which we honor and celebrate good will, generosity, peace, family, friends, and children derive from Christian traditions, they now have a life of their own independent of those traditions. Christmas trees, wreaths, colored lights, candy canes, carols and Christmas music, sleigh rides, presents, Santa Claus – though all of them have their origin in Christian traditions (or, at least, have come to us via Christian traditions), they don't put us in mind of any values or doctrines specifically Christian or religious.

The fact that for many who celebrate it, Christmas is an entirely secular holiday, irks many Christians. They resent that the symbols and practices by which they celebrate the birth of Christ and worship God have, for many people, lost the meanings that they have for Christians. Many Christians are not pleased that there are two holidays that go by the name "Christmas," one that has religious significance and one that doesn't. That the two holidays resemble each other in very many ways has a perfectly simple historical explanation: secular Christmas evolved from religious Christmas as religion declined through the generations. Interestingly, many of the multiculturalists who oppose public Christmas displays are Christians. For them, not only are public celebrations of Christmas insensitive to the non-Christian faithful, but they also confirm and extend the existence of non-religious Christmas. Their opposition to Christmas in the public square has two sources. It stems both from their multiculturalism and from their desire to restore a purely Christian Christmas.

We should note that those of us who celebrate and enjoy secular Christmas agree with the Christians that Christmas is prone to corruption. That corruption goes by the name of commercialization. Secular Christmas is about good will, generosity, peace, and children (it's about everything that religious Christmas is about, save religion); it's not about shopping or outdoing the neighbor's display of lights and ornaments. That's not to deny, of course, the importance that both shopping and lights have in the whole of the celebration, but it is to acknowledge the danger they can pose to the holiday when left unchecked. Christians who take a proprietary interest in Christmas are wrong to think that without religion at its center, Christmas must degenerate into a frenzy of shopping, but they are right that plenty of forces conspire to push it away from the values at its center.

Christmas, to repeat, is for many who celebrate it an entirely secular holiday, devoid of religious significance. So if public displays of Christmas trees or greetings of "Merry Christmas!" privilege some people or exclude others, it is not in virtue of their privileging Christianity or excluding non-Christians. Moreover, what we honor and celebrate at Christmas and through such things as Christmas trees, gift giving, and greetings of

"Merry Christmas!" – good will, generosity, peace, family, friends, children – are important in many traditions and ways of life current in multicultural societies. These values have wide and deep appeal.

Still, a multiculturalist might respond that though it is for many in her society a secular holiday that honors values to which almost everyone subscribes, Christmas is *someone's* particular celebration of these values and, so, maybe not someone else's. Christmas, secular Christmas, is a *particular* tradition of celebrating those values. And that fact brings us to the question what sort of multicultural society we would like ours to be.

We ought to distinguish between two sorts of multiculturalism that can be embodied in a society, *liberal* multiculturalism and *communitarian* multiculturalism. A liberal multicultural society is one that takes the individual person as the basic social unit and his or her flourishing as central to questions of social and political arrangements. A communitarian multicultural society is one that takes groups of people or cultures as basic social units and the wellbeing or rights of groups as central to questions of social and political arrangements. Christmas, as a secular holiday, can play a role in creating and maintaining a liberal multicultural society. But why should ours be a liberal multicultural society, or even multicultural in the first place?

Liberal multiculturalism is a wonderful thing – something to enjoy for its own sake and something to protect and extend. To see why, let us think for a moment about diversity, something which many who identify themselves as multiculturalists seem to cherish, but which, at least as I think, is something to which we should be indifferent. Diversity is not something that should matter to us one way or the other. For many people, the terms "multiculturalism" and "diversity" are synonymous. So let me explain the distinction I mean to mark by them. A liberal multicultural society is one in which people are free and able to live as members of the cultures with which they identify. To be liberally multicultural, then, a society cannot place barriers between people and the ways of life they wish to live. It must be a society that respects wide freedoms of thought and expression and assembly, and it must respect freedom of movement, freedom of dress, and freedom of manners. That is, it must be organized to honor traditional liberal values. But not only must a society, if it is to be multicultural, not interfere with people's choices how to live. It must also help people to live the lives they choose. That is, it must provide plenty of public space in which people can come together, it must support media such as newspapers and television programs, through which the people of a culture can talk to each other and to people outside their groups, it must support minority tastes in food, dress, education, recreation, and the rest. Without such help, social, political, and economic pressures might well push a society toward cultural homogeneity against the wishes of its people.

Diversity, on the other hand, is about having in each public realm people from many of the different cultural groups present in the society at large. Diversity in the workplace, then, consists in white, brown, and black people, men and women, straights and gays, atheists and Christians, people of Lebanese heritage and people of Ecuadorian heritage, old and young, working together in the same building or factory. Diversity in the university or in the classroom consists in people of lots of different types and cultures learning together. To support diversity in jobs, housing, education, and the rest, one must actively recruit and promote people from groups underrepresented in each particular sector of a society. Each university or fire department or softball league is at its best, for one who values diversity, when it reflects in the make-up of its members the demographic make-up of the larger society in which it is found.

A commitment to liberal multiculturalism comes directly as an expression of a commitment to three fundamental values. Those of us who value respect for individuals as individuals, who value equality before the law and equality of opportunity, and who value decency must be strongly committed to multiculturalism. We express our respect for individuals as individuals by acknowledging that their ends are as significant to them as our ends are to us and, then, by refraining from manipulating them as they pursue their ends. We express our respect for equality of opportunity by requiring that all public positions be available to anyone on the basis of fair criteria alone. Decency has to do with allowing another person's hardship or pain to take precedence over one's mere inconvenience or discomfort. We are decent when we do not hoard what others can use to make their lives better or when rather than use our resources to indulge our small desires we contribute them to alleviating suffering. If we respect others, we will leave them free to pursue whatever way of life they will; if we are also decent, we will happily contribute resources toward enabling each of us to live as he or she will. That is why we value multiculturalism. We want people to live as they will and we want that they have what they need to live as they will.

So why, then, would one value diversity? What reason could one have for thinking diversity itself a worthy goal to pursue? Partisans of diversity offer instrumental reasons for valuing it, reasons for valuing diversity that take it to be a tool useful in realizing other ends. One is that diversity makes for a dynamic workplace, one able to respond well to challenges and opportunities. Likewise, diversity in the classroom leads to a better education for all through the clash of values and viewpoints. The evidence seems, though, to be that diversity costs businesses more money than it produces. And if the clash of viewpoints and values promotes education, then what is at work are the values and viewpoints themselves, not the differences in skin color or manners. But perhaps these instrumental reasons for valuing diversity do after all have merit. The question is one for economists and other social scientists to settle. They might discover that the costs are low and the benefits high. In any case, instrumental reasons for valuing diversity do not amount to reasons for thinking it valuable in itself. There doesn't seem to be any reason for valuing diversity for its own sake.

Now certainly a multicultural society will be, at least in most areas most of the time, a diverse society. A commitment to a multicultural society, because it is a commitment to respect, fairness, and decency, would lead to diverse workplaces and universities and other institutions. That a workplace or whatever does not reflect the cultures of the society as a whole can be taken, though only *prima facie*, as evidence of a lack of commitment to multiculturalism. But that through a commitment to multiculturalism each workplace and public institution became as diverse as the society as a whole would mean nothing one way or the other to those of us who value multiculturalism. What matters to us is that each person is making a life for him or herself as best as he or she can without interference and without surrendering her values or identity.

Perhaps this difference can be brought out by an example. Suppose that a partisan of diversity for its own sake and a partisan of multiculturalism for its own sake are together at a gathering – a public lecture, for instance, or a political rally or a parade or a concert or a restaurant. Let's suppose that each notices that there are very few black people present. The partisan of diversity thinks "this gathering should be more diverse. There should be more black people here." The partisan of multiculturalism, though, has a more complex thought. "Are there black people," she wonders, "who would enjoy what is happening here but who are not here? If so, what are the barriers preventing them from being here? Let us identify those barriers and bring them down. But maybe," she continues, "people who aren't here simply don't want to be here. Maybe they would rather be elsewhere, doing other things. In that case, are they able to gather to do what they want to do as easily as the people here were able to gather?" Her goal is that no one who wants to be somewhere be excluded from being there.

I indicated above that I can't see why one would value diversity for its own sake, and I noted that instrumental reasons for caring about diversity are doubtful. Even more, though, I worry that valuing diversity has bad consequences. What's at stake is whether we are to value people as individuals or to value them as representatives of a type. The liberal multiculturalist is concerned about people as individuals. She understands, of course, that for many of us our individual flourishing is intimately connected to the flourishing of others within the groups with which we identify. Nonetheless, it is your flourishing as the particular person you are that moves her. The partisan of diversity, on the other hand, looks at you and sees a representative of a group. It is the flourishing of your group that moves her. You yourself don't matter.

Before returning to Christmas, let us summarize our discussion of liberal multiculturalism and diversity. Liberal multiculturalism, stemming from respect, equality, and decency, upholds the worth of each individual person, as the individual person he or she is. Because individuals are who they are to a large extent in virtue of their identifying with one and another culture, multiculturalists are interested in protecting and advancing the different cultures within their societies, but only as a means towards individual flourishing. So where does Christmas enter into this? What reason have we to think that Christmas has a role to play in fostering and maintaining a liberal multicultural society? We can imagine a multicultural society in which no celebrations or holidays are public celebrations or holidays. There are, perhaps, statutory holidays, such that everyone gets off work the first Monday of every third month. Or maybe each of us just gets a certain number of days off work each year to take when she or he chooses, so that people can coordinate with others of their culture to celebrate together their own particular holidays. Each of us, in that system, congregates with others of her group when according to her traditions or authorities it's time to honor something, and we engage in whatever activities our particular tradition or authorities would have us engage in.

In the sort of multicultural society we are imagining, some cultural groups might invite outsiders to be with them on certain celebration days; perhaps some groups have a fair that anyone who wants to attend can attend. Other cultural groups might instead just have one of the elders write an article for the city newspaper describing that group and its ways, and explaining what that group is honoring. We find a lot of this sort of thing in our society today – articles by local imams, for instance, explaining Ramadan, or features on the Hindu festival Diwali.

Multiculturalists advocate devoting public money and public facilities to assist people in conducting their celebration or observance, and not only for the economic gain of attracting tourists or creating good will. So, in the sort of society we are imagining, though various cultural groups may well engage in one or another sort of outreach to other cultural groups and to the society as a whole, nevertheless no celebration is by everyone for everyone.

This would, I think, be what we would find in a society that embodies the principles and ideals of communitarian multiculturalism, the sort of multiculturalism that insists on the separateness of cultural groups and values cultural groups for the ways of life they represent rather than as modes through which individual people seek to flourish. The groups are separate, and there is no common identity as citizens of a society. Indeed, for the communitarian multiculturalist, a common identity is impossible – perhaps not in principle, but at least in practice in contemporary societies, given the wide differences in traditions, if not also in values, that mark such societies. What might seem a common identity would really be just another particular identity, though one that imposes itself upon others. For the communitarian multiculturalist, then, a common holiday is a threat, a threat to the integrity of particular cultural groups. A common holiday – that is, a common celebration, a holiday with a particular meaning and not just a day off for everyone could not but be an imposition by one cultural group on all the others.

In another sort of multicultural society, though, a *liberal* multicultural society, some holidays or celebrations *are* common, public events – events funded and organized by or through civil authorities acting on mandates from governments. These holidays would, of course, have to honor values important to most people in the country and to honor them in ways people from various cultures find congenial, or else they would attract few participants. In this second sort of multicultural society, a few holidays, maybe only two or three a year, belong to *all* the people. They are times when everyone gets together to enjoy themselves and to enjoy each other – and to enjoy themselves and each other through participating in common traditions. In a liberal multicultural society some celebrations will be common celebrations because a liberal multicultural society will feature a common, or at least widespread, public life. This common life will be based on the liberal ethos, the three values of respect for individuals, equality before the law and equality of opportunity, and decency. The common life will first of all, of course, be lived in and expressed by important social institutions: schools, government, work places, the law, and the courts. And yet secondary manifestations of it in, for instance, communal recreation and celebrations, will play an important role in solidifying the liberal ethos.

This sort of multicultural society, the liberal multicultural society, is much more attractive than the communitarian sort. There are two reasons why this is so. The first is simply that the communitarian multicultural society is apt to breed envy and rancor within itself. Each cultural group will be concerned for its own wellbeing and see other cultural groups as hostile toward it. Communitarian multicultural societies will be marked by the ills of identity politics and the cult of the victim. A communitarian society certainly might evolve political, legal, and social mechanisms to prevent it from falling apart and to enable it to function. But such a society will not be able to generate loyalty to or love of the society itself, given that these mechanisms won't touch the fact that each group is envious of what the others possess and jealous of its own property and resources.

The second reason why liberal multiculturalism is more attractive is that liberal values, and the ways of life that honor them, are attractive just in themselves. The people in a liberal multicultural society enjoy whatever group identities they have, just as do those in a communitarian society. They are free and welcome to honor their distinct identities. But they also see themselves as citizens of a country and view their neighbors as fellow citizens. In a communitarian multicultural society, people see themselves merely as residing among their neighbors, not as connected to them through projects of citizenship. On the other hand, in a liberal multicultural society, the political, legal, and social mechanisms that evolve in order to deal with disputes and conflicts will not represent merely a *modus vivendi*, a method of securing the peace. They will, instead, encourage loyalty and love, for these mechanisms will be expressions of respect, equality, and decency.

So what might a holiday that all of us celebrate together look like? What traditions and practices would be appropriate to a holiday whose values touch all the members of a liberal multicultural society? An obvious candidate is the secular holiday known as Christmas. If we want to have a few holidays that belong to all of us and that all of us can enjoy, I say we make Christmas one of them. Christmas has been evolving into a secular holiday for decades. Now, though, there's pressure from both Christians and communitarian multiculturalists to reverse the trend. Some people would have us say "Season's greetings" rather than "Merry Christmas," or to say nothing at all to those outside our particular cultural

MARK MERCER

groups. They would deny us Christmas trees in public areas and Christmas music in the shopping malls. Some of them think, wrongly, that Christmas in countries such as the United States and Canada is properly a Christian affair, and they want to preserve it for the Christians. Many of these people are Christians themselves, upset at what they see happening to their holy day. Others recognize that Christmas isn't only for Christians anymore, but then object to it on the grounds that it is still a particular tradition of a specific culture. They espouse a communitarian form of multiculturalism, in which any common tradition within a society must be symptom and cause of one culture's dominating others. Both the Christians and the communitarians would undo the good work people have done over the decades to transform Christmas into a celebration that's moving and fun for everyone in our multicultural societies. Willingly or not, these people are helping to make all celebrations in our various countries small, sectarian, private affairs. I say we instead take up the noble task of continuing to offer Christmas to all as a delightful secular holiday that we enjoy together and at which we honor values we all cherish.

Let us, then, say "Merry Christmas" to each other and decorate Christmas trees in public places. And let us explain to anyone who worries that our behavior will offend or exclude someone that while Christmas does have its origins in Christian traditions, and was once the property of a particular, majority culture, the Christmas we celebrate is not at all a Christian or a religious holiday or even a specific culture's holiday. Christmas now belongs to all of us, no one is excluded from it, it privileges no particular religious or other tradition. Secular Christmas, we will tell them, expresses the liberal values that underpin our multiculturalism.

CHAPTER 7

CRUMMY COMMERCIALS AND BB GUNS
Son-of-a-Bitch Consumerism in a Christmas Classic

Movies are philosophically interesting in that they are indicative of trends in specific cultures. Movies provide a microcosmic snapshot of a culture. Movies can act as a foil for society as a whole and by examining film we can assess people and their ways of life much as we do when reading a textbook. By looking at media produced by popular culture, we can view a breadth of views about a certain time period, place, or group of people. We would be remiss in discarding these points of view because of an esoteric resistance to popular culture. Movies have lessons to teach us just as any other media.

The cult classic *A Christmas Story* is a fine example of movies revealing an aspect of our culture. This movie shows us a trend that is becoming increasingly apparent in modern society. The discussion of the secularization of society is one that has been underway since this country's inception. But our society is not simply moving in the direction of a generically secular way of life; rather, the religion of this country is being replaced. Consumerism has become the new American religion. *A Christmas Story* is an example of how that consumerism mimics the role religion plays and has played in the lives of most Americans. Remarkable similarities exist between the two phenomena, both in mentality and in practice.

But there is an undesirable side to a transition of this sort. The reverence paid to a consumerist lifestyle is alarming, even if we are not concerned with the erosion of religion. By examining this trend in the context of virtue ethics, we are able to identify just what is so troublesome about the drive to consume. Still, as much as consumerism seems to be an unstoppable force, we can avoid its overtaking our lives. With some help from the movie, we can see that the trends of society are not necessarily the trends that must be realized in our individual lives. The family in *A Christmas Story* is able to go in a different direction, as can we.

"Christmas is here. Lovely, glorious, beautiful Christmas ..."

For those unfamiliar with Jean Shepherd and Bob Clark's *A Christmas Story*[1] (1983) we will withhold our scorn and hopelessly try to capture some of its glory in a brief summary.[2] It is in this now truly American story that we find all of the makings for a genuine Christmas classic. *A Christmas Story* is set in the early 1940s and begins in the decked and garlanded, fictional downtown of Hohman, Indiana as an adult Ralphie (narrated by Shepherd) recalls a particularly memorable Christmas. We quickly meet the young Ralphie Parker who motivates the film with an unrelenting pursuit for the "holy grail" of Christmas presents: a Red Ryder air rifle. This interminable quest puts Ralphie at the center of a confluence of struggles with his parents, his teacher, Santa, and his neighbor's turkey-loving hounds. The fate of such a gift, however, constantly hangs in the balance. Around each turn and with every new possibility Ralphie is met with the persistent worry that he will shoot his eye out. Thus, as so many have come to cherish, the "glorious" *Christmas Story* ensues.

Ralphie's perilous journey begins with a modest adoration of Red Ryder and his "peacemaker" and an unassuming request from his mother for what he would like for Christmas. "Horrified, I heard myself blurt it out," adult Ralphie recalls, "I want an official Red Ryder carbine action 200-shot range model air rifle." Without a moment's hesitation his mother responds with the "classic mother-BB gun block ... 'You'll shoot your eye out!'" Although such a rejoinder is nearly "insurmountable," Ralphie quickly begins to "rebuild the dike" with his mother and turn his "BB gun mania" toward his teacher, Miss Shields.

In Miss Shields Ralphie finds a "light at the end of the black cave of doom" out of which he was looking. Miss Shields has given Ralphie's class a writing assignment with the theme, "What I Want for Christmas."

As the cogs in his young mind begin to turn, Ralphie believes when Miss Shields reads his "magnificent, eloquent, theme that she [will] sympathize with [his] plight [for the Red Ryder BB gun] and everything [will] work out." But unfortunately for Ralphie, Miss Shields ruthlessly expresses the same BB gun worry with a red "C+" and a "P.S. You'll shoot your eye out" for his theme. At last, Ralphie's "struggle for a way out of [his] impenetrable BB gun web" leads him to consider his last resort.

Ralphie's final hope to circumvent his mother's *irrational* worry rests in the hands of "the Big Man, the Head Honcho, the Connection" – Santa. Going to see Santa could not come fast enough for Ralphie, anxiously awaiting their auspicious meeting. When the fateful encounter finally comes, Ralphie stammers and forgets what he wanted for Christmas. Luckily, at the last moment he remembers, "I want an official Red Ryder carbine action 200-shot range model air rifle!" Alas, his last hope fades away as Santa utters the now all too familiar sentiments, "You'll shoot your eye out, kid." Then with a push from Santa's boot, Ralphie and his dreams of protecting his family from "insensate evil" end in a pillowy cotton snow at the bottom of Santa's mountain. But as we all know, the *Story* is not over. Christmas Eve passes quickly and Ralphie and his little brother, Randy, awake to a snow-covered Christmas morning. "Christmas had come, officially," adult Ralphie recalls. Wrapping paper begins to fly and the "cornucopia" of presents slowly recedes from around the tree without any signs of the Red Ryder BB gun. The reality begins to sink in to Ralphie. Until, urged by his Old Man, Ralphie discovers one last present in the corner. It is the Red Ryder BB gun! Eager to try out his new "blue steel beauty," Ralphie takes aim at a warped tin sign and pulls the trigger. "OH MY GOD, I SHOT MY EYE OUT!" Luckily, the shot merely broke his glasses. Though bad enough, this is only the beginning of a series of mishaps on what should have been the best of Christmas days.

While Ralphie is having his eye tended to by his unsuspecting mother, the smelly next-door neighbor Bumpass hounds ravish the Parker's Christmas turkey. The hounds destroy all hopes for the Parkers of having the traditional Christmas dinner. Not to be outdone, the Old Man summons his family to get dressed: "We are going out to eat." What could possibly be open on Christmas day but a Chinese restaurant? A Christmas, nonetheless, as adult Ralphie remembers it that "would live in our memories as the Christmas when we were introduced to Chinese turkey [and when] all was right with the world." Somehow, everything ended all right for the Parkers, though, there is more to be said about this truly American *Christmas Story*.[3]

"Some men are Baptists, others Catholics; my father was an Oldsmobile man"

A good deal of the nostalgic elements of *A Christmas Story* resonates in the hearts of millions of Americans. The film has such a universal appeal that one can wonder if the Parker family shares some Christmas ideal similar to that of most other Americans. So, we may ask, what is it that is really important to the Parkers about Christmas? Interestingly enough, we find a hint to this answer in the *absence* of a particularly common Christmas institution: religion. On the whole, the film itself only dares for a split second to enter into the religious history associated with Christmas.[4] As for the Parkers, the closest they come to associating religion with Christmas is adult Ralphie remembering his Old Man as an "Oldsmobile man." Strangely, in this same scene we hear the Old Man say, "That goddamned Olds is froze up again!" Surely those aren't the words of a religious man. Nor do those words bring about any real religious repugnance from the rest of the family.[5] We can only presume that this lack of concern simply corresponds to a lack of any real religious conviction in the Parker family. To be sure, we can go, exhaustively, a bit further.

As the film progresses, we are gradually introduced to more and more of the Parker home. From the space occupied by "electric sex gleaming out of the window" to Ralphie's decoding in the bathroom to the family meals in the kitchen, we can make sure that we have not overlooked any indication that the Parkers might in fact be religious. But, there are no such indications. There are no crosses and no Bibles or other religious symbols often associated with Christmas.[6] There is no obvious religion (in the classic sense) in the Parker family. Perhaps the absence of religion itself is one of those universally appealing elements in *A Christmas Story*. It cuts across whatever religious lines there might be. So, in attempting to figure out what the Parkers might share with most other Americans about what is important at Christmas, it seems that it is at least *not* religion. Consequently, as the summary above suggests, there is definitely a driving objective throughout the film to obtain the Red Ryder BB gun. It is to the nature of this objective that we will now turn our attention.

"There it is, the 'Holy Grail' of Christmas presents ..."

In the Parker family it is not necessarily the *absence* of religion that is so noticeable, but rather its replacement with a new American institution: consumerism. There can be no doubt that religion itself is becoming more commercialized; we have all seen television advertisements for the Latter Day Saints. A church near our hometown, in an attempt to fill seats in a period of lagging membership, decided to put a Starbucks coffee shop just inside its doors. This seems to be just another stop in the trend of commercialism writ large. These days every event has a corporate sponsor and product placement is everywhere from sitcoms to basketball games. As we become more exposed to media as a result of increased technology, we will be more exposed to, for lack of a better phrase, people trying to sell stuff. It seems naive to think that religion is somehow exempt from a trend that has infiltrated every other part of our lives. In other words, the increased commercialization of religion does not seem worthy of comment over and above a discussion of an increase in commercialization generally. It certainly does not seem especially relevant in the context of a movie that is, as we have discussed, remarkably secular.

It has been argued for some time that the world, and America in particular, is becoming increasingly secular. Another way to put this point is to say that we, as a society, are not becoming more secular, we are only shifting the focus of our reverence. Americans, and perhaps the rest of the industrialized world, have shifted their emphasis to a different system, that of consumerism. In a sobering article by Peter Wenz, he claims that this consumerism is the ideology of "industrial, consumer-oriented societies" and that it "dominates American politics."[7] Consumerism goes beyond mere consumption to "treating consumption as good in itself."[8] It is "the ideology that society should maximize consumption, pursue [it] without limit."[9] Of course, this is not an absolute proposition, people still exhibit fervor on behalf of their religion, but there are certain similarities between religious practice and the sort of commercial lifestyle to which we have all become accustomed.

Religious belief is something that is seen as an inextricable part of individual personality. Quite often, people identify their religion as something that makes them who they are. As an example of this, take the various online matchmaking sites. One of the first identifiers is not only what religion one considers oneself a member of, but also the extent to which religion is part of one's daily life. The reason for this, obviously, is the

ERIN HAIRE AND DUSTIN NELSON

"deal-breaking" nature of religion. If two people differ fundamentally on this particular matter, the assumption is that the relationship is doomed from the start. Religious belief is also seen as something that should infect every part of a person's life. A person's religion should affect how they treat people, who they associate themselves with, what pastimes they engage in, even what movies they see. Religion is socially significant, as an identifier of personality and also as a behavioral indicator.

The same can be said for the ways we consume and the very *things* we consume. The items we buy are as inherent to our personalities as anything else. Our clothes are seen as outward expressions of inner traits, the things we have in our homes are reflections of who we are. What we buy is indicative of what we believe. When someone makes a decision to buy a hybrid car over a large SUV, that indicates a value judgment. The purchase of a Prius is an outward manifestation of an inward belief, namely that we should reduce our fossil fuel consumption whenever possible. We indicate beliefs as much with our purchases as, say, choosing a church to attend.

In addition to being a personal identifier, religion is seen as a force that has the potential to change one's life. In the same way that religion may dictate the personal choices one makes day to day, it also has the power to change the course of one's life more generally. When we talk about "finding religion" or having a "religious experience," the assumption is that one's life is not the same as it had been previously. Something has changed fundamentally, and someone who drastically changes their religious beliefs might describe themselves as "not the same person" they were before.

Marketers and advertisers use the lure of this transformative power as a tool to move a product. We buy things that will change our lives for the better. Whether it is a cosmetic that will make a woman feel like a million dollars or a pair of running shoes that will make you into a world class athlete, advertisers know that they will be more successful if they sell more than just a product – they must sell an improvement on the status quo. Good campaigns are the ones that sell a way of life, not just a product. That purchasing things, not just self-examination or new ideas, can transform us, shows us that religion is, in some way, competing with a consumer mindset. If transformation can be achieved as easily as a trip to a department store, then there seems to be no reason to read my Bible diligently or attend church regularly.

Christmas is the paradigm example of the increasingly blurred line between the religious and consumerist tendencies of our society. It is far and away the biggest shopping occasion of the year, but the occasion behind all of it is one with terrific religious importance. The Parkers seem as susceptible to this trend as any American family; they identify themselves with the things they own and they believe in their transformative power. Ralphie's father is described as an "Oldsmobile man" as opposed to others who are merely "Baptists or Catholics." Ralphie's mother is concerned not with her son's Christmas wishes *per se*, only wishing to prevent him from "shooting his eye out." Randy, Ralphie's kid brother, is the stereotypical ungrateful child whose mother pleads with him to eat because "there are starving people in Africa."

Ralphie, of course, is all consumed with his desire for a "Red Ryder BB gun with a compass in the stock and this thing which tells time." All his time in the movie is spent scheming to get just what he wants for Christmas. Other plotlines (the Scut Farkus debacle, his father's major award) seem to be but hilarious distractions in Ralphie's quest for the perfect Christmas gift. In the first scene of the movie, Ralphie refers to the "twinkling display of mechanized, electronic joy" in the window of the local department store. It seems as if the Parkers' Christmas is motivated almost entirely by the pile of presents they will open. We see in the Parkers' *Christmas Story* the replacement of the religiously significant Christmas with the notion that happiness on Christmas morning will be had only if the right presents are received, the perfect tree is in the living room, and a wonderful Christmas feast is on the table.

At the end of the movie, however, things do not work out quite as Ralphie and the Parkers have planned. The Christmas tree causes nothing but problems and the Bumpass hounds destroy the perfect feast. Ralphie does finally get the Red Ryder, but disaster strikes when he nearly shoots his eye out, as his mother warns him he would. The consumerist ideal has failed the family. The reverse could be said as well: through all of the bumbling and mishaps, the family does not seem to live up to the ideal of the perfect American Christmas.

"We plunged into the cornucopia quivering with desire and the ecstasy of unbridled avarice"

Now, even though "all seems right with the world," don't forget that "Philosophy" is in the title of this book. After all, this is not entirely an exposé on the American Christmas as told by a consumerist named

ERIN HAIRE AND DUSTIN NELSON

Ralphie Parker. There *is* a distinct wisdom to be gained here. In fact, the insight we obtain from this exposé of the *present* era's Christmas has its roots in the *ancient* work of Aristotle (384–322 BCE), truly described as a founding father of philosophy.[10] So, as we descend into the realm of ethics, we must acknowledge that we will forever be indebted to Aristotle for the kinds of questions he raised, as many of those questions still perplex even the most astute philosopher.[11] Of those questions, one is important for our present (Christmas pun intended) considerations: "How should I live?"

The answer that Aristotle offered to this question over twenty centuries ago has been revived in contemporary philosophy in what is currently (and deceptively) called *virtue ethics*.[12] Modern virtue ethicists, not far removed from Aristotle when answering this perennial question, boldly respond: "Virtuously! You should live virtuously." They argue that there is a best kind of life, a flourishing life, for a person to live. Each of us should live fostering virtue within ourselves. These mysterious "virtues" become clear when we recognize them simply as ethically admirable character traits. For example, the person who regularly donates money or time to the local soup kitchen we call generous, charitable, or benevolent; the person slow to anger we call gentle, forgiving, or peaceful; the firefighter who saves the family dog from a burning house we might call courageous, strong, or compassionate; and so on and so on. We say that they possess a certain amount or kind of character trait – a virtue – that will bring about the good life for that person.

If the virtues help bring about the good life for a person, then their antitheses are the vices. These are the character traits that hinder one from fostering the virtues and ultimately encumber the good, or flourishing, life. Thus, the person who takes money from a small child we would call greedy or full of avarice; the person who lets food spoil or throws it away before giving it to a hungry neighbor we would call stingy, selfish, or mean; and so on. Typically, the vices are seen as moral failings in one's character rather than as ethically admirable character traits. It becomes quite difficult then, or at least morally questionable, to promote such vices. Hence, virtue ethicists encourage living life according to the virtues.

Avoiding the vices and fostering the virtues, however, is not restricted from any particular time of day, day of the week, or specific holiday. Christmas, for example, does not exempt one from living according to the virtues while avoiding the vices. Moreover, it is quite possible that there are virtues and vices distinctly associated with this Yuletide holiday.[13]

In our discussion so far, we have come across at least three candidates for Christmas virtues. First, it is possible that *being religious* could be a Christmas virtue. Fostering this virtue would honor the holiday's history (to a degree) while simultaneously valuing the holiday itself. Secondly, *being traditional* might count as a Christmas virtue by not only honoring the holiday's history but also its local and regional customs. Fostering this virtue helps preserve the roots of Christmas and provides it with a reliable future. Thirdly, *being family-centered* has recently emerged as a candidate for Christmas virtue.[14] By fostering this Christmas virtue, a person reconnects with their family and loved ones and propagates the holiday as a special time of forgiveness, remembrance, and love. Although this is merely a sketch of what Christmas virtues might look like, we can also make sense of at least one ferocious Christmas vice thanks to the Parkers: consumerism.[15]

Consumerism, as we have argued, is slowly permeating and even replacing vital aspects of people's lives. It should be uncontroversial to view this drive to consume as a vice, in general, to living a good life. It incites worry and fear and leads to greed and avarice. Indeed, *being consumerist* is a character trait worth avoiding. Peter Wenz claims that out of all the traditional vices, "the linchpin is consumerism."[16] It harms the environment, the poor, and even the wealthy.[17] This is no more true in general than it is at Christmas. If there are indeed virtues and vices associated with Christmas, then consumerism is an obvious vice. From the three potential Christmas virtues discussed above to the more obvious such as charity, benevolence, and compassion, consumerism seems to be an adversary to each and all of them. For the religious, as we have also seen in the Parkers, it has the potential to overwhelm religious meaning, replacing it with reverence for bigger and shinier objects. Consumerism hinders the traditional, calling into question the sentimental with a manufactured need for things new and improved ("plastic trees" rather than real, for example). Finally, for family centeredness, the vice of consumerism moves the value of Christmas from togetherness to worry over giving the right, and big enough, present. And though the Parkers fall into this pervasive vice, we also see them overcome it.

Though the potential is there, the Parkers cannot, or do not, overcome consumerism by being religious. This promising Christmas virtue is out of the purview of the Parker family. Subsequently, their attempts at tradition disappoint through no fault of their own. Their traditional Christmas turkey dinner gets destroyed and the tree (though real) just does not seem to work out and Ralphie, receiving a BB gun like his father's, does

ERIN HAIRE AND DUSTIN NELSON

indeed nearly shoot his eye out. Nonetheless, they press on. It seems as though when all else fails, and the BB gun is left lying in the snow, they have each other. As the Parkers sit down for Christmas dinner at the Chop Suey Palace, it is the Christmas virtue of *being family centered* (promoting fond memories, forgiveness, humor, and love) that overcomes the vice of consumerism. It is this virtue that allows adult Ralphie to recall, "All was right with the world."

The Parkers do not turn to religion to salvage their holiday – in the last scene the family does not stumble into a church where they are welcomed in from the cold night with open arms. Clearly, for this family, the holiday does not exist just within the competition of consumption versus religion. They are forced, when the one fails and the other has long been ignored, to develop a new paradigm within their own family. When the Parkers have their dinner at a Chinese restaurant where the Christmas carols are not quite perfect, they are forced to see humor in the situation and eventually quite enjoy their holiday. After all is said and done, we learn from the Parkers that there are options outside of just consumption or religion. These options are open to us, but they require a change in character.

We now stand at the precipice of this consumerism takeover. The Parkers have shown us that we can overcome it, even at Christmas. In some small sense, the Parkers represent for us a fictional moral role model. Not only are they a reflection of our current circumstances, but they are also an example of how to foster those character traits, the virtues, that allow us to relinquish our consumerist vices. There is hope, too, beyond the few prospective "Christmas" virtues we have previously discussed. Wenz concludes in his essay that those "who reject consumerism in favor of [or, by fostering] the traditional virtues … will flourish better than people whose lives are dominated by envy, greed, work, money worries, and separation from family and friends."[18]

NOTES

1   *A Christmas Story*. Dir. Bob Clark. Writer Jean Shepherd. Perfs. Melinda Dillon, Darren McGavin, Peter Billingsley. Nar. Jean Shepherd. 1983. DVD. Warner Brothers, 2003.
2   How is this even possible? It is literally on television for 24 hours every Christmas Eve.
3   There is obviously much left out of this brief summary. Beyond the central plot are numerous subplots: the Old Man and the battle over his "major award,"

run-ins with the school bully Scut Farkus, Flick's tongue stuck to the flag-pole, and Ralphie's slipping of the "queen mother of all dirty words" among others. These bits fit neatly and often humorously into the main film and make *A Christmas Story* a true classic. However, these instances would do little more for the task at hand than bring back fond feelings for the movie.

4   In the opening scenes the camera pans through downtown Hohman, catch-ing a glimpse of carolers singing "Go tell it on the mountain, that Jesus Christ is born. Hallelujah!"

5   The mother does mildly scorn the Old Man, but not on the basis of religion. "Little pitchers," she says, most likely referring to Ralphie and Randy sitting at the table. Seemingly, this is a warning to the Old Man about cursing in front of the boys, not for being blasphemous.

6   It being a "Christmas" movie should surely rule out any Hanukkah symbolism.

7   Peter Wenz, "Synergistic Environmental Virtues: Consumerism and Human Flourishing," in *Environmental Virtue Ethics* (Lanham: Rowman and Little-filed,, 2005), pp. 197–213.

8   Ibid., p. 198.

9   Ibid.

10 T. H. Irwin, "Aristotle," in E. Craig (ed.) *Routledge Encyclopedia of Philosophy* (London: Routledge, 2003). Available online at www.rep.routledge.com/article/A022 (accessed July 7, 2009).

11 J. L. Ackrill, *Aristotle the Philosopher* (New York: Oxford University Press, 1981), p. 8.

12 Roger Crisp, "Virtue ETHICS," in E. Craig (ed.) *Routledge Encyclopedia of Philosophy* (London: Routledge, 2003). Available online at www.rep.routledge.com/article/A022 (accessed July 7, 2009).

13 Distinguishing Christmas virtues and vices, as such, from the more general virtues and vices should not be controversial. Environmental virtue ethics, for example, advances similarly by distinguishing environmental virtues and vices from the more general categories.

14 There is a great section concerning Christmas and the family in Daniel Miller (ed.) *Unwrapping Christmas* (Oxford: Oxford University Press, 1995).

15 A complete discussion of "Christmas virtue ethics" would surely contain much more than these three potential virtues. For example, charity, generos-ity, benevolence, and so on. The sketch here is more focused on the potential virtues we find in the film, but the resulting vice would undoubtedly affect even the most complete account of Christmas virtues.

16 Wenz, "Synergistic Environmental Virtues," p. 197.

17 Ibid., pp. 197–205.

18 Ibid., pp. 211–12.

PART III

SANTA: A DEEPER LOOK

CHAPTER 8

THE MIND OF SANTA CLAUS AND THE METAPHORS HE LIVES BY

What's in Santa's Mind?

Who is Santa Claus? Where does he come from? How does he know so much about everyone else? On the one hand, he appears to be an extremely generous, eccentric, married, older gentleman of uncertain nationality. On the other hand, his place of residence, his lifestyle, his behavior, his magical ability to overturn the laws of physics the rest of us are subject to, and his prodigious mental insights all strongly suggest a being that is superhuman. There seems to be no better way to explain who or what Santa Claus is.

Whoever he is, it is no mystery that Santa Claus is our figurehead for a season in which we (ideally) emphasize charity, good will toward others, forgiveness, peace, understanding, and love. He seems to have superhuman powers of knowledge and moral judgment. Santa is the icon for our season of giving, peace, and justice because he has cognitive abilities that are seemingly divine rather than human. The mind of Santa intuits our intentions, knows the consequences of our actions, and makes immediate and accurate assessments of our annual moral performance.

Santa physics is a topic unto itself and the physical evidence all points to a superhuman entity. He lives in an inhospitable area of the world, the North Pole, a place where most of us would quickly perish in the average December temperature of −45 °F without more than a red velvet outfit:

striking, but of dubious protection from the winter cold. But the fact that Santa thrives in a frigid arctic climate doesn't mean he is not human. His flight acrobatics, however, are a different matter.

Santa flies in an open sleigh without oxygen or a pressurized cabin – requirements for a human being soaring to the heights achieved by Santa Claus on his annual December delivery. He also flies at speeds not possible for conventional aircraft, yet Santa's sleigh is powered only by nine flying reindeer. According to estimates, Santa has to fly remarkably – some would say impossibly – fast in order to deliver presents to the world's children (those that have been good, anyway) in what we humans perceive to be the span of a single December evening. In fact, because of the date and time lines he passes through, and the speed with which he travels, Santa Claus has 34 hours to make his deliveries. A Fermi Lab researcher estimates that in order to accomplish this feat, Santa must be traveling at close to the speed of light.

But we are philosophers and cognitive scientists, not physicists, so as superhumanly impressive as Santa's flying feats are, his mental abilities – in particular his God-like moral omniscience – present equally intriguing reasons for surmising that Santa is not conventionally human; that perhaps Santa's brain is structured differently from the brains of other humans. And he has this certain knowledge without personally knowing or experiencing the people he judges. Rather, his knowledge is gained at a distance: he knows all from his vantage point at the North Pole, a feat not possible for human beings – if, in fact, Santa Claus is human.

Santa has certain moral knowledge while humans do not. This mental capability means that Santa knows the moral status of the world's children; that is, he knows if they have been naughty or nice. The mind of Santa intuits our intentions, knows the consequences of our actions, and makes immediate and accurate assessments of our annual moral performance. Santa has access to the behaviors of all children (and perhaps all people) on an ongoing basis; perhaps at a disturbing level of detail, for he knows when we are sleeping and when we are awake. Indeed, singers from Eartha Kitt to Madonna to the Pussycat Dolls ask "Santa Baby" to reward their belief in him with sables and convertibles, and Run DMC celebrate the reward (a large wad of cash) Santa magically left for them on the night before "Christmas in Hollis" for their intentions to return a lost wallet.

Santa rewards good behavior and also responds to us when we are not so good. So, not only does Santa know the details of our actions, but he accurately evaluates their moral status. He knows when we've been naughty and nice, and, as a result, whether we deserve candy or coal in our Christmas stockings. He appropriately rewards moral behavior, and so understands what actions are deserving of toy trucks, trips to Las Vegas, and lumps of carbon. He knows what is needed to make the world aright, to reward good with desired objects and recognize bad with coal, he apportions out justice to every individual, and flies away. No wonder he is jolly!

So Santa knows better, judges more rightly, and rewards more perfectly than any human. He is omniscient, has perfect judgment of good and evil, and the ability to determine and mete out appropriate rewards and punishments, is someone whose mind is not marred by ignorance or bias, who's understanding of the moral world is clear and accurate, and whose generosity is balanced with a perfect sense of justice. Regular people have none of these.

How We Know Anything

The nature of moral knowledge and moral decision-making has become a topic of scrutiny in cognitive science. Notions of "knowing," "moral judgment," and "just reward" are grounded in metaphor. When we know things, we discuss our knowledge in metaphorical ways. We say things like "I've grasped the real issue now" or "She finally got it through her thick skull." So we understand knowledge through our physical actions, such as holding or grasping something in the hand, or putting something in the head. Knowledge is taken to be some sort of special object, and the mind is a container for that object. But we also say things like "He suddenly saw the truth" or "A light switch went on in my head." Knowing something is often cast as seeing something, or having it illuminated. When we don't know something, we say "I am in the dark" or "I can't see how you got that answer." Sometimes we talk about knowing something as having the right perspective, or vantage point, as in "I had the answer in view." Further, knowledge is often talked about in terms of something we can control or have an advantageous position over. For example, we might say "I am on top of it." So knowledge is something *grasped* or *held* in a *mind container*, something *seen* or *illuminated*, and something *controlled*, especially from *above*.

We Know Santa as a Moral Exemplar

Metaphorical representations of Santa's good moral judgment and incredible knowledge are found in our common mythology about him. First, Santa views us from above, as he lives on top of the world, at the North Pole. Santa also flies high above the earth to deliver his gifts to us. He is a tall, large individual, towering above elves and children alike, metaphorically able to "see" further than we do, to observe our actions with the perspective of someone above us – someone who can see farther (and know more) than we can. Further, Santa lives in a cool climate, which suggests that he makes decisions with "cool" reason rather than "hot" emotion.

But, you might object, Santa is jolly, so he is hardly unemotional. Interestingly, recent research in cognitive science by, among others, Joshua Greene and Jonathan Haidt, suggests that we cannot make moral judgments without some emotional response involved.[1] These studies provide evidence that counters the idea that moral knowledge is gained through rational thought. Instead, as Greene and Haidt demonstrate, we are much more likely to have an emotional response first and then, after the fact, generate an explanation couched in the language of rational thought for why we felt the way we did. I might, for instance, have a very negative emotional response to murder that only afterwards do I explain in terms of "it is wrong to kill other human beings" or "God commands that we not kill." Traditional moral philosophy does not deny the importance of emotion, but holds that human beings have the ability to come to objective moral knowledge through the application of a transcendent rationality to human actions and their consequences. From this traditional view, rationality is primary and affect is secondary. The newer cognitive science perspective reverses this process and says that when we have a strong response to some action – say, physician assisted suicide – our moral evaluation, whether positive or negative, is guided by our feelings (or what cognitive scientists and moral psychologists call "affective intuition") rather than by some process of rational reflection. To the extent that we do engage in rational reflection, it is after the initial emotional response has already occurred. So Santa's jolliness shows us that he has emotional responses too – and nice ones at that. However, a good moral judge would not let his emotions run wild. Does Santa?

WILLIAM E. DEAL AND S. WALLER

A famous metaphor for controlling one's emotions is found in Plato's *Phaedrus*. Here, Socrates recommends that the truly good and happy person is one whose rationality governs his emotions just as a chariot driver governs her horses. Socrates has us think of the horses that pull the chariot as animal examples of human *will* and *desire* (literally, *appetite*). Good drivers control their chariots. For example, I know that Christmas cookies are both delicious and fattening, and I desire them. If I am guided by reason, I can bake them, enjoy a few to satisfy my desire, but also have the willpower to give the rest away to friends, neighbors, or needy children. Thus, I share the wealth in a just way while keeping myself healthy. If my reason guides my will, and steers how I feel, then I will be good, healthy, and happy. Reason makes me balanced on the inside, and so I behave justly and kindly. Given this 2,000 year-old story of happiness and goodness, it is no surprise that Santa drives a sleigh with nine reindeer. His control of the beasts is a metaphor for his mastery over his own desires and emotions that might interfere with his perfect morality and generosity.

Of course, you might object that Santa is rather large and so clearly does not abstain from Christmas cookies. After all, he eats the cookies left for him by families all over the earth; no wonder his laughter makes his belly shake "like a bowl full of jelly." He seems to have the girth of a man governed more by appetite than reason. But his girth, too, is a metaphor for wealth. Santa is literally bigger than the average person, so he has much that he can give away without impoverishing himself – he has plenty to spare. We would feel uncomfortable taking gifts from a scrawny man. Just as the voluptuous women in paintings by Peter Paul Rubens (1577–1640) – whence the term "Rubinesque" to describe large, beautiful women – symbolized fecundity and sensuality, our huge, happy Mr. Claus is a metaphor for magnanimity and the ability to give freely.

In his happiness, Santa lives a relatively solitary life with Mrs. Claus and his workshop elves. This suggests that Santa does not consult with many other people when he compiles his list of naughty and nice children. This solitude, endorsed by Descartes (in the *Discourse on Method*, chapter 2) as the path to perfecting one's thoughts and avoiding interest and bias, assures us that no one else influences Santa's decisions. Santa has not been bribed or persuaded; he is not engaged in arguments with peers, friends, or enemies about the moral worth of your actions. He has no special interests or self-serving ambitions. God-like, Santa sees all and needs nothing. He alone decides, and he alone is the ideal man to make the decision.

Santa the Moral Accountant

Regardless of Santa's standing as a human being or as some other kind of creature or god, we have no choice as people but to approach him, to try to understand him, to speculate about his intentions, through very human ways of thinking and conceptualizing. The sense we have that Santa stands in moral judgment of us is thought about through very human metaphors. We utilize figurative language to conceptualize who or what Santa is and to understand how Santa's moral system operates. By knowing who Santa is and the ways that he metes out moral justice, we can strive to fall morally in line with the prescribed ethical agenda. We understand Santa's thoughts, judgments, beliefs and decisions through their grounding in conceptual metaphor, a ground that is human through and through.

A conceptual metaphor is one in which the content of one domain of knowledge is overlaid – mapped – onto another. Conceptual metaphor theory, pioneered by George Lakoff and Mark Johnson in 1980, posits the ideas of a source domain, usually connected to our embodied experience of the world, and a target domain, often something much more abstract.[2] So, for example, when we say "She *shot down* all of my arguments against the plan" or "The senator *attacked* the policies of his opponent and *won* the debate," we are utilizing the "argument is war" conceptual metaphor. The source domain is our knowledge and experience of war, battles, and other military actions. The target domain, in the examples cited here, is the world of arguments and debates. What is extremely important for our discussion here is that conceptual metaphors are powerful precisely because they structure how we understand the target domain. We really do come to feel that arguments are battles to be won or lost; this is not just simply flowery language. If, for instance, we said something like "the two debaters pirouetted around the issue," then we would be utilizing an "argument is dance" conceptual metaphor. Thinking about arguments as a dance as opposed to a war sets us up for a very different understanding of our experience. And it is precisely within the conceptual metaphors we use to think about Santa's moral system that we can locate our understanding of how this system operates, how we are positioned within it, and how we are expected to behave as a result of its ethical requirements.

Santa provides a classic example of the "moral accounting" conceptual metaphor whereby morality is understood in terms of commodity

  WILLIAM E. DEAL AND S. WALLER

transactions. The moral accounting metaphor conceptualizes moral interactions as economic transactions. Mark Johnson provides an explanation of the source domain, the economic or commodity transaction, and how it is mapped onto the target domain of moral interactions.[3] For example, commodities in economic transactions tend to represent deeds or actions, so by doing good actions we accumulate "goods" that we can trade for other rewards. When children are good, they exchange this goodness for gifts. Similarly, when we behave in good ways often, we are very good, and achieve a state of wellbeing that is not unlike being financially wealthy as a result of selling many objects. And, if being good is analogous to being wealthy, then being evil or doing evil things is akin to losing one's money or incurring a debt. Our goodness is decreased when we are naughty.

This moral accounting metaphor is, in turn, derived from the "social accounting" metaphor. In the latter, we think of social relationships and social status in terms of finances. So, someone who is popular has a "wealth of friends"; we "invest" in relationships, have social "cash" and "value" our families. The notion here is that the more money and material comforts we have, the better our life is. Similarly, getting money is often mapped onto the idea of having achieved one's purpose, or having wellbeing. Here, we have the idea that we get paid when we have accomplished something of worth, and so life satisfaction is "earned."

If all of this seems hopelessly abstract, applying it to an analysis of Santa ethics and to stories about Santa should help to clarify how these metaphors operate in human thinking about Santa ethics and the logic by which Santa ethics makes sense to us – sensible enough that stories of Santa's omniscience and his function as a bringer/conveyor of reward and punishment are sufficient, at least sometimes, to get children to consider the potential effects of their actions.

If wealth and material possessions make us feel good and contribute to our sense of wellbeing, then Santa's gift-giving improves our wellbeing, signifies our worth, and alerts others to our goodness. Santa has, through his gifts, certified our moral standing. By extension, children who get gifts have achieved goodness that has been earned through good behavior. Also at work here is a sense of reciprocation: if you do good, then you deserve, and should get, a gift. If you are bad, then you do not deserve a gift, or you receive the non-gift – a lump of coal – a symbol of your bad character. Either way, the notion of reciprocity sets up the expectation for something in return for our actions, good or bad. According to Santa ethics, it is the fear of retribution, that Santa will know we've been naughty and gift us accordingly, that keeps children good.

Santa as Moral Authority

Santa has moral authority over people in the world, much as a parent has moral authority over a child. Just as a parent can compel a child to do certain things, so Santa has control over who receives gifts and who does not at Christmas time. This is absolute authority: a child can ignore the warnings about what will happen if he or she is bad, but the moral obligation to obey the rules of Santa ethics remains and Santa will dish out justice accordingly. From this perspective on Santa ethics, it is clear that children are being treated as moral agents responsible for the consequences of their behavior. Though we cannot know for sure since we cannot directly know Santa's mind, it appears that there is a certain point in the development of the very young child when Santa begins to apply moral accountancy to the child's actions and makes evaluations of naughtiness and niceness.

Santa's moral system can be understood, in part, through the "moral authority is parental authority" metaphor. Typically in this metaphor, the one holding the moral authority is depicted as a strict father figure. Although Jolly Old St. Nick does not present outwardly as a strict father figure, he nevertheless fulfills that role in the logic of the moral accounting conceptual metaphor. This metaphor maps parental authority on to moral authority: the idea of the caring but protective parent – typically, the father – concerned with the best interests of his children. The parent's strict and stern demeanor and actions are directed at what is best for the child even if the child does not understand it that way. The child, though, is expected to respect and obey the parent's decision. In the case of Santa, children do not have the same kind of intimate relationship with him as they do with a strict father figure. Nevertheless, Santa Claus requires that children obey the moral rule to be good, lest they pay the negative price.

Santa is not only a moral authority, like a strict father, but he is also like a nurturing parent, traditionally, a mother. When we think of Santa in this way, we are utilizing the "morality is nurturance" metaphor. The idea that Santa is a nurturing parent, a mother, derives from the view of Santa as a caretaker of the needs and wants of children all over the world. In popular American culture, children are excited when Christmas season arrives because this also means the appearance of Santa Claus. The throngs of children that line up to meet Santa at department stores across America are not afraid of Santa (at least most aren't), but rather look to him as a source of comfort, as a nurturing parent who will see to it that the children's desires are realized.

WILLIAM E. DEAL AND S. WALLER

Example of Santa in Action: *A Christmas Story*

The popular 1983 holiday film *A Christmas Story* provides a more concrete way into how these metaphors operate in American popular culture
and how they frame how we understand Santa ethics. In the film, Ralphie
wants a BB gun for Christmas, and two moral problems emerge. First,
Ralphie is not particularly good; in fact, he is quite naughty. He uses the
"F" word, gets into fights with the neighborhood bully, and lies to his
mother about how his eyeglasses were broken. And if children are not
good, then Santa will not give them their desired gifts for Christmas.
From the logic of the social accounting metaphor, Ralphie has not earned
a good gift by enacting goodness, and seemingly has earned a lump of
coal because of his bad actions. Of course, Ralphie is not entirely bad
either – he wishes to capture villains with the BB gun, to make it an
instrument of goodness.

This leads us to the second moral issue: How much can a BB gun be
an instrument of goodness, or a truly just reward, even for a good child?
Since guns have great capacity to cause bad things to happen, one might
think that a gun might be an appropriate gift for a bad child. Of course,
Ralphie's elders are encouraging and expecting him to be good, and
simultaneously, trying to dissuade him from even wanting a gun. Words
from his mother, his teacher, and a department store Santa all warn
Ralphie: "You'll shoot your eye out." Santa, in his literal agreement with
mother and teacher, is clearly representative of the parental figure as
moral authority. Thus, even if Ralphie is good, his goodness cannot earn
him the desired gift, because the desired gift is itself not good, i.e., the
social accounting metaphor would be violated if good children got evil
gifts. However, Ralphie persists in wanting the gun; a morally ambiguous
boy wishes for a morally ambiguous gift.

From Santa's moral perspective, the moral concern is that Ralphie
does not understand (cannot see) how dangerous the gun might be for
him. Thus, as a figure that not only delivers rewards and retributions, but
also metes out justice, Santa's job here is to teach Ralphie why the gift he
desires is not really desirable. Ralphie has earned a lesson because he
desires to be good, and Santa relies on Ralphie's consistently devilish
actions, in combination with the gun, to reveal the truth.

The plot unfolds: "Santa" does indeed deliver the BB gun. A ricochet-
ing BB hits Ralphie just below the eye, his glasses fall off, and he steps on
them. Ralphie has not lost his vision permanently by shooting his eye

out, but the BB gun has still managed to stop him from seeing as well as he could. Ralphie has gotten his gift, his punishment, and his lesson – BB guns are indeed dangerous.

Santa as Karma Embodied

If Santa is truly all-knowing, similar to ways that God is conceptualized in Western monotheistic traditions, we also have to acknowledge that he appears dispassionate in his judgments while, for instance, the biblical God can seem quite angry when humans act immorally. This dispassion, this idea that Santa metes out justice correctly, but without some personal response – such as anger, disappointment, or disapproval – to the wrongdoer is reminiscent of Hindu, Buddhist, and Jain notions of karma: actions and their consequences. According to these karma systems, any intentional human action has a specific consequence. Do good deeds, and good consequences are the result. Do bad deeds, and the appropriate bad or unpleasant consequence are the result. While the consequence can be immediate, it is also true that the consequence is sometimes not realized until a subsequent life (remember that the concept of karma is part of a larger worldview that says human beings experience multiple lives until liberated from the cycle of birth, death, and rebirth, a cycle known as *samsara*). This law of karmic consequence is impartial and impersonal. It is impartial because it applies to everyone without exception, and it is impersonal because there is no deity or other entity doing the judging. It is just the operation of the laws of the universe without the intrusion of human or human-like emotion.

Though it is not our popular view of Santa Claus, it can be argued that Santa Claus is like the law of karmic consequence in human form. Santa, though having corporeal form, seems to know when we are naughty or nice. The judgment, if we can call it that, occurs without any apparent appeal to self-interest or to the social, economic, or other standing of the one being judged. Because it is not typically the case that people are all bad or all good (think of Ralphie), weighing of the overall good or bad performed over the year would seem to be required in order for Santa to make a judgment of the kind of present deserved – the just consequence – for the sum total of one's yearly behavior. This, too, mirrors the law of karmic consequence where it is the net sum of good and bad that determines the consequence one will experience immediately or in a future life.

WILLIAM E. DEAL AND S. WALLER

Conclusion

Santa's apparently God-like knowledge and good judgment have been viewed through the lens of a variety of metaphorical structures. His near-omniscience has been discussed through metaphors of *seeing* clearly, and viewing from *above*. His decisions are *cool* and rational rather than *hot* and emotional, though they are tempered by emotion, and so more human than we might have thought originally. We have considered his moral judgments and actions through these metaphorical structures: *moral authority is parental authority, moral accounting, morality is nurturance,* and *social accounting*. All of these metaphorical structures are ultimately human, rather than superhuman. Santa, at least as we understand him, does think with a human mind, though he does have some amazing abilities.

NOTES

1 Joshua Greene and Jonathan Haidt, "How (and Where) Does Moral Judgment Work?" *Trends in Cognitive Sciences* 6, 12 (2002): 517–23. See also Jonathan Haidt, "The Emotional Dog and Its Rational Tail: A Social Intuitionist Approach to Moral Judgment," *Psychological Review* 108, 4 (2001): 814–34.

2 George Lakoff and Mark L. Johnson, *Metaphors We Live By* (Chicago: University of Chicago Press, 1980). See also George Lakoff and Mark L. Johnson, *Philosophy in the Flesh: The Embodied Mind and Its Challenge to Western Thought* (New York: Basic Books, 1999); George Lakoff, *Women, Fire, and Dangerous Things: What Categories Reveal about the Mind* (Chicago: University of Chicago Press, 1987); Mark L. Johnson, *Moral Imagination: Implications of Cognitive Science for Ethics* (Chicago: University of Chicago Press, 1993).

3 Mark L. Johnson, "How Moral Psychology Changes Moral Theory," in Larry May, Marilyn Friedman, and Andy Clark (eds.) *Mind and Morals* (Cambridge, MA: MIT Press, 1996), pp. 45–68.

CHAPTER 9

MAKING A LIST, CHECKING IT TWICE

The Santa Claus Surveillance System

 During a central moment in the 2004 movie *The Polar Express* a group of children wandering through Santa's factory in the North Pole encounter Santa's elves overseeing a massive surveillance operation. As the children watch from a balcony over the immense control room, the elves call up different children on a wall of television monitors, remarking on their behavior and the implications that behavior holds for Christmas. The screens show each child's name and allow for stop action and rewind, underscoring their omnipresent surveillance. One child, who has put gum in his sister's hair, is seen pleading, most likely to a parent but almost directly into the elves' monitor, "I didn't do it, I didn't do it." The elves confer with each other over whether they should report the child, and the supervisor even picks up the candy-cane striped hotline to Santa before announcing, in a thick Brooklyn accent, that he'll cut the kid a break since it is Christmas Eve. However, he admonishes the elves to put the kid on the "check twice list" for the following year. Later, when the elves discover the children among the presents in Santa's sack, they remark, "We knew you were there all along," reinforcing to the children that Santa – directly or via his elves – truly does know everything about their actions.

Like many American Christmas programs made for a young audience, *The Polar Express* refers a number of times to the 1934 song, "Santa Claus is Coming to Town." The song, which contains the lines, "He sees you when you're sleeping, he knows when you're awake, he knows if you've been bad or good, so be good, for goodness' sake!" and "He's making a list and checking it twice," has become such a standard at Christmas time that multiple generations of artists – from Ella Fitzgerald to the Beach Boys to the Cheetah Girls – have kept it alive in popular music. Indeed, the song jumped genres powerfully when Rankin/Bass produced the television special *Santa Claus is Comin' to Town* in 1970. The show asserts a creation myth, or myth of origins, for Santa Claus that turns many of the song's lyrics into dialogue. In *Santa Claus is Comin' to Town* Santa's surveillance operation is a bit less complex than in *The Polar Express*, consisting of a magic snowball that allows him to monitor children's behavior to see who's naughty or nice. The popularity of the song's lyrics has meant that it's contributed heavily to – perhaps even created – one of the major roles that Santa plays in Christmas mythology in the United States: arbiter of good behavior.

Santa, Genealogy, and History

To understand the historical development of Santa Claus in general and the surveillance model that accompanies these stories in particular, we could turn to the work of French philosopher Michel Foucault (1926–84). Foucault held a chair at the Collège de France in "History of Systems of Thought," a title that attempted to encompass his concerns with contemporary social formations and their historical development. Taking inspiration from the work of Friedrich Nietzsche (1844–1900), especially his approach in *On the Genealogy of Morals* (1887), Foucault attempted to trace the development of broad concepts and practices, such as the definition and treatment of mental illness or the punishment and reformation of criminals. His investigations into these specific areas led him to draw conclusions about values in society at large.

One of Foucault's most famous works is *Discipline and Punish: The Birth of the Prison* (1979), an exploration of disciplinary and surveillance systems starting within the confines of prison walls, but extending far beyond that arena. For Foucault, the central object – in this case, the prison – is interesting not in and of itself, but for what it can tell us about society at large. Therefore, when he examines the development of punishment from the time of the French monarchy through the twentieth century, he wants to know how components of the legal apparatus both reflected and impacted social practices and beliefs. For instance, how did the criminal confession function as a model for other truth-telling or knowledge gathering? What did the scaffold – that final stage upon which the condemned appeared before the crowd – represent in terms of state power? How did surveillance models filter through other social arenas, such as schools and factories? Very briefly, albeit complexly, he sums up his text as an attempt "to study the metamorphosis of punitive methods on the basis of a political technology of the body in which might be read a common history of power relations and object relations."[1] In short, he is interested in the ways punitive methods both reflect and shape behaviors and interactions across society.

Foucault's investigation of the prison illustrates his general technique of analyzing "discursive practices," which he sees as statements, or systems of statements, that claim to reveal or hold truth. The concept of the discursive practice is so central to his thought that he devoted his first-year lecture series at the Collège de France to an elaboration of the concept, arguing:

> Discursive practices are characterized by the delimitation of a field of objects, the definition of a legitimate perspective for the agent of knowledge, and the fixing of norms for the elaboration of concepts and theories. Thus, each discursive practice implies a play of prescriptions that designate its exclusions and choices.[2]

So one function of discursive practices is to give order to things, but more importantly they establish the ways in which we can think about things; discursive practices provide the methods and limits for understanding the world. These discursive practices, he reminds us, are everywhere: "embodied in technical processes, in institutions, in patterns for general behavior, in forms for transmission and diffusion, and in pedagogical forms which, at once, impose and maintain them."[3] In short, discursive practices surround us and frame our reality.

Power/Knowledge: The Gift That Keeps on Giving

One way to understand discursive practices is through another important concept for Foucault, Power/Knowledge. Foucault joins these two terms because in his view knowledge production is intimately related to power: keeping records, making lists, segmenting tasks, and categorizing objects all contribute to an extension of power relations between and among individuals and systems. An easy way to understand this relation would be to think about a patient's process of filling out his medical history. While there's certainly a practical application in doing so, the process of completing the medical history reveals the patient as an individual not only to the doctor, but also to the medical system that includes office staff and insurance companies. In other words, they know much more about the patient than the patient does about them, a fact that implicitly structures a power relationship. Taken together, the medical forms, the division of labor from receptionist to doctor to insurance company, and the physical structure of the office with waiting room and consultation rooms and billing area all contribute to the discursive practice of medicine.

For Foucault, knowledge production never ceases, constantly expanding to lay bare further corners of individuals and societies. He traces the development of knowledge through prisons, medicine, sexuality, schools, factories, and the military, to name a few. The knowledge produced in these fields allows for ever more specialization, ever more minute distinctions, and therefore ever more areas for the spread and grasp of power. Furthermore, as the medical records example above indicates, power isn't entirely or even primarily about domination or repression, because it can be deployed to prolong or improve life.

In fact, Foucault argues that power is productive and not repressive, by which he means that power doesn't shut down discourse, but multiplies it. Foucault asserts: "We must cease once and for all to describe the effects of power in negative terms.... In fact, power produces; it produces reality; it produces domains of objects and rituals of truth. The individual and the knowledge that may be gained of him belong to this production."[4] The mechanisms of power – the courtroom, the confessional, the school exam, the medical history – all call us to account for ourselves. Power disciplines the subject through knowledge production: the proper technique for efficiently putting objects together in a toy factory, the revelation of our desires in the form of gift lists, as well as the painstaking work of determining who remains on, is added to, or deleted from the Christmas card list shape our experience of Christmas and remind us that even holidays are a lot of work.

"He sees you when you're sleeping": Foucault's Theory of Panopticism

One of the most discussed sections of Foucault's *Discipline and Punish: The Birth of the Prison* is the chapter entitled "Panopticism." Here, Foucault discusses the Panopticon, an idealized prison designed by Enlightenment-era thinker Jeremy Bentham (1748–1832). Bentham is best known as the founder of utilitarianism, a philosophical school based upon the idea that actions should be judged by their utility, or what brings the greatest good or pleasure to the greatest number of people. Bentham formed his social and legal theories in the late eighteenth and early nineteenth centuries, a time when the newly emerging democratic ideals of equality, liberty, and brotherhood were taking hold in America, France, and other Western countries. Thus, his ideas were progressive for his time, an attempt to improve the general conditions of everyday people, as in his design of the Panopticon, a prison that would be clean, safe, and free of physical punishment.

In developing his theory of panopticism, Foucault examines how nineteenth-century ideas for discipline are reflected in Bentham's architectural drawings for the Pantopticon. The plans of the prison building itself feature a tower in the center of a circular surrounding building divided into cells. The inhabitant of each cell is separated so he can see the tower, but cannot see any other prisoner. In this way, Bentham says, a single observer can watch all prisoners, while the inmate never knows for certain whether he is being observed, knowing only that he may always be observed. The key point for this form of discipline, Foucault observes, is that "one is totally seen without ever seeing."[5] This produces, Foucault argues, "the major effect of the Pantopticon: to induce in the inmate a state of conscious and permanent visibility that assures the automatic functioning of power."[6]

Though Bentham's prison was never built, Foucault argues that the panoptic surveillance systems he described have become a regularized part of contemporary culture, disciplining us to be "good" citizens. "The panoptic schema," he writes, "was destined to spread throughout the social body; its vocation was to become a generalized function."[7] In fact, he argues, the panoptic surveillance method is so effective that it is now used far beyond the prison setting:

> Whenever one is dealing with a multiplicity of individuals on whom a task or a particular form of behavior must be imposed, the panoptic schema may be used.... It is polyvalent in its applications.... It serves to reform

  RICHARD HANCUFF AND NOREEN O'CONNOR

prisoners, but also to treat patients, to instruct schoolchildren, to confine the insane, to supervise workers, to put beggars and idlers to work.[8]

Thus, Foucault asserts, surveillance systems are now used in many settings to train or "discipline" people into behaviors that the larger culture finds acceptable. Many have noted that this surveillance model of discipline – for example, the use of cameras in stores to both control shoplifting and observe the workers, at automatic teller machines, and on public streets – has grown in usage in contemporary times. Like Bentham's prison, which was designed to elicit good behavior without obvious punishment, these methods of surveillance are used to discipline people into automatic obedience.

"He's making a list, he's checking it twice"

Once we understand the social history that Foucault traces, it is not surprising to find that the Santa Claus myth, with its nineteenth-century roots, includes strong references to the use of surveillance methods for disciplining children. This aspect of the myth is captured for Americans in the words of the Christmas standard, "Santa Claus is Coming to Town"; as alluded to before, the song has enjoyed continuous popularity over the past 75 years. No matter what era or genre, the song admonishes those who would "pout, cry, or shout" to behave well because the all-seeing Santa, the bringer of gifts, can see, and presumably pass judgment on, their behavior.

The popular song is so ubiquitous and forms a basis for the Santa myth to such an extent that few American Christmas programs aimed at children fail to refer to it. Santa is, in almost any of these programs, immediately capable of knowing whether children have been bad or good. Santa's actual methods of surveillance, of seeing but not being seen, have been depicted in widely varying and inventive ways. We need only to return to our opening example of *The Polar Express* to get a sense for the prevalence of this representation of Santa's function. The cutting edge computer graphics produced for the 2004 Robert Zemeckis film, adapted from the Caldecott-award-winning 1985 children's picture book, go hand in hand with the film's images of Santa's equally technology driven surveillance systems: a crew of Santa's elves oversee a vast, complex control center featuring walls of cathode ray tube era screens showing individual children, and a candy-striped hotline telephone for important decisions. Except for the scale of the chamber, which underscores the immensity and completeness of the surveillance, the scene immediately calls to mind images of security guard stations, a familiar staple of thrillers; however, in Santa's system, there's no disabling cameras or relying on a dozing security guard.

In comparison, the 1970 television special *Santa Claus is Coming to Town* depicts a character named the Winter Warlock showing Kris Kringle how to create a magic crystal snowball, a surveillance device that allows Kris to see whatever he wishes. While the Warlock uses it to show Kris that the town's schoolteacher, Jessica, is searching for him, Kringle almost immediately devises a much more disciplinary way to use it. When he rushes from the Warlock to Jessica, who is soon to become Mrs. Klaus, she brings him letters from children asking for more toys because their evil mayor, Burgermeister Meisterburger, ordered all toys destroyed. Life under the dictator Burgermeister, in this Cold War era program, resembles many other Western depictions of life behind the Iron Curtain, and casts Kringle – who will soon adopt the name of Santa Claus as an alias to avoid persecution from the vindictive but comically inept Burgermeister – as a freedom fighter.

Kringle promises Jessica that Burgermeister's edicts won't stand in his way. "You tell those young'un's there'll be plenty of toys, but only if they behave themselves," he tells her. "No cryin' or poutin' or … oh I'll know. I've got ways of knowing," he says, showing her his magic crystal snow ball. As the tune to "Santa Claus is Coming to Town" plays in the background, the pair recite the words to the song as dialogue: "Yes sir," he says, "I can see when they are sleeping and I know when they're awake." "My goodness! You know if they're bad or good?" she asks. "So you tell them to be good for goodness' sake," he replies. Kringle's reply seems to imply that, just as in the *fin-de-siècle* slogan of "Art for Art's Sake," good behavior should be divorced from any system of rewards. To put it another way, being good should be its own reward. However, Kringle undermines this message through constant resupply of material goods, in this case the toys he brings the oppressed children of Somberville.

Naughty or Nice: The True Meaning of Discipline

Santa's surveillance systems may seem at first, as Kris Kringle tells Jessica, to be aimed toward disciplining children to be "good for goodness' sake," and rewarding this good behavior with Christmas gifts. However, the system does not produce those effects. American children have gotten the message that their Christmas presents are coming regardless of behavior

RICHARD HANCUFF AND NOREEN O'CONNOR

and they understand that threats to the contrary are complete humbug. Santa may be checking up on them, but their presents will be under the tree on Christmas morning.

The children's programs *Santa Claus is Coming to Town* and *The Polar Express* both include key scenes that drive the point home. For example, despite their elaborate monitoring center, Santa's elves in *The Polar Express* are disinclined to mete out the ultimate punishment for children on the naughty list, instead cutting breaks for miscreants on account of Christmas Eve. In *Santa Claus is Coming to Town*, the narrator, warmly voiced by Fred Astaire, tells us "Kris made a list of all the children and the toys they wanted. He checked it over once, then checked it over twice. He tried to figure out just who was naughty and who was nice." The images that accompany these words are of Kris Kringle puzzling over a long list of children's names, struggling to decide what to do. "Well, I guess they are all pretty nice," he says, before bundling up his bag to go deliver Christmas gifts to all the children. In these programs, as in lived experience, children rarely receive any punishment for naughtiness.

In the end, Santa's surveillance systems and double-checked lists do not produce children who are "good for goodness' sake." These imagined systems are but parts of a larger set of what Foucault calls the disciplines: "tiny, everyday, physical mechanisms, by all those systems of micro-power that are essentially non-egalitarian and asymmetrical."[9] Through the Santa story, children are disciplined to participate fully in the com-modification of the Christmas holiday and to become "good" consumers in late capitalist culture. The list we imagine Santa maintaining – the one that enrolls each child separately and pairs each individually with a toy – is part of a much larger set of lists that the adult must produce and main-tain as a part of a capitalist Christmas ritual. Through stories about Santa, children are disciplined in the logic of capitalist consumerism; trained in the knowledge that the receiving and giving of consumer prod-ucts is the ultimate aim of the holiday season. They are therefore trained to create lists of products that they desire, and finally thereby trained to understand products as possible to fulfill desires.

The Archeology of Christmas

Although widely acknowledged as a major Christmas figure, Santa Claus is not the only individual associated with the holiday. In fact, often competing on front lawns with illuminated sets of Santa and his reindeer, one will find illuminated sets of Jesus in the manger, surrounded by adoring humans, angels, and animals. As a holiday, Christmas occupies two seemingly contradictory spaces in our culture: it is both a highly religious celebration of the birth of Jesus Christ and a spectacle of secular mass consumption. The tension between these two poles can generally be summed up by a few slogans that reappear during what we've come to call the "holiday season": "Happy Holidays," "Season's Greetings," "Jesus: the Reason for the Season," and the more recent "Keep Christ in Christmas."

The first two express a secular inclusiveness that not only acknowledges the presence of other holidays such as Hanukkah, but also implicitly invites non-Christians to take part – or at least feel included – in the frenzied festival spirit that lasts roughly from Thanksgiving until New Year's. The second two acknowledge and oppose the secular interpretation of Christmas as a consumer holiday, and they are lone voices crying in the wilderness marked only by the ever-earlier appearance of store Christmas displays featuring reindeer, elves, and Santa Claus. While you may be able to purchase a light-up nativity scene, you're far less likely to see a smiling image of Jesus imploring you to find that perfect gift.

Moreover, the consumer Christmas, the Christmas marked by a cheerful fat man in a fuzzy red suit stealthily entering the homes of sleeping residents and leaving untold riches around a gussied-up evergreen, dominates popular culture from the mid-nineteenth century forward. Many critics cite Clement Moore's 1823 poem "'Twas the Night Before Christmas" as the origin of the development of our current ideas about Santa Claus, and while Moore may not have invented the traditions themselves, he represented them in a way that captured the popular imagination. The cultural products that follow the poem, from *Santa Claus is Comin' to Town* to *The Polar Express*, not to mention the crassly commercial but utterly honest song "Santa Baby," take their lead from Moore's imagery. The development of Santa Claus' dominance over Christmas iconography coincides with the rise of consumer culture through the late nineteenth and early twentieth centuries, as production models demanded expanded consumption and marketing experts refined their ability to identify and develop new markets, sometimes with the help of Kris Kringle.

In addition to delivering all those toys at Christmas, Santa moonlights as a corporate spokesperson, lending his image to holiday advertising campaigns and "collector's edition" soda cans. Iconic representations of Santa enjoying a Coke – left out as a treat for him by some particularly thoughtful family – have entered America's popular imagination to the extent that what began as an advertising campaign has turned into a tradition, a component of the nostalgic force of Christmas, yet still remains effective in its original role of promoting a product. Even in instances where Santa does not appear personally in the advertisements, the ads work on the basis of their reference to elements of the Santa mythology, as in the Budweiser Clydesdale campaign, in which the company's iconic horses, outfitted with harnesses bedecked with jingling bells, pull the company's wagon full of beer through idyllic snowy landscapes, presumably to eagerly awaiting – and of legal age – girls and boys. Perhaps not coincidentally, just as eight reindeer pull Santa's sleigh, eight horses pull the Budweiser wagon.

Santa as pitchman underscores the contradiction between his role as judge of the good and the bad and his role as representative of holiday generosity. In countless ads, Christmas is about giving and receiving; it is about the wonder that new objects from dolls that wet themselves to luxury cars wrapped in oversize ribbon can bring to young and old. While we may not take Santa's surveillance very seriously as a system of rewards and punishments – very few children find their stockings empty on Christmas Day – our culture has learned the disciplinary lessons well. From a Foucauldian perspective, the lesson isn't that Santa is watching, but that we are meant to consume, and with a nod and a wink to the division between "naughty and nice," we heartily check off the names on our list as we load our shopping carts under the dancing snowflakes of the local big box store.

NOTES

1 Michel Foucault, *Discipline and Punish: The Birth of the Prison* (New York: Vintage, 1979), p. 24.
2 Michel Foucault, "History of Systems of Thought," in *Language, Counter-Memory, Practice: Selected Essays and Interviews* (Ithaca: Cornell University Press, 1977), p. 199.
3 Ibid., p. 200.
4 Foucault, *Discipline and Punish*, p. 194.
5 Ibid., p. 202.
6 Ibid., p. 201.
7 Ibid., p. 207.
8 Ibid., p. 205.
9 Ibid., p. 222.

CHAPTER 10

YOU'D BETTER WATCH OUT …

Ho, Ho, History

Santa Claus is not purely a fantastical invention of modern Western society, since the well-known Christmas figure is based on a historical person. The character of "Santa Claus" is based on Saint Nicholas of Myra, a third to fourth century bishop from Asia Minor, modern-day Turkey. Long before he became Santa Claus, Nicholas had an interesting appearance at the famed Council of Nicaea.

But before we can talk about that, let's first get some background. Back in the early fourth century, Constantine (272–337) was on the throne of the Roman Empire. As emperor, Constantine had immense power to influence Roman culture as he saw fit. Fortunately for the Christians in the Roman Empire, Constantine considered himself a Christian, too. In fact, he was the very first emperor of Rome to be a Christian.

The very early Christians underwent periods of persecution from the Roman Empire. Think, for example, of stories of crucifixions and being thrown to the lions in movies like *Quo Vadis?* and Cecil B. DeMille's *The Sign of the Cross*. The Romans persecuted Christians for a number of reasons, but one of the biggest reasons is that Christians refused to revere the Roman emperor as a divinity. They already had their own divine human to worship: Jesus Christ.

Christians were pretty unpopular within the Roman Empire, and some political leaders exploited this fact. For example, when Emperor Nero had ideas for a grand building project in the middle of Rome, he knew that the only way he could free up space for the new buildings was if some "accident" like a fire burned down large sections of Rome. Well, a number of historians think that Nero had his own capital, Rome, set on fire in order to make his building dreams possible. It worked, but, as you might expect, people were furious and outraged at the fire that destroyed their homes and businesses. Someone must be held responsible for this! Nero took advantage of the situation and blamed those unpopular Christians for the devastating fire. Everyone hated them already, anyway. Outrage against Christians grew, and this resulted in another Roman persecution of the early Christians. In fact, Nero was so ruthless in his dealings with the Christians that he had a number of them nailed to crosses, covered in oil, and then set on fire. Nero arranged these suffering Christians so that their flaming bodies would provide light for his evening parties. If those Christians wanted fire, his cruel message seemed to say, then let's give them fire.

Why mention these Roman persecutions of Christians? It is important to realize how radically *different* things were for Christians when one of their own became emperor. "Imagine," they thought, "now we can be free to worship without fearing political pressure, persecution, or martyrdom!" After all these years, could it be true that a *Christian* was the emperor of Rome? Yes, and Emperor Constantine made certain to protect the freedom of Christian worship by advocating freedom of worship in the Empire. How Constantine must have been loved by his Christian citizens!

Constantine took an active interest in promoting Christianity. He did this through large funding and countless building projects. He even sent his own mother to go touring the Holy Land in order to find places important to Christian history, like the tomb that Christ was buried in, and where he might have been born in Bethlehem. She would build churches on these sites so that no one would forget what had happened there. This was long before the days when people would discuss ideas like the separation of church and state, so Constantine did not hesitate to appoint Christian priests and bishops to places of influence and political power within the Roman Empire. Constantine wanted Christianity to grow in his empire, and he did what he could to make that happen.

Arius and Theological Controversy

As an emperor, Constantine wanted to maintain a unified and healthy empire. As a Christian, Constantine wanted to maintain a unified and healthy church. These two interests combined when theological turmoil started brewing that led to political turmoil for Rome. The theological issue was over the nature of God as Trinity.

Early Christians had the guidance of their local churches and bishop, the Old Testament of the Bible, the set of holy books that would be canonized as the New Testament of the Bible, and various other admired inspirational writings. These resources were enough to answer many questions for the early Christians, such as basic points of theology and questions of how to make ethical decisions in order to live in accordance with God's will for them. This did not mean, however, that the Christians had an answer to every single question they would *like* to have an answer to. Like many Christians today, they would often simply come up with answers on their own to questions that occurred to them, and not every one of those attempts at answers would be equally approved by the wider Christian community.

One puzzle concerning the nature of God occurred to several early thoughtful Christians. From the Bible it was clear that Christians, like Jews, worshipped only one God. For example, in Deuteronomy we read, "Hear, O Israel: The LORD our God, the LORD is one." On the other hand, when Jesus came he explained that there is also some kind of threefold nature to God. For instance, in the Gospel of Matthew Jesus commanded his disciples to "go and make disciples of all nations, baptizing them in the name of the Father and of the Son and of the Holy Spirit." So, which is it? Do Christians worship one God or three? Who exactly are the Father, Son, and Holy Spirit, and what is their relationship to one another? If Father, Son, and Holy Spirit are all divine, can that be reconciled with the Christian's confession that there is only one God? What does it even mean to be "divine"? Something needs to be explained here.

One fourth-century figure in the church at Alexandria had a suggestion about how to make sense of this confusion. He focused specifically on the relationship between God the Father and the Son, Jesus Christ. This man, Arius, held firmly to the idea that there was only one God. Since the Father was that one God, that meant the Son could not be fully God. Arius had no problem admitting that the Son was in some way "divine," but for him the Son was more like a great angel than God himself. Arius taught that the Son was the first and greatest thing ever created by God the Father. Since the Son was created by God, though, that means that while God the Father had existed from all eternity, the Son could not have been eternal. The Son had to have been created at some point in time. Arius popularized his theological understanding of the nature of God using a happy little jingle: "There was a time when the Son was not." This short phrase, set to a catchy tune, began spreading widely across the Roman Empire. Many people liked it because it gave an understandable explanation to the confusing topic of the nature of God, promoting Arius' view that the Son had not existed eternally and so was not fully God as the Father was.

Not everyone was satisfied with Arius' explanation, however. For instance, Alexander, who was Arius' own bishop in Alexandria, had strong concerns that the solution proposed by Arius reduced Jesus Christ to being less than God. That would not be an acceptable position for someone who confesses to be a Christian. Eventually, the issue spread, sides were drawn, and turmoil resulted. The controversy grew to the point that Egypt, which provided much grain for the Romans, threatened not to ship their grain supply to Constantinople because of disagreement about this issue! Such a state of affairs was unacceptable for the Christian emperor Constantine, and even before things progressed that far he had decided to intervene in order to settle the dispute.

The Council of Nicaea – a Jolly Occasion

Constantine decided to settle the controversy by calling for a Christian council in 325 at the city of Nicaea in northwestern Asia Minor, not far from Constantinople. Now, there had been local councils called by bishops before, but never a Christian council that was universal (or "ecumenical") in scope. Since this council was called by the emperor himself, it would hold special prominence in people's minds. The idea behind having a council was that pressing concerns for the Christian communities could be brought to a place in which well-informed and thoughtful Christian bishops could rule on what would be best for all. The controversy with Arius rose to the level that a council was needed to address it. (The Arius controversy was not the only issue dealt with at Nicaea, though. For example, it was also decided at Nicaea how churches should calculate the date on which Easter would be celebrated ... but that's another holiday altogether. Back to Santa's story.)

Practically everyone at the Council of Nicaea agreed that the Son was divine in some way, but it was much more controversial to spell out just what that meant and what the Son's relationship to the Father was. On one side stood Arius and his followers, who wanted to make a strong distinction between the Father and the Son, with only the Father being truly uncreated and eternal. On the other side were Alexander and his supporters, who rejected Arius' strong difference between Father and Son in the Trinity. They are both God and should be spoken of as such. Eventually, Alexander and the anti-Arian party prevailed, and the Council of Nicaea, led by Emperor Constantine, ruled that Arius' theology was unacceptable for Christians. Indeed, Arius was even exiled as a result of his heresy. One result from this council was the famous Nicene Creed, still recited in churches to this day.

Float like an Acolyte, Sting like the See

So where does Santa Claus fit into all of this? According to legend, as bishop of Myra at the time, Nicholas was invited to attend the famed council at Nicaea. Nicholas was on the side of Alexander and what would become Christian orthodoxy, so he was strongly opposed to Arius' teachings, which denied the full divinity of Jesus Christ, not to mention the coherence of the Holy Trinity. Emperor Constantine sat on his throne, governing over the council, and permitting each group to have its say. As Arius spoke his heretical account, Nicholas observed him, growing angrier and angrier all the while. Soon, Nicholas had had enough of Arius' dangerous prattle. Unable to contain himself any longer, Nicholas got up, went over to Arius, and smacked him in the face! Now that's a Santa Claus with some guts.

Imagine the scene: 'twas the fight before Christmas. As Constantine looked on, Arius roamed before the assembled bishops, explaining his controversial ideas: "Sure, Jesus isn't fully divine, but think how much cleaner and nicer my account of things is!" Meanwhile, Nicholas, seated nearby, began clenching and unclenching his mitten-covered fists in frustration. His eyes – how they twinkled! "How could the Father and the Son both be God, anyway?" Arius continued, "It's just confusing.

And if there's one thing we know, it's that the nature of the Almighty God should be perfectly comprehensible and transparent to our human minds." The tiny bells on Nicholas' hat began to jingle as his muscles quivered. His cheeks were like roses, his nose like a cherry – in fury! "You see," Arius explained, "Jesus Christ wasn't really truly God at all. He certainly hasn't existed for all eternity. I'm sure that part in the Gospel of John that says, 'In the beginning was the Word ...' wasn't even talking about him." The passion was mounting within Nicholas, as if rising up a snow-covered chimney. A slight smoke emerged from his ears, and it encircled his head like a wreath. Arius said, "It is much better just to stick with my handy little catch phrase, 'There was a time when the Son was not.' Everyone be sure to go teach that to all your churches, okay?" Out among the bishops there arose such a clatter. It was Saint Nick, cracking his knuckles. "So," Arius added, "That means Christmas isn't really about God becoming human, after all. Since Jesus wasn't fully God, Christmas probably isn't more special than any other day." That did it. Nicholas stood up and walked directly over to the heretic. He spoke not a word, but went straight to his work. One can almost hear the Byzantine ring announcer calling into his microphone, as Nicholas moved, "And in this corner, weighing in at 318 pounds – the very number of bishops assembled today at Nicaea – we have a man who brings the Donner and the Blitzen (German for thunder and lightning). It's the bishop with his fists up ... Ol' Saint Nick with a right like a brick ... the patron saint of quaint restraint, he ain't ... ladies and gentlemen, Santa Claus!" Arius looked over to see what was going on – but too late. Sock! Arius' head turned with a jerk. The blow shook him like a bowl full of jelly. It was the fight of the fourth century, and it finished as quickly as it started.

What would the council do now? Most of the bishops stared in shock at Nicholas, though a few quietly cheered the decking. Arius' supporters immediately complained, and the point was raised that it was illegal for anyone to lift his hand in violence in the presence of the Emperor. The penalty for such an infraction was for the offender's hand to be cut off. Uh-oh. How would Nicholas fill out his naughty and nice lists then? But Constantine was feeling generous and left the decision of penalty to the bishops themselves. They had Nicholas arrested and he spent a night in jail for his rash behavior. Later, though, Nicholas had his full standing as a bishop restored in dignity, and the Emperor even asked Nicholas' forgiveness for punishing him! He was only acting in defense of the Christian faith, after all.

Does Theology Really Matter?

Why did Nicholas feel so passionate about this theological controversy that it brought him to smack Arius in the middle of the council? It's all so abstract and strange sounding to us. Did it really matter who won the debate? Sometime later, Athanasius, who had been a young secretary to Alexander at the council and would eventually succeed Alexander as bishop, explained why Arius' theology had been so unacceptable for Christians. Athanasius pointed out that even if the Son had been the first and greatest creation of the Father, as Arius said, the Son would still have been *created* rather than being the *creator*, as God truly was. In other words, he argued that Arius' position meant that Jesus Christ could not be truly God since, no matter how great, wonderful, or holy he was, he still would have been placed on the wrong side of the creator/creature distinction. Imagine God the Creator on one side of the divide, with everything he made in the universe on the other side. By Arius' account, the Son would have been on the wrong side of that divide to be truly God. Jesus would have been on the same created side with us regular humans, ice cream, dung beetles, Detroit, and every other created thing in the universe. That implication is unacceptable for Christians, who confess that Christ is truly God. Jesus is not merely a really wise person or very holy prophet, but is God himself who has become human!

Why is it and was it so important for Christians to confess the full divinity of Christ? Why was it seen to be so important that it became an empire-wide controversy that required the emperor himself to intervene? The deep, driving motivation behind this controversy and many other seemingly abstract theological controversies is the issue of *salvation*. Many people, especially non-Christians, may be confused by what the big deal was with all of these fancy-pants, abstract, and complex arguments about theology. People were passionate about it because they felt that their salvation was at stake. They reasoned that we would be dead in our sins and destined for eternal Hell except for the fact that Jesus Christ, who was both fully God and fully man, died on the cross in order to atone for our sins. On the third day, Jesus was raised from the dead, finalizing his triumph over the powers of sin and death. Because Christ lives, we, as his followers, can live as well. Now consider this: What if Jesus were not truly God after all? Even if he were a very moral and nice man, it would be a sad thing that he died on the cross, but how would that affect us and our salvation? Nice people die every day. In order for

Christ's atoning death to matter for us all, he must be more than just a man. He must be God, for only God can save. Thus, the controversy about whether the Son and the Father were both equally God relates directly to the issue of whether Christians are indeed saved by the sacrifice of Christ. No wonder St. Nick was so passionate about this issue that he struck out at Arius. For him, Arius was spreading a heresy that wasn't just wrong, it was endangering people's eternal salvation! This man must be stopped, and quick.

Here Comes Santa Claus – into the Twenty-First Century

Fast forward to our modern Christmas celebrations. It seems hard to imagine that our modern representation of Santa Claus would take theology as seriously as Saint Nicholas did. We can't imagine Santa concerned about much of any kind of theology, really. Even morally, the most Santa stands for is a certain discernment between the vague categories of "naughty" and "nice." (It is likely that having violently settled Arius' brains for a long winter's nap would have gotten Santa placed on his own naughty list). After illustrators Thomas Nast and Haddon Sundblom, we can imagine a portly Santa sharing a Coca-Cola with some huggable polar bears, but would he have an opinion on the nature of God or of our salvation in Jesus Christ? How different Santa has become over the years.

The point is that the "Santa" of history was a Christian *bishop*. That means he was charged to care for and protect the souls of those in his diocese. Theology mattered to him, and it mattered deeply, because what we believe about God will change what we believe about ourselves and how we should live in this world. It also will affect our relationship to that God, which has eternal consequences. "Santa" was not a magical bundle of jolliness and vague moral gestures. He was explicitly and particularly Christian, which doesn't fit as nicely with our modern assumptions about openness to other worldviews. I bet you know many people who celebrate Christmas without even being serious Christians. What does this say about the current version of the holiday that such a thing is even a possibility?

To illustrate the point of how non-theological Santa has become nowadays, notice that on the rare occasions when Santa is paired with Christian theology it strikes us as a very strange thing. For example, take the popular Christmas song, "Here Comes Santa Claus." It is familiar enough to all of us, but read over the lyrics very carefully and you will notice some peculiar ideas in it that blend Christian theology together with the popularized depiction of Santa we all know and love. For instance, the song includes the line, "Santa knows that we're God's children, / That makes everything right." He does? Are *all* children here understood as "God's children"? Or are non-Christian children not supposed to sing, "Here Comes Santa Claus"? The line is so striking that some renditions of the song, uncomfortable with such explicit theology, leave it out altogether. The song also puts popular fable and Christian worship right next to one another with the line, "Hang your stockings and say your prayers." Are the children's prayers supposed to be for the safe arrival of Santa? For generous gifts in their stockings? Are they praying to God for these things, or to Santa himself? This peculiar blending of two different belief systems is sometimes called "syncretism," and the song "Here Comes Santa Claus" is a great example of the syncretism of Christian belief and the popular secularized holiday season. Perhaps the best example of Christian syncretism comes at the end of the song, with the words, "Peace on earth will come to all / If we just follow the light. / Let's give thanks to the Lord above / 'Cause Santa Claus comes tonight." The phrase "Peace on earth" is not just a happy wish, of course, but a reference to the coming of Christ as declared by the heavenly angels in the Gospel of Luke. Is the light we are to follow the light of Christ and his truth, then? Is it the star that leads us to the young savior at Bethlehem? Or is it just one of the many happy Christmas lights that can mean any warm feeling we want it to? Finally, that we should thank the Lord above for the coming of Santa is a strange suggestion. Presumably, most Christians do not actually believe that a magical Santa will visit their house to deliver presents, so what exactly are they supposed to be thanking the Lord for, again? This kind of syncretism is likely to make non-Christians, who still want to celebrate Santa with the kids, uncomfortable because of the references to Christian doctrine. And it is also likely to make Christians uncomfortable too, since they confess the Lord and his Son Jesus Christ to be true while taking fables about Santa Claus to be cute holiday silliness. The fact that it appears odd to us to associate Santa with Christian theology just goes to show how non-Christian we take Santa to be nowadays. Most of the time, though, Santa has become so thoroughly de-Christianized that he doesn't even appear syncretistic to us – just magical and delightful.

The Nicholas of History and the Santa of Faith?

Given his strong feelings at the Council of Nicaea, imagine the many problems Saint Nicholas would find with what we have done to Santa and to Christmas today. For one thing, the Christian bishop would never stand for our describing him as "a right jolly old elf." An elf, seriously? That's pagan superstition! Also, southwestern Asia Minor isn't exactly overrun with reindeer, and I'd bet that whatever reindeer might happen to be there can't fly. And Saint Nicholas certainly never visited the North Pole.

Even making Christmas about Santa Claus would have annoyed him. The original Santa Claus was willing to risk himself and his good standing for the sake of the integrity of the gospel of Jesus Christ. It is not Santa who is the chief giver of Christmas; it is God, who gave his Son to us. We are recipients but not consumers, as the secularization of Christmas would have it, for God's grace is inexhaustible, and it was bought at a price far beyond the power of our credit cards. Nicholas would have understood Christmas to be more about salvation than consumption or even sentimentality. As fun as it is to exchange gifts, it is not Santa but the nativity that should be the dominant symbol of our holiday. The nativity points to the marvelous confession that God became human in order to save us from our sins. That theological truth was just what Nicholas was fighting for at Nicaea.

Sometimes our modern Christmas appears very far removed from the incarnation of Christ that started the celebration in the first place. Indeed, our ways of celebrating might even make our holiday season more like a rival to Christmas than a celebration of it. After all, the word "holiday" literally means "holy day," which is not often remembered when we use the word simply to mean any excuse to get a day off from work. It seems clear that, even if done in Santa's own name, Santa himself would never put up with a celebration that detracted from the Christian gospel.

If Ol' Saint Nick was willing to take down Arius because of a perceived threat to Christianity, we must be bold enough to ask what violence Nicholas might be tempted to inflict on we moderns for what we have made out of Christmas, all tarnished with ashes and soot. Perhaps he would dole out noogies for saying the bland "Season's Greetings" instead of "Merry Christmas"? Maybe a kick to the shins for thinking that leaving milk and cookies can substitute for receiving the body and blood at a Christmas Eve service? Or perhaps an elbow to the gut for being more concerned about purchasing a lavish gift than for investing our resources in churches and in charities? Would he "dash away all" attempts to remove the public display of Christian symbols, like nativity scenes? Maybe a slap on the head is in order for our being more interested in Rudolf or in filling out wish lists than in sitting down to read the Gospel of Luke together with the family. After all, Luke recounts the birth of the God-man Jesus Christ, whose divinity Nicholas would not permit to be down-played at the council.

Some think that a Christian shouldn't enact the mildest violence or hurt even the smallest thing. Not even a mouse. But it is evident from his willingness to forcefully lay his fingers aside of Arius' nose that Saint Nicholas did not agree with the pacifist's position. We'd better watch out, indeed.

CHAPTER 11

SANTA'S SWEATSHOP

Elf Exploitation for Christmas

Imagine Christmas morning: a young tot wakes up with jubilation and tippy-toes downstairs to discover presents under the holiday tree. Mom and Dad, roused by the early morning racket, shuffle groggily from their bedroom and nod in permission that he may open up his presents. Flinging off wrapping paper, the exultant lad discovers a red fire truck! Just what he asked Santa for in his letter! The child is overjoyed; his parents pleased. Merry Christmas.

An idyllic scene, to be sure. But where did that red fire truck come from? Little does the child know that fingers as tiny as his own built it: the toil of a work-elf in Santa's sweatshop.

Some have argued that elfs are made for such brutal labor: their crafting abilities unparalleled by human hands. Others contend that elfs are benefited by Santa's sweatshop, for what else would they do – work in a tree, baking delicious cookies? And isn't any elfish misery outweighed by the happiness of children on Christmas morning?

Elf labor, harnessed by Santa's billion-dollar Christmas industry, needs to be investigated. Only then can we determine whether Santa's labor practices are ethical or unethical. Such an exposé will prove difficult, however, as Santa is shrouded in myth and secrecy. His workshop's exact location is undetermined. His labor practices are undisclosed. His financials are off-book. And like Thomas Pynchon or J. D. Salinger, photographs of the man seem non-existent. Indeed, some skeptics naively assert that Santa doesn't actually exist. What better way for Santa to effectively dodge business regulations, taxes, and international law!

Given the dearth of biographical and operational information on Santa, one is left to engage in educated deduction. For instance, since Santaland doesn't appear on any global map, in governmental tax documents, or even on Google Earth, we are left to assume that it must be a sovereign estate. As such, Santa's workshop evades the purview of any national or global business regulations. Our evaluation of Santa's labor practices, then, cannot be a legal evaluation, but must be an ethical one. Is Santa exploiting elf labor? Is the Fat Man keeping the little man down?

By criticizing Santa, I am not trying to be a Scrooge, who pooh-poohs children's joy. Nevertheless, I fervently believe we have a moral responsibility to consider where these "free" toys are coming from. Nothing in this world is free. And even low-cost toys are sure to have a hidden high price. Ultimately, Santa must account for his labor practices. Mr. Claus: take down this candy cane wall!

The Myth of Christmas Elfs

According to the traditional myth, "christmas elfs" (as opposed to make-believe "elves") are magical creatures that live with Santa Claus in the North Pole. Contrasting with Santa's jollily corpulent stature and cherubic rotundity, elfs are a diminutive race with pointy ears and noses. They wear green outfits and contentedly craft the toys for Santa. Does anyone else find this paltry narrative dissatisfying? Naively idealistic and suspiciously deficient? Who *are* these elfs? Where did they come from? What do they think?

As to their exact origin, I can offer no speculation. Nonetheless, one thing is clear: elfs cannot be indigenous to the Arctic. Their small legs and feet would inhibit locomotion on a snowy tundra. Moreover, elfs have no fur or other means of thermal insulation. We can infer, then, that Santa brought the elfs to his workshop via magical sleigh, presumably as indentured servants to Santa – much like the Oompa-Loompahs of Willy Wonka's chocolate factory.[1] Both Santa and Wonka brought a diminutive race of people to work for them on-site. Ingeniously, this is an optimal way to attain cost-effective labor.

To date, no investigative reporting has managed to obtain a verifiable quote from any of these elfish workers. This leaves one with the burden of piecing together the most reasonable story of their labor conditions. For instance, given the lack of voice of these elfs, we can assume that they're not unionized, and would be afraid to speak ill of their work conditions, lest they lose their jobs. Also, they must have families, as both male and female elfs constitute Santa's workforce. So not only are these elfs captive workers, with little negotiating power, but they're under economic pressures to provide for not only themselves, but their dependents as well.

Ho-Ho, Ho-Ho: Off to Work Elfs Go

Elfs are the lifeblood of Santa's business. They labor for Santa throughout the year, with crunch-time arriving after Thanksgiving. The expanse of the North Pole provides a lot of space for storage of the toys and trinkets elfs make, until they can be later offloaded under Christmas trees around the world.

How might these elfs be compensated for such year-round labor? The toys that elfs make, we know, are given away by Santa. This might seem magnanimous of Santa toward the world's children, but what about these *other* little people, in his very own workshop? Santa can't pay them much, as he's not directly making any money from what they produce. However, Santa *does* compensate them, in part, by providing room and board for these elfs. This shouldn't necessarily reassure us, though, as house-slaves in the pre-Civil War South were also provided "free" room and board.

Elfs don't make much and probably don't keep much. From the lack of stores in the North Pole we can assume that Santa holds a monopoly on the sale of staple goods. Similar to the Joad family portrayed in John Steinbeck's *The Grapes of Wrath*, disenfranchised elfs likely pay their wages right back to Santa, through overinflated prices on essential goods.[2] Sure, the elfs can try to find a Wal-Mart somewhere, but the nearest store is hundreds of miles away. On foot. With very, very small feet.

A defender of Santa might justify the elfs' low wages via entitlement theory. Santa owns all of the resources and means of production. He offers elfs wages in exchange for their efforts. No one is *forcing* the elfs to work. Santa simply offers the elfs an opportunity that they otherwise wouldn't have. If the elfs don't like the terms of the exchange, they can choose not to enter into the contract. This is just an instance of free-market capitalism: a business owner holds absolute property rights to the capital and means of production. That means Santa can do whatever he wants with his property – after all, it's his. While it might be *nice* for Jolly Saint Nick to provide the elfs a living wage, dental benefits, and the like, he is by no means obligated to do so. His only obligation is to his stockholders.

Santa's publicist might identify children as Santa's sole stockholder group: he is merely an agent working for them. If he were to pay the elfs more, sure it might make some elfs happy, but these diverted resources would produce fewer toys for the tots. And who wants that? Christmas is for all of the world's children, and do we want some child, anticipating a bright shiny toy in his stocking, only to discover coal?

Ho-Ho Hopelessness: The Failure of Entitlement Theory

Several flaws lie in this entitlement reasoning. Elfs willingly accept their low wage, but what reasonable alternatives do they have? Once ensconced in Santa's workshop, they have little bargaining power. What are their choices? Work for whatever wage they can get, or be exiled into a frozen tundra, where they'd surely perish? That isn't much of a choice. Clearly, they don't have the ability to exit their employment contract, and they possess just as little leverage to renegotiate the terms.

Why did elfs agree to this indentured servitude to the SantaCo. machine? I will charitably assume that Santa didn't abduct them from their native land, as slave-traders did in colonial America. If Santa acted ethically and fully disclosed to the elfs, up front, the measly compensation package awaiting them, then surely their indigenous economic opportunities were scarce and bleak; otherwise, Santa wouldn't have gained their employment in such large numbers.

Oompa-Loompahs, the resident employees of Willy Wonka's chocolate factory, faced a similar choice. They signed on to Wonka's workforce because they otherwise would have been eaten by large predators indigenous to Loompahland, their island home. Without irony, Mr. Wonka paints himself a savior, rather than exploiter, of his orange-skinned laborers.

Is it truly generous, though, for an employer to give low wages to workers just because it provides them an alternative that is slightly less bad? Are elfs *really* free in their acceptance of Santa's labor contract? No, they're coerced into acceptance: not directly forced by Santa, but forced by their dismal conditions. Santa and Wonka, both, are taking advantage of their workers' bad initial circumstances. Their entitlement justification is based on a false dichotomy: the unvoiced third alternative is to pay them a fair wage. Consider the Wonka chocolate factory: If Mr. Wonka offers to save the Oompa-Loompah from the mouth of a preying beast *only if* they divest themselves entirely of all their possessions and freedom, wouldn't that be exploitive even if "freely" agreed to?

Absolute property rights are not absolute – not even Santa's. Entitlement rights are suspended if there isn't enough common property to go around. Consider philosopher John Locke's analogy to a water hole in the desert. If a person owns the only water hole in a desert, he must allow reasonable access to the water to others around him. After all, they would otherwise perish. Though the North Pole is a frozen tundra, it is much like that desert in Locke's example. And elfs, without reasonable access to essential goods in this tundra, would likewise perish. "Reasonable access" here means that the person is to be provided access to such resources without exploitation by the owner of the resources.

Santa is exploiting his elfs by precluding them the opportunity to exit their employment contract, and by begrudging them a living wage. Perhaps, at the very least, Santa's little helpers can negotiate for better terms. While a logical possibility, this doesn't seem likely, for what leverage do disenfranchised elfs have? If Santa's elfs were unionized, perhaps they'd have a fighting chance, but Santa – master of his sovereign domain – holds all the bargaining chips.

Elf-Self-Deception

The Christmas myth portrays elfs as contented, even happy. Even though divested of wealth and freedom, the elfs perhaps fully acquiesce to their low station. But would that suffice as an ethical justification? Consider reports of some contented house-slaves in the South before the Emancipation Proclamation. Some slaves, disenfranchised on the plantation, would also claim domesticated contentment – and would even refuse the possibility of freedom. This seems an anemic justification of their exploitation, nevertheless. Contentment and even happiness needs to be in the context of the subjects' full cognizance of other alternatives. This phenomenon was coined by Karl Marx as "false consciousness": "a failure to recognize the instruments of one's oppression or exploitation as one's own creation, as when members of an oppressed class unwittingly adopt views of the oppressor class."[3]

Consider the "Society for the Promotion of Elfish Welfare" (SPEW) in the Harry Potter book series.[4] Albeit a fictional example, Hermione

Granger's arguments for the liberation of house-elfs is illustrative for our purposes. The organization's task is to liberate house-elfs – even though the house-elfs whom she is trying to liberate do not want to be free. Nevertheless, Hermione recognizes their oppression, even though they do not recognize it themselves. And we, the thoughtful reader, recognize that Hermione is right: the domination of house-elfs by wizards must stop. These house-elfs are not even allowed to own property! We might assume the same of Santa's elfs. The house-elfs of the Potter series are frequent subjects of verbal lashings, as well as physical and magical violence. Like abused dogs, the house-elfs cower by the side of their owners. They are so conditioned by domination and terror that they would never even think of vying for liberation; most are uncomfortable when it is mentioned, and some even actively denounce it.

The "false consciousness" that elfs possess – in the Potter series as well as in real life – undermines any alleged consent by them to their servitude. True consent requires not just knowing alternative ways of life, but also requires full cognizance as to what these alternatives *are like*: experiential knowledge rather than mere propositional knowledge, if you will. If the elfs truly realized what it would be like to live full lives – no longer under the fat thumb of Santa – then I imagine they would surely prefer liberation: not just for themselves, but for their elfin families.

Elfs: Magically Exploitable

Across our culture, elfs are characterized as magical creatures. They make our cookies magically delicious. They make our cereal snap, crackle, and pop. They make our Christmas toys. It's a seductive fantasy. It almost seems empowering to elfs: after all, who wouldn't want to be magical?

Calling elfs magical is actually disempowering. Similar to calling a woman "sexy," this supposed compliment sounds elevating, but, really, it's objectifying. What does "magical" mean in relation to elfs? Implicitly, it means that they were made for the work they do: it is their natural purpose. Thus, we can ignore any rights they have or any goals they might have. Being magical, they're not like you or me. They're a special breed, much like Santa's reindeer that – while fantastical – are still slave to the mounted rider across the sky.

If elfs are magical, why aren't they out doing something fantastic? Why are they trapped in a cookie-baking tree, on a cereal box, in Santa's workshop? I guess what makes them magical is their complacency. Attributing the adjective "magical" to something turns it into a tool, rather than a person. Consider magical characters in fairy-tales: Cinderella's godmother was merely a tool – turning a pumpkin into a chariot, mice into horses – all of this just so Cinderella could enjoy an evening out.

We should be wary when something is put up on a pedestal: it excuses us from considering it as an equal, as real. It allows us to oppress that "magical" being. Consider the history of sexism against women. On one hand, wives were regarded as madonnas: near-holy, domestic goddesses of the home, worthy of awe and admiration as they carry out their little duties, as only they could do – as only they were "fit" to do. On deeper investigation, however, these women were near-slaves: exalted yet subjugated.

Elfs are shackled by the same idealization: they are carrying out duties that only they can do – that only they are "fit" to do. After all, intricate toys and dolls are best fashioned by elfish hands, aren't they? Why is that? Sure, elfs have small hands, but that's not magical. Is there something magical about being short? Next time you're near a short person, I suggest you call them "magical." You'll get a swift punch to the knee for the compliment.

Santa's Little Helpers: A "Magical" Mere Means

Since elfs are "magical" and thereby fit for thankless toil, Santa takes license to exploit elfs as mere tools to produce his cheap goods. German philosopher Immanuel Kant (1724–1804) would denounce Santa's treatment of these elfs, citing the second formulation of his categorical imperative: "Act in such a way that you treat humanity, whether in your own person or in the person of any other, always at the same time as an end and never merely as a means to an end."[5]

Elfs, like other humanoids, possess rationality, autonomy, and free will. As such, elfs have unconditional, intrinsic value. Santa's business enterprise is morally deficient in failing to distinguish between humanoid and non-humanoid means of production. After all, this is one reason we recognize slavery as repugnant: it treats persons as mere chattel, as property to be owned and traded. Elfs are not property. They are not tools. They are not machines. They are humanoid beings: with feelings, and emotions, with hopes and dreams.

Kant reasons that no individual could consistently universalize the rule that everyone treat each other as mere objects to further their own ends. Every individual wants to have their intrinsic value to be recognized and respected. Employing elfs as mere tools to his own ends, Santa is acting on a rule that he himself would not endorse. He would not want himself to be used as a mere means to someone else's end. He recognizes himself as having intrinsic and unconditional value, worthy of respect rather than exploitation.[7]

Treating elfs with respect requires providing them a moral minimum: namely, a living wage, affordable healthcare, freedom to negotiate terms of labor, and a right to meaningful work and meaningful lives. Respect also requires not frustrating their humanoid needs, such as a right to privacy.

"He knows when you are sleeping"

Santa is sure to disregard elfin workers' privacy rights. Like Mr. Wonka's Oompa-Loompahs, Santa's elfs have been secreted away, only to live and work in a sprawling industrial complex. Why are they cloistered and isolated from the outside world? Primarily, this protects the owner from having to submit to any negative publicity or work regulations. Second, this protects against any "leaks" of proprietary information. Before he indentured Oompa-Loompahs, Willy Wonka had his fantastical secrets betrayed to a competitor who bribed one of Wonka's workers. The rebirth of Wonka's chocolate factory exclusively used on-site Oompa-Loompah labor to ensure industrial espionage could never occur again.

The magnitude of Santa's secrets parallels those of Wonka. Not only does Santa's internal operations teem with valuable proprietary information, but the very location of his workshop is a secret! Think about the danger of an elf rolling over on rolly-polly Santa – whether to the media or a competitor. SantaCo. could come tumbling down.

How could Santa quash defection or liberation? Not only by isolating his workforce, but by surveilling them 24/7, as do many sweatshop corporations overseas. The close monitoring of employees would also prove in Santa's general economic interest: it goes hand-in-tiny-hand with keeping an obedient, productive workforce. For these reasons, we can assume that Santa's surveillance of his workers is extensive. As the song ominously forewarns, "He knows when you are sleeping / He knows when you're awake / He knows when you've been bad or good / So be good for goodness' sake!"[6] Sounds like a merry jingle that belongs in George Orwell's *Nineteen Eighty-Four*.[7] All hail Santa: a.k.a. Big Brother.

MATTHEW BROPHY

If Santa has the goods (and bads) on kids throughout the world, surely he knows about those under his own roof! Monitoring employees may be reasonable to a point, but workers live on-site, they lose all personal respite. All workers need a private life. Imagine if your entire life was broadcast to your employer, 24/7. Even in bedrooms and bathrooms!

Free of any laws and regulations, Santa has no reason to provide such allowances. We can reasonably assume, then, that Santa's provisions of elf safety and comfort are sure to be minimal. Injuries woodworking, sewing, and assembly are among the most dangerous in cottage industries. The frequency and degree of these injuries increases with the long hours. Paid work-breaks, mandated in many countries, would not need to be observed by Santa. So elfs could toil in the workshop for 15-hour days (without bathroom breaks). The elfs' only reprieve would be to collapse, exhausted, on their tiny bunk beds to sleep a few winks until the workday starts again. Not exactly a "magical" existence, is it?

Christmas Joy = Elfploitation

Ursula K. Le Guin's short story "The Ones Who Walk Away from Omelas" paints a picture of a utopian society where everyone is happy, content, and flourishing.[8] The dirty little secret, it turns out, is that the happiness of Omelas is magically dependent on the squalid enslavement of a child – hidden away in the basement of a town building. This small being is isolated, alienated, and unaided. If the child is liberated, the happy society will quickly degenerate.

The ethical theory called utilitarianism would fully endorse such exploitation. Utilitarianism only cares about maximizing net happiness: maximizing the greatest good for the greatest number. Utilitarianism asserts that the ends justify the means – even if the "means" to optimal happiness is the sacrifice of a few innocents. But doesn't such exploitation – even of a single child – strike us as wrong, greater happiness be damned? Imagine that *you* were a citizen of Omelas. Would you participate in the exploitation of this child to further your own happiness? Or would you "walk away from Omelas," like some in Le Guin's story do, refusing to be complicit in such dirty deeds?

The elfs in Santa's workshop are like the child in Le Guin's story: trapped in cramped, squalid conditions – all for the greatest good for the greatest number. Children around the world might be made happy due to exploitation of elf labor, just as the Omelian citizens were made happy by a child's exploitation. Yet is "greater happiness" a sufficient ethical justification for enslavement?

Consider that it could be *you* in the elf's place. Imagine that you were behind a "veil of ignorance" where you didn't know what person you would end up being in society – including a child in the basement being exploited, or an elf shackled on the factory line. Would you endorse such slave-societies, where a few were sacrificed for the benefits of the rest? Or would you choose a non-exploitative society, where the minority wasn't sacrificed for the "greater good" of the majority? I presume that no rational person would freely exploit a child, or an elf, directly themselves. I offer that we should make ourselves as happy as we can by our own efforts and devices, and shouldn't build our bliss on the shoulders of slaves or servants.

Elfs work hard and make the products that children enjoy on Christmas morning. Santa may give these products away for free, but don't be fooled. Santa's sleigh is full of cash at the end of the year due to product placement and marketing revenues. All the fruits of elf labor are split between Santa and the children. Elfs, on the other hand, get scrooged. In similar industries overseas, a worker under such conditions as the elfs might get 3 cents for every shirt they produce, or 18 cents for every toy they produce. That's mere dollars a day. Don't the workers that make these products from raw materials *deserve* more than 1 percent of its value? Shouldn't they be partners in the creation? Elfs put in a hard day's work for Santa – year in and year out – and they deserve reciprocation from him. They deserve to share in the fruits of their hard labor. Shouldn't Santa's attitude be gratitude? Shouldn't he treat his workforce better?

Sleigh the Myth of Santa: Boycott Christmas

Santa is the Kim Jong-Il of the North Pole. Santa disseminates exaggerations, similar to those of the North Korean dictator, of his own origins and abilities. And Santa's public relations machine not only keeps all of his elf-exploitative operations under wraps, but purposefully orchestrates positive myths about the jolly fat man.

Yet when we remove the jingling bells, take off the bow, and unwrap the "gift" of Christmas, we are disabused of the illusion. We see the truth. Christmas is a holiday burdened upon the frail shoulders of elfs. Only through the exploitation of elf labor can Santa give toys away for free.

While excited tots may be jubilant on Christmas morning, parents need to be aware of Santa's scam.

We all need to make the moral decision to not participate in Santa's suspicious gift give-away. Nothing in this world comes for free. And like the Omelian citizens in Le Guin's short story – or the wizards in the Harry Potter series – we should not benefit from another's misery.

This essy is my call to action: boycott Christmas this year, and every year, until Santa is held accountable for his business practices. Santa must make his business operations transparent. He must abide by the global regulations of the Caux Roundtable Principles and UN Global Compact. Both documents call for respect of workers, freedom of association, the abolition of compulsory labor, and the ability for employees – as stakeholders – to voice complaints and negotiate contracts. Santa needs to abide by the same moral rules other businesses should respect, rather than cleverly circumventing them.

But I leave it up to you, the reader, to decide where your morality lies. Before you make your decision, all I ask is that you please think of the elfs: those little workers toiling with Sisyphean effort, day in and day out, isolated in the wastes of the North Pole. I trust your conscience – your *true* Christmas spirit – will move you to be a deliberate Scrooge this holiday, and resist Santa's seasonal seduction. Whatever you may decide, though, one thing is clear: I won't be getting any gifts from Santa this year.

NOTES

1   *Willy Wonka & The Chocolate Factory*. Dir. Mel Stuart. Perfs. Gene Wilder and Jack Albertson. Videocassette. David L. Wolper Productions, 1971.
2   John Steinbeck, *The Grapes of Wrath* (New York: Viking, 1939).
3   Freedictionary.com.
4   J. K. Rowling, *Harry Potter and the Goblet of Fire* (New York: Scholastic Press, 2000).
5   Immanuel Kant, *Groundwork of the Metaphysics of Morals (1785)*, trans. H. J. Paton (New York: Harper and Row, 1964).
6   "Santa Claus is Coming to Town," written by J. Fred Coots and Haven Gillespie, 1934.
7   George Orwell, *Nineteen Eighty-Four* (London: Secker and Warburg, 1949).
8   Ursula K. Le Guin, "The Ones Who Walk Away from Omelas," in *The Wind's Twelve Quarters* (New York: Bantam, 1973).

PART IV

THE MORALITY OF CHRISTMAS

CHAPTER 12

AGAINST THE SANTA CLAUS LIE
The Truth We Should Tell Our Children

American adults encourage their children to believe that an all-knowing, all-seeing, rosy cheeked fat man in a red suit named "Santa Claus," pulled in a sleigh by flying reindeer, will come down their home's chimney and give them presents on December 24 – but only if they are good and sleeping. And the adults go to extreme lengths to keep their children ignorant for as long as they can. They tell and re-tell the stories, assuage doubts with "magical explanations," and even concoct false evidence. There is a standing non-verbal agreement to keep other people's children naïve of the truth – violation of which can get you fired.[1] And when the kids earnestly ask for the truth, adults flat-out lie. "Yes, Virginia, there *is* a Santa Claus."

Why do we tell the Santa Claus lie? Where does it come from? I don't have time for all the details, but in short …

Centuries after the "death" of St. Nicholas, people began to believe he visited small rewards onto the faithful annually on his death's anniversary. Why? Because Christianity appropriated pagan myths for conversation purposes, and pagan gods – such as Odin, Thor, and Hold Nickar – were already believed to be December gift givers. Eventually, Nicholas was given a sidekick – someone to dole out the punishment for being bad. Krampus, as he was often called, was originally a pagan goat man fertility god, but the church demoted him to "Santa-Sidekick" to prevent pagan converts from continuing to worship him. When Protestants came to America they left Catholic saints like Nicholas behind, but they did enjoy scaring their kids into obedience. The few who still celebrated Christmas modified the demonic Krampus by mixing in a few of St. Nicholas' non-saintly features, called their creation "Pelznichol," and had him visit on Christmas Eve. (Watch out; if you're bad, he might carry you off in his sack ... to hell.)

Clement Moore – in an attempt to make Christmas more about children and less about poor people trying to get into his house – borrowed from the Pelznichol tradition and published (but probably didn't write) " 'Twas the Night Before Christmas." Moore got his wish when the poem caught on as a fad and soon everyone (even the poor) spent Christmas tricking their children into believing "St. Nick" would deliver presents on Christmas Eve. St. Nick changed over time. Some claim that his name's Dutch pronunciation – Sinter Klass – was butchered by Americans into "Santa Claus." Thomas Nast turned him from "a right jolly old elf" into a full grown and rotund person with a drawing for *Harper's Weekly* in 1881. And Coca-Cola solidified his dress into a Coca-Cola-red suit with their ad campaign that started in 1931. But the lie Clement Moore promoted is basically the Santa Claus lie we tell today.[2]

But what's the big deal? Isn't it all in fun? I know it's a lie, but some lies are okay, right? Right. But the Santa Claus lie is not one of them. It's not that the Santa Myth should be forgotten or removed from Christmas. But we should stop teaching and encouraging our children to believe that the Santa Myth is *literally* true. Why? I'll give you three good reasons.

Reason 1: It's a Lie, and Lying is Wrong

Many parents will try to excuse their behavior by suggesting the Santa Claus lie isn't a lie. "Santa is real; he's my husband." But your husband does not live at the North Pole, own flying reindeer, nor is he all-knowing. Either you are lying about Santa's existence, or you are lying about your husband's mailing address, livestock, and cognitive abilities. Others say, "I don't lie. I just don't tell them the truth. I read the story, label the gifts and let them draw their own conclusion." But lying is wrong because it is a form of deception, and deception is wrong. Engaging in deception – half-truths and false evidence – to make your kids believe in Santa is just as bad as lying about it. "I didn't lie; I just didn't tell the whole truth" doesn't excuse anything.

DAVID KYLE JOHNSON

Immanuel Kant (1724–1804) argues that lying is always wrong. He suggests that any action that would lead to a contradiction if universalized is immoral. Since, if everyone lied, communication would be impossible, and thus no one could lie, lying is always immoral. But that can't be right. If a simple lie can, say, save a life then that lie would seem morally justified. So, maybe the Santa Claus lie has justifying consequences that make it okay. What are the consequences and do they justify it?

The Santa Claus lie is supposedly fun for children because it creates awe and excitement during the Christmas season. Even if this is true, it is hardly noble enough to justify lying. (It's not like saving a life.) Besides, usually we don't think "lying to get people to believe what they want" is justifiable. Cult leaders do that to their followers; the government does it to its citizens. Plato (429–347 BCE) called such things "Noble Lies" – he proposed one to keep his republic in line – but people usually don't think they are very noble. As a professor, I would be doing my students a disservice if I simply let them believe what they wanted. Parents are doing the same with Santa.

In any case, I don't think it is a literal belief in Santa that creates the awe and excitement; it's the presents. What would happen if kids had to choose between St. Nicholas bringing a single gift that fills their shoe and parents buying loads of presents? And if it's "awe" you want, how about throwing some Krampus into your holiday traditions? Literal belief in Santa is not necessary for kids to possess the "Christmas Spirit" – in fact, it would be much better if we produced awe and excitement without literal belief in Santa (and without presents). How about some generosity to the less fortunate, instead?

Another consequence of the Santa Claus lie is the fun parents have watching their kids get all excited. But I've never known "it's fun" to legitimately excuse an immoral action. It would also be fun to trick your children into believing you bought magic beans, watch them plant them in the back yard and wait for a beanstalk. But wouldn't you feel bad about lying to them and exploiting their *naïveté*?

There are other proposed justifications for the Santa Claus lie. Some think parents *are* justified in lying to their children to create an illusion of security. For example, a parent may lie to their children about a national security crisis or corruption in politics. Maybe the Santa Claus lie can play a similar role. But only if the Santa Claus lie were necessary for such an illusion could it be justified on the grounds of creating one – and it is not. Even if torture could provide information vital to national security, if there are other less morally objectionable ways to acquire the same information, torture would obviously not be justified. In the same way, even if you could create an illusion of security with the Santa Claus lie, that you can create one without it nullifies this defense.

In addition, I think this line of reasoning overstates the impact of the Santa Claus lie. It creates awe and wonder, sure – maybe even warm fuzzies. But such things should not be confused with a sense of security. It is entirely unclear how the lie that a stranger will invade your house in the middle of the night makes one feel safe and no parent I know says they tell the Santa Claus lie for this purpose. In fact, for some children, the Santa Claus lie has the opposite effect. The children of one of my colleagues would rather Santa just leave the presents on the porch and a student of mine recollected always being very worried about her parents leaving the front door unlocked for Santa because they didn't have a chimney.

Reason 2: Santa Doesn't Have Your Best Interests in Mind

There are some practical reasons to avoid telling the Santa Claus lie as well. For one, Santa steals the credit you should be receiving for gift-giving and robs your children of an opportunity to learn how to show appreciation to real people who deserve it. The Santa Claus lie can also hinder a child's moral development. We learn to be virtuous by imitating virtue, even if the imitation is motivated, at first, to avoid punishment.[3] But prompting obedience through bribery? If a child comes to think that material reward is the main goal of good behavior, what will s/he think once s/he learns that, in the real world, material reward is most often the reward of bad behavior? Good behavior should be seen as its own reward, not something used to get a reward. And when family finances prevent your child's good behavior from being rewarded (but the class's spoiled brat gets lavish reward), a child's understanding of good behavior can be warped.

But the most important practical concern involves the consequences of finding out the truth. It can be upsetting and even damaging, not only because, to the child, Santa just "died" but because s/he learns that s/he has been lied to, systematically, for a long period of time by those s/he trusted most: his/her parents. I canvassed my friends, relatives, and students for stories about this defining moment. I was surprised how many negative stories I received. This was my favorite.

DAVID KYLE JOHNSON

Jay got into an argument at school with his best friend about Santa. He defended Santa's existence profusely, and eventually the entire class was involved. Jay's main argument was that Santa must exist because his mother told him he did, and his mother would not lie to him. To settle the issue, Jay sought out the classroom encyclopedia. Upon reading the words "Santa Claus: A fictional character ..." in front of the whole class, he looked up at his teacher, wanting her to tell him it wasn't true. "But I could tell by her slumped shoulders and the look in her eye she couldn't. I remember that moment like it was yesterday. I was so embarrassed because my ignorance was revealed in such public display, in front of all my friends. I had said my mother would never lie to me, but clearly she had. Mrs. Stubblefield was apologetic, but I realized that she was in on the deception too. I, seriously, still get upset when I talk about it."

But I received countless others. Many viewed it as conspiracy to deceive them. Julie was so upset, she refused to open her presents. Sara's brother is still openly hostile to their parents every Christmas. Caleb's mom caught her dad in the act and was so upset she vowed to never teach her children to believe (she kept her word). Parents think that the Santa Claus lie is worth the "magical wonder," but most kids think differently. Sure, belief in Santa is fun, but they would rather not be the victim of perpetrated grand delusion. They are learning about the world, and they trust their parents to tell them the truth about it. When that trust is violated, they feel betrayed.

The most famous example of a child wanting to know the truth about Santa is Virginia O'Hanlon. We all know the famous answer to her 1897 letter to the *New York Sun*: "Yes, Virginia, there is a Santa Claus." But her question reveals much about her childhood mindset and desires. "I am 8 years old. Some of my little friends say there is no Santa Claus. Papa says, 'If you see it in The Sun, it's so.' Please tell me the truth, is there a Santa Claus?"[4] She is not seeking someone to tell her what she wants to hear. Her friends say one thing, her parents another; she is tired of not knowing what to think. She wants the truth and with "Please tell me the truth," she reveals that she trusts the *Sun* to give it to her. Francis Church's reply violates that trust.

Of course, not everyone's story is traumatic, not everyone remembers, and some I surveyed said they missed the wonder that belief in Santa brought. A study (1979) showed that, upon learning the truth, although 39 percent of kids were disappointed, only 6 percent felt betrayed.[5] But given the severity of the possible consequences, I would consider that significant. You would avoid an action that risked a 6 percent chance of crippling your child. Obviously, losing your child's trust is not as severe, but are the benefits really worth the risk?

Reason 3: The Damage to Credulity

There is yet another reason telling the Santa Claus lie is immoral. In "The Ethics of Belief" William Clifford (1845–79) argues "it is wrong always, everywhere, and for anyone, to believe anything upon insufficient evidence."[6] He tells the story of a ship owner who believes without evidence, but at the peril of his crew and passengers, that his ship is seaworthy to avoid being required to have it inspected and repaired.[7] Clifford concludes that any belief like the ship owner's – belief without evidence that risks harm to others – is morally wrong. But, Clifford argues, all belief without evidence risks harm to others. Whether your belief is true or false, if you believe without evidence you promote credulity – a mental laziness, a lack of critical thinking – in you and others that promotes false belief and superstition, and holds back the progress of humankind.

I think Clifford goes a bit too far. As William James (1842–1910) argued in "A Will to Believe," sometimes belief without evidence is unavoidable. Since we can't be morally blamed for something that can't be avoided, belief without evidence is sometimes morally permissible. However, since the evidence for Santa's non-existence is overwhelming, James's argument can't be used to defend belief in Santa. In addition, Clifford does seem to have a point about credulity: it's bad and promoting it is immoral. But isn't this exactly what teaching your kids to believe in Santa does?

When children begin to doubt, parents often suggest the child continue to believe despite the evidence – like Laurie, who loved Santa so much she continued to believe in Santa even after she found out the truth. But stifling doubt and ignoring evidence to continue to believe what is comforting is an extremely bad thinking habit. Parents will also try to explain the doubts away with false explanations for Santa's Christmas Eve worldwide excursion, or chimney entries, for example. But thinking these explanations are good ones can't be good for the child's developing logic skills. Worse yet, parents may simply appeal to magic. But do you really want your kids believing in magic; do you want them believing that magicians are supernatural rather than illusionists? (Think they'll grow out of it? Some of my critical thinking students believe Chris Angel really can

DAVID KYLE JOHNSON

walk on water.) Not only does this encourage bad thinking skills, but you also lose the opportunity for a lesson against them.

Then there is *making up false evidence* for Santa Claus. One of my students' parents made "ash boot-prints" from the chimney to the tree. Jason's father made a fake video that "caught Santa on tape." Another student of mine left a note asking Santa to take a picture of himself with his camera; the parents photographed a friend in a Santa suit, and the student carried the picture around for a whole year showing it to his friends as "Santa Proof." Funny, sure – but this distorts a child's ability to decipher good evidence from bad and encourages the child to find bad evidence convincing – obviously, again, distorting critical thinking abilities.

Something that lights up, like a neon sign, most of what is wrong with tricking your children with lies and false evidence is a "movie" called *Search for Santa*.[8] It is a 30-minute *mockumentary*, intended for children with waning belief in Santa. Actors playing archeologists, physicists, and explorers present faulty arguments and fake evidence for Santa, in the name of "Santa Science." The "evidence" includes a planted 800-year-old sleigh runner found in "the desert," a shaky faux bigfoot-style video that shows, for a frame, what appears to be Santa delivering presents, and a staged trip to "the magnetic north pole" to find Santa's workshop. The actors make false statements, are highly speculative, equate "gut feeling" with "empirical evidence" and claim that their findings undeniably prove Santa's existence. Could anything be more poisonous to a mind seeking examples of how to think and reason?

Of course, you may not think critical thinking skills are that big of a deal. But a perusal of Gallup, Pew, and other polls reveals that many Americans believe the sun revolves around the earth (18 percent), in creationism (42 percent), spiritual healing (55 percent), ESP (41 percent), ghosts (32 percent), telepathy (31 percent), UFOs (24 percent), clairvoyance (26 percent), communication with the dead (21 percent), astrology (25 percent), witches (21 percent), and reincarnation (20 percent). Other myths include that Obama is Muslim and not a US citizen, that the world will end in 2012, and conspiracy theories like that the US government perpetrated 9/11. Most of these beliefs can lead to harm, but one can know they are false if one simply has the critical thinking skills to evaluate the evidence. I don't think the Santa Claus lie is completely responsible for our ignorance, but it certainly isn't helping improve our critical thinking abilities.

Richard Dawkins has recently expressed concern about children's exposure to Harry Potter and other fairy tales, thinking they might produce "insidious affect on [children's] rationality."[9] No studies have been done yet, but if merely reading or hearing fairy tales is harmful to a child's critical thinking skills, how much more harmful is tricking children into really believing one? I am not saying that we should do away with fairy tales, Harry Potter, or the Santa Claus myth. But in the same way that we tell children that fairy tales and Harry Potter are not real, we should tell children that Santa Claus is not real either. We need not announce it upon every fairy tale's first reading – until they are about two-and-a-half, they don't know the difference between reality and fantasy anyway.[10] But as soon as they are old enough to understand the difference, and ask for the truth, we should give it to them. "No, Virginia, Santa Claus is pretend."

Having Faith in Santa

Some will argue belief in Santa encourages faith in children, and the ability to have faith is a skill most parents want their child to have. This, in fact, was the point that Francis Church was trying to make in his reply to Virginia's question in the *New York Sun*.

> Virginia, your little friends are wrong. They have been affected by the skepticism of a skeptical age. They do not believe except they see ... Yes, Virginia, there is a Santa Claus.... How dreary would be the world if there were no Santa Claus!... There would be no childlike faith then, no poetry, no romance to make tolerable this existence.... Not believe in Santa Claus! You might as well not believe in fairies.... The most real things in the world are those that neither children nor men can see.... Only faith, poetry, love, romance, can push aside that curtain and view and picture the supernal beauty and glory beyond.[11]

Church thinks we should encourage our children to believe in Santa because the faith belief in Santa calls for is necessary to "view and picture the supernal beauty and glory beyond" because "the most real things in the world are those that neither children nor men can see."[12] But he has given us a false dichotomy (presented only two options when there are more), a classic logical mistake: either we embrace the kind of faith required for belief in Santa, or we are condemned to believe in only what we see, thus rendering life meaningless. But one can have faith, and even believe in the invisible, without embracing the kind of faith necessary for belief in Santa.

DAVID KYLE JOHNSON

He makes this mistake because he fails to distinguish between the two kinds of faith. The first is *belief despite sufficient evidence to the contrary*. This is the kind of faith that belief in Santa requires. Virginia's friends were not victims of a skeptical age, unable to believe in what they couldn't see. They had learned the truth; either their own eyes or their parents had provided conclusive evidence. To continue to believe, they would have to ignore that evidence. The second kind of faith is *belief without sufficient evidence*. This is the kind of faith that scientists have in the reliability of induction and Ockham's razor (favoring the simplest explanation), that the religious have in God's existence, and that we, as Americans, have in our inalienable rights to life and liberty. You can't prove such things, you just assume them. And this kind of faith is sufficient for belief in those things Church holds dear (like poetry, romance, and love). Such things cannot be proven or disproven, so you don't have to ignore evidence to believe in any of them.

Of course, maybe parents want to encourage *believing despite evidence to the contrary*. But I wouldn't advise it. This is what Islamic fundamentalists do when they continue to believe that God wants them to kill innocents. It's what Mormons do as they continue to believe that the Garden of Eden is in Jackson County, Missouri and that black skin is punishment for sin. It's what Scientologists do as they believe, literally, science fiction writer L. Ron Hubbard's story about the intergalactic lord Xenu. This is what creationists do when they still believe the earth is only 6,000 years old. This is what some Hindus do as they believe that the Ganges river is not polluted, because it's a goddess, despite the evidence it is.[13] Of course, belief in Santa is not as harmful as these beliefs, but it's the same kind of belief. If we want our kids to be rational, shouldn't we discourage it? Do we really want our children, literally, believing in fairies?

Ironically, if you want your kids to believe in God, you might want to skip Santa. Tennille tells her story:

> When I was real young I was told to believe in this Santa.… My mom tried real hard to get us to believe in him, but … one year my mother made a goof and wrapped a Barbie for my brother. I knew that this all awesome Santa would not make such a mistake and my mom explained that she was in fact Santa. I was mad because she tried so hard to lie to me and it made me wonder what else she lied to me about.… Unfortunately it also lead [*sic*] to my questioning of God. It made sense now why I did not always get what I asked for for Christmas because Santa did not exist, so when I prayed to God and things did not come true I figured my mother made him up too. It made a very big impact because I spent years being mad at God when I could have had faith and lightened my load.

Cut It Out, Wrap It Up

Since I first started talking about writing this essay, I have heard more objections than Santa has elves. Let's very quickly deal with the most common ones.

The fact that *everyone does it* is certainly no excuse. If your friends jumped off a bridge, would you? Some claim that Santa belief encourages imagination; but among all those I know that never believed in Santa, not one of them lacks imagination. The fact that "they are only kids" doesn't make the damage less severe, but more severe; those are our formative years. Those who get made fun of are not those who eschew belief but those who believe for too long. Others claim "It is every child's right to believe in Santa Claus!" But are Jewish parents violating their children's rights? One person claimed that telling children the truth will lead them to a universal doubt about adult veracity. But all kids find out eventually, and when they do this doesn't happen. And if it did, that would seem to be a good reason for doing away with the lie altogether.

Of course, some kids who grow up believing in Santa turn out to have good critical thinking skills; but such evidence is merely anecdotal. My argument is only that encouraging belief in Santa risks retarding or preventing those skills. Some have resorted to name calling. "You're just a loveless killjoy that hates children." My critical thinking students know such replies are called "ad hominems" and that calling someone who presents an argument a name does not invalidate their argument – even if the name is accurate, which by the way it's not.

Lynda Breen has argued that the benefits of belief in Santa include "family bonding and pro-social behavior, including sharing" and "enhanced fantastical thinking, expansion of the internal object world and purposeful play." I can't argue with the results of her studies, but I can point out that none of the benefits she mentions are gained exclusively by promoting literal belief in Santa Claus; teaching children *about* Santa Claus would bring about the same benefits. I think educating your children about the myth of Santa, promoting the spirit of Christmas, encouraging emulation of Santa's generosity and establishing Christmas traditions are all fantastic. But none of this – including gift giving in Santa's name – requires literal belief in the Santa Claus Myth.

I hope I have convinced you to avoid it and that you won't let your desire for your child to be cute to stand in the way of doing the right

DAVID KYLE JOHNSON

thing. If your children already believe, hopefully you will tell them the truth as soon as possible. If nothing else, I hope I have convinced you to voluntarily reveal the truth to them at an early age – 5 or 6 at the latest. If there is one thing I have learned, it's that too many parents simply let the belief in Santa go on for far too long.

If you are worried about damage that you have already done and are wondering how to reveal the truth to your children, perhaps you can kill two birds with one stone. Turn your child's lesson into a critical thinking game. Try the Socratic Method: lead them through a series of questions that lets them figure it out on their own (then agree). This way they get a miniature logic lesson, they won't feel like you lied to them, and they will know the truth. But I don't suggest telling the Santa Claus lie for the purpose of creating a critical thinking lesson opportunity; the entire process would do more harm than good and there are better, less damaging ways to teach reasoning skills.

Of course, there is the issue of how to have your child interact with other children who believe. One story I received was about Ingrid who tried to tell her 1st grade class that Santa wasn't real. The teacher pulled her outside and yelled "Let the other children believe what they want to believe." Once again, telling children it's okay to believe what you want, despite the evidence, simply because you want to is a really bad critical thinking lesson. Then there is my college roommate Kush who, as a high school freshman, told an annoying neighborhood five-year-old there was no Santa, just to spite him. That seems a bit far. I encourage you, however, to encourage your child not to lie about it. How about, "Santa is just pretend at my house."

Santa is an agglomeration of ancient mythical beings – from Norse deities to pagan goat-gods. We abandoned literal belief in such beings long ago as we matured as a species. But, for some reason, we have allowed it to survive as a strange lie we tell our children every Christmas. It's finally time to mature once more, and let these beings fade into the past – for our own good, and for the sake of the children.[14]

NOTES

1   Daily Mail Reporter, "Primary school teacher who told children: 'Santa does not exist' is fired," December 11, 2008; available online at www.dailymail.co. uk/news/article-1093535/Primary-school-teacher-told-children-Santa-does-exist-fired.html.

2 I have not done justice to the entire story here, and I have not given you many citations – I just didn't have room. Please, go to me webpage – http://staff.kings.edu/davidjohnson/ – and download (for free) my "history of Santa" paper. You won't be sorry.

3 Andre Comte-Sponville, *A Small Treatise on the Great Virtues* (New York: Holt Paperbacks, 2002), ch. 1.

4 "Is There A Santa Claus?" *New York Sun*, September 21, 1897, p. 6.

5 All these numbers were up from the 1896 study, however. I wonder what they would be now? "Why Do We Believe in Santa?" Université de Montreal, News Digest, December 8, 2008; online at www.nouvelles.umontreal.ca/archives/2007-2008/content/view/2121/248/index.html.

6 William Clifford, "The Ethics of Belief," in Michael Peterson, William Hasker, Bruce Reichenbach, and David Basinger (eds.) *Philosophy of Religion: Selected Readings* (New York: Oxford University Press, 2007), p. 109.

7 Ibid., p. 104.

8 CustomFlix, August 24, 2006.

9 Martin Beckford, "Harry Potter Fails to Cast Spell over Professor Richard Dawkins," Telegraph.com, updated July 5, 2009; online at www.telegraph.co.uk/news/3255972/Harry-Potter-fails-to-cast-spell-over-Professor-Richard-Dawkins.html.

10 Jane Meredith Adams, "Imagination vs. Reality"; online at www.parenting.com/article/Mom/Development/Imagination-vs-Reality/3.

11 "Is There A Santa Claus?" *New York Sun*, September 21, 1897, p. 6.

12 A similar argument is made by Tony Woodlief, who hesitates to tell his children the truth about Santa because he wants to encourage their belief in the "impossible," which he sees as necessary for belief in God. See Tony Woodlief, "OK, Virginia, There's No Santa Claus. But There *Is* God," Wall Street Journal Digital Network, December 19, 2008; online at www.online.wsj.com/article/SB122963990662019887.html.

13 "Ganges River – Tremendous Pollution," online at www.ecologicalproblems.blogspot.com/2008/05/ganges-river-tremendous-pollution.html.

14 A special thanks to all those who submitted their "Santa stories."

DAVID KYLE JOHNSON

CHAPTER 13

LYING TO CHILDREN ABOUT SANTA

Why It's Just Not Wrong

 Lying is generally considered to be wrong. At the same time, the vast majority of people who lie to their children about the existence of Santa Claus do not feel they are doing anything wrong. Why is this? There seem to be two possible reasons for this belief. Either engaging in the custom about Santa Claus is not really lying, or lying to children about Santa Claus is actually not wrong. I think that parents who lie to their children about the existence of Santa Claus need not lose sleep for fear of having wronged their offspring. Simply put, lying to children about the existence of Santa Claus is not wrong. Parents' natural instinct or intuition on this matter is correct. Why think this is so? And why might parents feel that they are not doing anything wrong when they tell their children about Santa?

"Talking about Santa is not lying"

Parents might feel they are doing nothing wrong because they do not feel they are really lying. For example, there seems to be a distinction between cases in which we are faced with a clear question about the existence of Santa Claus, as a result of a child's natural inquisitiveness or as the result of an older sibling's spilling the beans, and cases in which one simply "goes along" with the custom. Now, while it seems clear that anyone who answers the direct question by affirming the existence of Santa Claus is lying, it might be questioned whether going along with the custom constitutes lying. This, it seems to me, is a mistake. Going along with the custom might be a less obvious form of lying, but it is lying nonetheless. Consider what goes along with the custom: sweet treats and drinks being left for Santa Claus, presents miraculously appearing overnight, stockings being filled, letters being sent to the North Pole and sometimes even being answered, the occasional home visit and such like things. These are all cases where a child is encouraged to believe in the existence of something which does not in fact exist, a case in which a false belief is encouraged, without the need for an actual statement about the existence of Santa Claus.

I personally had what I considered at the time to be hard evidence for the existence of Santa Claus, since he visited my paternal home without fail after lunch on Christmas day. The fact that one does not announce the existence of Santa Claus but instead provides evidence of his existence (say in the form of a half-eaten mince pie) is no different from the case where one does not officially announce the existence of a distant relative but provides evidence of his or her existence in the form of, say, presents from her. In both cases a belief in the existence of that person is encouraged and in the case of Santa Claus this is – there is no way of getting away from it – a false belief.

There is an interesting question one could ask at this point: Where should one stop in terms of providing evidence for Santa Claus' existence? For example, is it permissible to provide "photographic evidence" of the existence of Santa Claus and how long should one persist in the business of evidence provision? I shall return to this question in the final section of this essay, but for now my focus is on determining whether going along with custom really constitutes lying.

At this stage, the weight of evidence seems to tell against the person who might want to claim that going along with the custom is not the same as lying. Is there any avenue available to such a person? Could he claim that going along with the custom is not lying if one does not engage in the "spurious" business of evidence provision? He could, for instance, allow the child to find out about Santa Claus at school, but not encourage the belief in any way at home. There are two things we could say about this: first, not saying anything does not mean that one is not complicit in allowing the perpetuation of a lie, a lie one is clearly uncomfortable with. Second, this scenario is largely untenable from a practical perspective. Consider the likely outcome: a child will naturally begin to wonder why Santa Claus visits other houses, why other children get presents from him and write him letters though nothing of the kind occurs in his or her home. This is very likely to lead to the direct question, which the parent clearly wishes to avoid, and either the unravelling of the lie or its confirmation. You might as well have gone along with the custom to begin with. After all, we might rightly feel that such a half-hearted engagement with the Santa Claus custom defeats the whole point of the exercise.

What of the parent who engages in the custom, but protests that its interactive component, midnight cookie eating for example, does not place it in a different category to that of other stories? We talk to our children about a number of imaginary characters in stories: unicorns, Snow White, fire-breathing dragons, and Alice, to name but a few, and we certainly do not see this as lying. We might even make believe that these characters actually exist as part of making a story vivid and engaging. No parent would start telling a story by saying: "Now Johan, I am going to tell you a story about some people and creatures that are not real." Both child and parent can fully engage in a story and nonetheless retain a sense that what they are pretending is real for the purpose of a story or game is not *actually* real. Engaging in the custom regarding Santa Claus is no different than this, my imaginary parent might claim.

This claim is not quite accurate. Although it might be clear to the parent that he is engaging in make believe when he tells his child about Santa Claus, this is not necessarily clear to the child. Young children, though generally quite good at it, are not always able to distinguish between make believe and reality. Making the distinction in this case would be particularly hard for them because it appears that Mom and Dad expect them to *believe*, not just make believe. This is evident by the fact that (unlike normal make believe) the child has no control over the pretend scenario, everything that occurs in the pretend scenario which the child observes (eaten cookies, presents being left, letters returned) are solid features of reality, and information is passed on as fact rather than in the form of storytelling. Even though make believe and storytelling would be spoiled if it was announced that we are "merely playing a game" or only "pretending," it is still implicitly clear that we are playing a game at the outset. So if the child is not certain whether he is engaging in make believe (indeed, parents might often rely on this kind of confusion precisely to avoid having to come down on either side of the question), then it is not clear that the parents' awareness that they are playing make believe extends to the child. In this case going along with the custom can still be safely construed as lying.

If, on the other hand, it is clear to children that the whole Santa Claus business is a game played with their parents on a yearly basis, then the question regarding the existence of Santa Claus has already been answered in the negative. In this case, parents have made it clear that discussions about Santa Claus and his actions are a game and so have effectively told their children that Santa Claus does not exist. Here parents are not going along with the custom, they have in a sense created their own custom. Whether or not this is a good alternative, it is surely beyond the question we are actually examining here: whether going along with the custom in its original form constitutes lying.

So it's clear that parents have two options: either go along with the custom regarding Santa Claus, and to this extent lie, or abandon the custom, and not lie. If one chooses to go along with the custom regarding Santa Claus, lying is unavoidable. This much is clear. However, the underlying thought parents are trying to express in claiming they are not actually lying to their children seems valid. This is that nobody intends to harm their children by telling them about Santa Claus. There are three different ways of thinking about whether lying to children about Santa Claus is wrong and thus three ways of justifying the intuition of parents who lie to their children about Santa Claus that they are doing nothing wrong.

Why Might Lying Not Be Wrong?

The first way we can think of deciding the question of whether lying to children about Santa Claus is wrong is by looking at the action itself. For example, we could consider whether lying to children about Santa Claus, in the sense of going along with the custom, is something that we, as rational beings, would be happy for everyone to do. If we rationally arrive at the conclusion that this is something that it would be good for everyone to do then, the argument might go, it is good to lie to children about the existence of Santa Claus. In philosophical terms, this would constitute a deontological analysis of the question of the kind advocated by the philosopher Immanuel Kant (1724–1804).

Deciding the question in this way would partly depend on whether lying to children about Santa Claus falls under the general prohibition against lying or not. If lying is always wrong, as Kant claimed, can it be permissible to lie in some situations and not in others? And if so, can a Kantian analysis still capture the intuition that in lying to their children about Santa Claus parents are doing nothing wrong?

Consider the following thought experiment, referred to in philosophical circles as the "murderer at the door" example. A murderer presents himself at your door and asks you if your friend is inside. If you tell the truth, that your friend is inside, then he will be murdered. If you lie, then the murderer will go away and your friend will be unharmed. The intuition most people have is that lying is not wrong in this case. This goes against the Kantian analysis and might incline us to think that lying to children about Santa Claus is a case in which lying is simply not wrong. Such a conclusion would be tantamount to a rejection of this analysis of the question. Can something more be said to help Kant here? A Kantian theory can be refined to say that lying is always wrong but that in some cases what is wrong can diverge from what is best, and in the case of the murderer at the door it is best to lie, as the lesser of two evils. Extending this to our analysis of lying to children about the existence of Santa Claus would imply that we treat lying as wrong but at the same time as a necessary feature in the education of our children. If we lived in an ideal world, or if children were fully rational at birth, one might argue that lying would not be necessary. Treating the permissibility of lying to children in this way does not make lying good, just less wrong. It is wrong but permissible. However, this violates the key intuition we started with, namely that lying to children about Santa Claus is *not* wrong. Parents do not treat telling their children about Santa as regrettable precisely because they do not think they are doing anything wrong. This leads to the conclusion that a Kantian analysis does not constitute a promising avenue for resolving our Christmas puzzle.

But all is not lost. There is an alternative theory, one which considers the consequences of lying to children about Santa Claus and treats this calculation of consequences as the ultimate determinant of the goodness of an act. For example, one could argue that leading children to believe in the existence of Santa Claus causes, on balance, more happiness than unhappiness. Such a calculation would be part of a consequentialist analysis of the question, an ethical theory associated with the philosopher John Stuart Mill (1806–73). But consequentialism does not simply state that in determining whether an action is right or wrong we need to look at consequences. This is something that reasonable people will do anyway, whether or not they are consequentialists. The theory states that consequences are the *only* thing that matters in determining if an action is right or wrong. These consequences are evaluated in terms of their effects in trying to maximize an unconditional good. Mill, whose version of consequentialism is called utilitarianism, sought to maximize pleasure over pain. This approach, sadly, is as problematic as the Kantian approach outlined above. Apart from the difficulty of calculating consequences and comparing them, one has the sense that a utilitarian analysis does not account for all we care about when we tell our children about the existence of Santa Claus.

This point becomes clearer when we consider the potential educational effects of going along with the custom about Santa Claus. A plausible effect of stories about Santa Claus is that they make children act better. But it is not sufficient, in educational terms, that children only act well because they will get presents, because we want them to act well even when there is no reward attached to being good. We want the stories to make our children be better in some sense rather than simply buying us good behavior. For if our peace of mind was all we sought in engaging in the custom, then our claim to benefit our children by going along with the custom would be severely weakened. A utilitarian can claim that part of what is good about going along with the custom is that it gives children a good character, in the sense of a disposition to act well. It is in this respect that we might feel that utilitarianism fails to capture what we really care about in telling our children good stories. A utilitarian's interest in the development of character only treats it as a tool for the production of good action. If there were other more effective methods of getting children to act appropriately, a utilitarian would be equally happy with those. But is it true that all we should ultimately care about is good action? Is what we care about when we educate our children simply that they act in good ways, or rather that they become good people? Is getting them to act well important to us in an "impersonal way" because it leads to more goodness in the world, or is it important to us in a "personal way" because it leads them to be good people? And, surely, becoming a good person means something more than simply doing good things, for a bad person can also do good things, as can someone who has been indoctrinated to act in various ways, but we do not consider either of them to *be* good.

A different way of expressing the questions posed above would be to ask whether the primary focus of telling our children stories about Santa Claus should relate to the production of good action or to the development of their character. Ethical theories that put weight on

ERA GAVRIELIDES

character as the ultimate aim of our ethical thinking fall under the label "virtue ethics" and are associated with the Greek philosophers Plato (429–347 BCE) and Aristotle (384–322 BCE). A virtue ethicist is certainly not interested in character simply because it leads to good actions. He is interested in character in itself. A virtue ethicist is interested in determining whether a person is kind, charitable, and courageous. Character and living a good life are the ultimate things we should concern ourselves with and while it's true that a good *person* will act well, we should not get the order of priority the wrong way round. It is not the case that a person is good because he acts well (someone can do something good without being a good person), but rather that a person acts well because he is good. Good action is important in the development of a good character, for example in teaching children to act kindly, but it is not the end goal; the end is a good character (becoming a kind person).

Stories about Santa Claus fit more naturally within a plan of character education rather than a plan the end goal of which is the production of kinds of action. It is certainly true that prizes and punishment encourage a disposition to act well, and this is a key part of the educational process, as we have said. Yet we should not ignore the fact that an equally important, if not more important, function of stories about Santa Claus is that they lead children to view certain character traits like kindness, charity, and joviality as desirable in themselves, and encourage them to adopt those traits. If all we were trying to achieve by telling our children stories about Santa Claus was to get them to either mechanically adopt certain forms of conduct, or develop an instrumental interest in those kinds of conduct, then storytelling would be pretty pointless. It is a lot simpler to simply state the rules and require compliance. On the other hand, if our aim is character formation so that our children develop into the kind of people who act well even when there is no rule of conduct to follow, or no prize at the end of the process, then stories introducing good role models are a much more apt educational tool. Such an approach more fully captures the intuition that when we tell stories about Santa Claus to our children the aim of this exercise is something that is good *for them* rather than as an exercise in bringing about more good in the world.

So a virtue ethicist's approach to the question seems better able to capture the idea that parents are doing nothing wrong when they lie to their children about Santa Claus and that this activity benefits their children. To back up this judgment, let's go back to the work of Plato.

The Platonic Account of Why Lying is Not Wrong

Why turn to Plato? Plato's views on the education of young children in the *Republic* are particularly relevant for our purposes because he thinks of storytelling in a similar manner to that which I outlined in the opening section. He takes storytelling to often involve lying (*Republic* 382c–d) and thinks of this as a perfectly acceptable, even desirable, mode of education. Plato appreciates the force of stories that might involve falsity in the education of children and treats false elements in stories as a way to make those stories more vivid and effective. Falsity can present itself in various ways, for example through describing things that did not, or could not, actually happen and through the storyteller imitating the voice of one of the characters in the story, or pretending to be that character. Lying in this sense of involving untruths in one's stories and engaging in make believe during their telling can be administered, according to Plato, in the same way that a doctor administers medicine for the benefit of the patient.

Moreover, the effect of the education that Plato prescribes is one directed at developing the character of young children. Aiming to foster in them correct likes and dislikes and provide them with role models can create dispositions to behave and react in the way a good or excellent person would in different situations. In a nutshell, their education and the telling of stories are aimed at making them good people. So storytelling is important in Plato's system of education because it is one in which education is primarily directed at character rather than the production of certain kinds of conduct.

So, do Santa stories fit this pattern? Stories about Santa Claus are, of course, only a small part of the stories available to us for the education of children, but it is relevant for our purposes to examine the consequences of these stories alone. What is it that children are exposed to in these stories? The figure of Santa Claus that we all know and love is a happy and kind figure distributing gifts. Santa Claus distributes these gifts solely on the basis of merit, regardless of race or social class. He rewards good behavior and punishes bad behavior. At its simplest stage the educational process starts by encouraging good behavior just for the presents. However, at the same time it shows children good character traits as expressed in action: kindness, charity, fairness, and joviality. It also positively disposes children towards these traits, making them appear desirable to them. This tendency can work in tandem with a desire for Santa

ERA GAVRIELIDES

Claus' approval, leading children to develop a positive attitude towards kindness, joviality, and giving to others. It encourages a positive attitude towards acting well and being good, so that children become, in their estimation, people Santa approves of. In a sense, then, stories about Santa Claus follow a pattern similar to Plato's educational plan of breeding the correct likes and dislikes and making children desire to be good.

There is also another reason, related to the development of character, why stories about Santa Claus can be considered to be good. Engaging in the customs about Santa Claus with our children encourages self-reflection from a fairly young age. A child who writes her annual letter to Santa Claus is encouraged to think about whether she has been good or bad, what she can do better, and how she can improve. Such self-reflection is central to thinking about our character and moral worth, and determining how our character can improve. This reflection is certainly something we should do even after we have passed the stage of writing letters to Santa.

Moreover, any remaining worries related to lying to children about Santa Claus can be dispelled by considering the self-destructive nature of the lie. What do I mean? Simply that stories about Santa Claus involve numerous elements that naturally lead children to question their validity as they grow older. For example, a child is sooner or later going to start wondering about the possibility of flying reindeer, delivering gifts all over the world in the course of a single night, about the ability of a fairly rotund man to squeeze down chimneys – when they are available – or to gain access to a locked house and other "irregularities." In my particular case a key irregularity was my father's yearly absence during Santa Claus' visit and indeed the striking resemblance between them. Many children, unless a sibling or school friend has interfered ahead of time, will start questioning the possibility of Santa Claus, and of course this is a desirable development in that it shows that they are starting to use critical thought rather than taking everything on trust. So not only do Santa stories have beneficial effects in terms of developing a good character, the story has a mechanism which makes it the case that the lie which it involves is unlikely to be self-perpetuating.

This relates to a worry raised at the beginning of our discussion regarding the limits on "evidence provision" for the existence of Santa Claus. In particular, I raised the question whether it was acceptable to provide "photographic" evidence of the existence of Santa Claus in one's living room for the purpose of putting a child, who has started asking questions, off the scent a bit longer. The uneasiness many of us feel at such a proposal is easy to explain within the context of an account which takes developing good character to be the primary aim of going along with the custom about Santa. The reason for this is that critical thought and inquisitiveness are key elements of what we would consider a well developed character. If children display these characteristics then they should not be lied to, as that will have no further beneficial effects on their character. Indeed, being told that they are clever and praised for their inquisitiveness might act as a further spur in their development.

We have reached the conclusion that telling children about Santa Claus is indeed lying. There is no way out of that. However, it is a kind of lying, like the sort involved in storytelling, which can be beneficial in developing a child's character. One could ask whether the development of character can be as well served by other stories, perhaps that involve a less interactive component. Maybe it can. But asking this question to an extent misses the point. It is true that we have a number of ways of educating our children, but our question was this: Given the existence of stories and custom about Santa Claus are such stories good? Is the intuition of a large number of parents that they are doing nothing wrong in going along with the custom correct? The answer to both these questions, I have argued, is a resounding: Yes! Midnight cookie eating can continue unabated.

CHAPTER 14

PUTTING CLAUS BACK
INTO CHRISTMAS

A Christmas season wouldn't be complete without the annual complaint that the holiday has become too commercialized and that we need to put Christ back into Christmas, that he is the reason for the season. This gripe is not only misguided but has things backwards – Santa Claus is a better representative of the true spirit of Christmas than Jesus ever was or ever could be. As we will see, Christmas was a commercial enterprise in its very origin. Since it was a Christian sales job from the start, it is rather hypocritical to condemn its current retail qualities. But perhaps such hypocrisy isn't all that bad. In his book *Beyond Good and Evil* (1886), the great German philosopher Friedrich Nietzsche inquires into the value of truth and decides that there may be considerable merit in untruth, uncertainty, and ignorance. Nietzsche argues that there is no problem with believing and promulgating fables; the issue is simply which myths are outdated and obsolete, and which ones are socially useful and enhance our lives. I'll consider Nietzsche's thoughts on why it was once valuable to believe in God, and why he thinks that is no longer true. Then I'll argue that the myth of Santa Claus is a finer modern fairy tale, and a truer exemplar of the spirit of Christmas, than the story of Jesus Christ. Santa may be no more real, but he is a more useful fiction.

Nietzsche's Useful Fictions

A lot of ink has been spilled over whether the religious claims of Christianity are true, or its historical assertions accurate. But does it really matter whether Christmas is really Jesus's birthday or a fabricated mythology? So long as Christianity is a nice story about the world, a social lubricant that performs a helpful role for us, or a narcotic that deadens the sense of our inevitable non-existence, perhaps that's all that's really important. In his book *The Gay Science* (1882), Nietzsche cautions against conflating truth with the idea of social necessity or usefulness. In section 121 he writes, "we have arranged for ourselves a world in which we can live – by positing bodies, lines, planes, causes and effects, motion and rest, form and content; without these articles of faith nobody could now endure life. But that does not prove them. Life is no argument. The conditions of life might include error."[1] Of course, even granting Nietzsche's point here, one might still reasonably maintain that while Christianity is a proof-free article of faith, it is still something that helps us "endure life." Is belief in the Christian God, Jesus, the virgin birth, the resurrection, and all that other stuff – is it useful for us?

Nietzsche argues that the answer is no, it's not. When he declares, famously, that God is dead (originally in *The Gay Science* section 108, and then also in sections 125 and 343), he does not mean that a real, immortal God is literally deceased. His statement is metaphorical. Nietzsche means that we no longer need to believe in God; such belief is no longer helpful to us. God has gone the way of typewriters, monarchies, and gas guzzlers. But if God is no longer valuable to believe in, this suggests that there may have been a time when we needed to believe in the Christian God, or, at least, belief in some kind of god was needed for our lives.

Nietzsche thinks that's absolutely right; in antiquity there was a vast pantheon of tribal gods. These ancient gods – Yahweh, Baal, Odin, Isis, Jupiter – were once symbols of community pride and celebration. They represented the ideals of the tribe, and like modern sports mascots, were rallying points under whose banner people would go to war. In *The Anti-Christ* (1895) section 25 Nietzsche describes Yahweh as a decent sort of god, an expression of national self-confidence, a god who helps, who devises means, who is fundamentally a word for every happy inspiration of courage and self-reliance.[2] He was the Hebrew ideal. Over time, the concept of Yahweh began to change. The new idea was that God had entered into a legal arrangement with his people and was bound by conditions. All

STEVEN D. HALES

good fortune was interpreted as a reward, all bad fortune was interpreted as punishment, and the idea of sin was invented. God is now someone who demands.

In *The Anti-Christ* section 26 Nietzsche argues that with the advent of a priestly class the down-to-earth social-mascot sort of deity was finally replaced with an abstract, aloof, transcendental god who must be approached only indirectly through the priests. The priests alone are the final authority on the will of God. Now God is everywhere, and everything must be made holy, divine, denaturalized by the priest. Everything naturally decent needs "sanctification" – meals, relationships, birth, death, marriage, the administration of justice, brotherhood. Finally, Nietzsche maintains, 1,900 years of Christianity finished off anything decent left in the idea of God. Now we have a God "who cures a head-cold at the right moment, or tells us to get into a coach just as a downpour is about to start" (*The Anti-Christ* section 52). The only thing left to God now is to be a "domestic servant, a postman, an almanac-maker – at bottom a word for the stupidest kind of accidental occurrence." Instead of a symbol of community self-esteem, God has become trivialized and personalized. Nietzsche thinks this kind of a god is a bad joke, and is so absurd that he would have to be abolished even if he existed.

So Nietzsche is no fan of the modern notion of God. But what about Jesus? Surprisingly, Nietzsche had a grudging respect for the historical Jesus; he even says that, with some qualification, Jesus could be considered a free spirit (*The Anti-Christ* section 32). What Nietzsche excoriates is the religion about him that sprang up after his death. According to Nietzsche, what Jesus offered was his practice – a new way of living, not a new belief system. Jesus criticized the rigid, rule-bound, priest-ridden system of religion that the Jews then had. But this is exactly the kind of religion about him that arose after his death. Jesus was an original, an iconoclast who lived outside of his society and offered a new perspective on how to live one's life. Yet Christianity became the official state religion and brooked no heresies. Jesus promoted brotherhood on the basis of sharing food and drink together after the Hebrew-Arabic custom, and Christianity turns it into the miracle of transubstantiation. Jesus offered a way of living, a way that was indifferent to dogmas, cults, priests, church, theology, and sacrament. As soon as he is dead, Christianity develops and propagates those very things.

Under Nietzsche's interpretation, Jesus proposed that the kingdom of God is in the hearts of persons. The kingdom is a this-worldly outlook and attitude. Yet the early Christians never understood Jesus. First, they agree with Jesus that the kingdom is of this world, but they falsely give it a political meaning. They expected God to come and set up a new Jerusalem shortly after Jesus's death. When that didn't happen, they made their second error: they invented the idea of an other-worldly kingdom of God, something abstract and remote. Thus Nietzsche wrote that "In reality there has been only one Christian, and he died on the cross. The 'Evangel' died on the cross. What was called 'Evangel' from this moment onwards was already the opposite of what *he* had lived: '*bad* tidings', a *dysangel*" (*The Anti-Christ* section 39).

In short, Jesus had his good points, but, in Nietzsche's view, Christianity doesn't.[3] The issue is *not* whether the religion is true or false, but whether it is something still useful in our time or instead is it legacy code, a vestigial tail, or – as Nietzsche thinks – chronic appendicitis. While Nietzsche's interest was in all of Christianity and the Christian God, here my focus is on Christmas. How did we get this holiday, and is Jesus the right deity for our modern Christmas?

The Commercial Origins of Christmas

In many ways, Christianity is composed not only out of the festivals and holidays of earlier rival religions, but also their rituals, myths, and sacred texts. Consider Christian symbolism. The religious connotations of the cross predate Christianity; it was a symbol of Bacchus and versions also appear in the Hindu swastika and the Egyptian anhk. While the cross is the most famous Christian totem, prior to about the fourth century the ichthys ○ and the labrarum were their prominent icons. And while the labrarum ⚹ formed by the superposition of the Greek letters χ (chi) and ρ (rho), was a monogram for Christ (Χριστός), it was earlier a monogram for the Greek god of time, Chronos.

The divine myths are also recycled by Christianity; for instance, many prior religions had conceptions of judgment and an afterlife. The Egyptians embalmed their cats by the hundreds of thousands in preparation for the afterworld, and the Greeks placed coins in the mouths of their dead to pay the boatman Charon to ferry the departed to Hades. The idea of resurrection isn't new either. The Sumerian agricultural god Tammuz, the Roman wine god Bacchus, and the Egyptian sky god Osiris (all predating Jesus) died and were reborn. In fact, all the major Christian tropes are present earlier and elsewhere, such as

STEVEN D. HALES

escaping from the underworld (Greek Persephone) and a virgin birth (Greek Perseus). Even the sacrament of eating the dead god, or theophagia, was commonplace, as neolithic worshippers ate the grain of the harvest that represented the fertility/harvest deity whose death saved the community from hunger and who would be reborn in the spring. A well-known version of this idea is in the medieval English folksong "John Barleycorn" in which the barley grain is personified. John Barleycorn is buried, slain, beaten, and ground, only to be reborn as whiskey and in that form triumphs over his oppressors.

Christians have been sensitive about these antecedents. In his *First Apology*, the second-century writer Justin Martyr declared all those earlier religious stories to be fictions promulgated by Satan. The "when in doubt, blame Satan" strategy was redeployed at the end of the nineteenth century to reject a fossil record that supported evolution and an ancient Earth. Of course, creating your own religion from scratch, without relying on a few tried-and-true models, is tough work. Ancient religions established their bona fides among the general public by claiming roots in deep antiquity; there was widespread suspicion of anything new or recent in religion. This is one of the reasons the version of Christianity that claimed continuity with Judaism was the historical victor over the Marcionites who rejected all things Jewish and insisted that Jesus established a religion *de nuovo*.[4]

Christmas, too, was essentially heisted from other religions and other traditions. Actually, the celebration of Christmas wasn't on the Christian radar for a few centuries; the earliest mention of Christmas as a feast or festival wasn't until 354 CE. The Romans often deified their emperors and celebrated their birthdays, and the first Christians didn't want to be associated with such a practice. The early Church Fathers Origen and Arnobius both condemned birthday parties for the gods. In the third century, writings start to appear that assign a specific date to Jesus's birth, including May 20, April 19 or 20, and January 6 or 10. According to *The Catholic Encyclopedia*'s entry on Christmas, "there is no month in the year to which respectable authorities have not assigned Christ's birth." So how did we wind up with December 25 as the universally accepted day of Christmas?

December 25 had long been a holy day in the Roman Empire. That date was the legendary birthday of the light god Mithras, a deity originally of Persian origin, but very popular in Rome, especially among the imperial legions. The 25th also marked the end of the week-long Saturnalia festival, a raucous party that celebrated the harvest god

Saturn. Gifts were customarily exchanged and the sacred holly used as decoration.[5] Finally, December 25 was the festival of *Dies Natalis Solis Invicti*, "the birthday of the unconquered sun," which is to say the sun god Sol Invictus. Under the old Julian calendar, December 24 was the date of the winter solstice, when the day was shortest and the night longest. On the 25th the days began to grow longer again, proving that the sun god was indeed unconquerable and would gain in strength.

Sol Invictus was a hugely important god, endorsed as an authorized state deity by Emperor Aurelian in 274 CE. Later, Emperor Constantine would declare the day of the sun to be an official Roman day of rest, in honor of Sol Invictus. At the fourth-century Council of Laodicea, Christians decided to borrow this idea and declared Sunday to be their holy day too. With respect to Christmas, since Christians claimed that it was Jesus who was the Light of the World, what better day to celebrate his nativity than on the sun god's birthday?

It's not hard to see why Christians decided to overcome their initial reluctance and start coopting Roman holidays. The Roman gods were a hit with the masses and Sol Invictus was particularly popular at that time. The difficulty was that since Christianity had taken so much from other religious traditions that people kept getting Jesus confused with Sol. In the third century Tertullian had to deny that Sol was the Christians' god, as did St. Augustine in the fourth century and Pope Leo I in the fifth. Clearly, it was a durable confusion.

The incorporation of other religious traditions into Christianity didn't stop in antiquity. In the Middle Ages, as Christianity began to radiate out of the Roman epicenter, it absorbed local religions along the way. Christians referred to their competition as "pagans," a word derived from the Latin *paganus*, meaning rural or country folk. "Pagan" is not ethnographically precise and is best considered an epithet akin to our "hick." Paganism was what backwoods hicks believed. While the pagans were proselytized (and worse) out of their religious beliefs, Christians saw that their quaint customs were worth keeping and, like so many prior sacred ideas, repurposing. Kissing under the mistletoe is connected to the plant's longstanding service as a fertility symbol, something that dates back to the ancient druids, who (according to Pliny the Elder) considered it a cure for infertility.[6] The midwinter Norse Yule celebration, with its festive feasting, drinking, singing, and burning of the Yule log, was also swept up into Christmas. Todd Preston's essay in this volume, "Putting the 'Yule' Back in 'Yuletide'," gives more details.

These modest historical observations are not a knock against Christianity. Improving one's sales by stealing ideas from competitor products is a time-honored tradition. Where would the Windows operating system be if it weren't for Apple's prior development of the graphical user interface for the Macintosh? But let's be honest – most of Christianity is the result of either reinventing various ideas of the sacred, cobbling together assorted bits and pieces of other religions' symbols and sacraments, or out-and-out plagiarism. As far as Christmas goes, Christ wasn't the reason for the season; no one has any idea when Jesus was really born, and basically no one cared for 300 years after he died. Christmas has always functioned as a religious sales tool, and fortunately a more benign one than the *auto-da-fé* and the *Malleus Maleficarum*. It should come as no surprise that the more secular, but at least culturally Christian, public should recognize this commercial quality and run with it.

Christmas has nothing to do with the actual, historical birthday of Yeshua bar Yosef, a troublemaking Jewish carpenter executed by Imperial Rome, and a great deal to do with promoting the latest model of messiah. Of course, that model year was a long time ago. "Almost two millennia and not a single new God!" Nietzsche laments (*The Anti-Christ* section 19). What I want to suggest is that there *is* a new god, one hiding in plain sight, one that, like the original Yahweh, might even muster Nietzsche's respect: Santa Claus.

Santa Claus and the Social Compact

The story of Santa Claus is a pocket-sized Christian allegory. Like God, Santa lives in an exotic and inaccessible place surrounded by magical helpers, he is omniscient, passes moral judgment, gives rewards for good behavior, and performs miracles by violating the laws of nature. While God may come in for criticism from free thinkers, cultural critics, and killjoy philosophers, there is a vast social edifice, erected with a wink and a nod, devoted to ensuring that the legend of Santa Claus respectfully endures. One of the founding documents in this genre is Francis P. Church's editorial in the newspaper the *New York Sun* (September 21, 1897) in which he responds to the letter of eight-year-old Virginia O'Hanlon, who asks quite sincerely whether there is indeed a Santa Claus. Church's response is to take a left-hand turn into the abstract, the same approach condemned by Nietzsche in the case of ancient religions. The aptly-named Church writes:

> Not believe in Santa Claus! You might as well not believe in fairies! You might
> get your papa to hire men to watch in all the chimneys on Christmas Eve to

catch Santa Claus, but even if they did not see Santa Claus coming down, what would that prove? Nobody sees Santa Claus, but that is no sign that there is no Santa Claus. The most real things in the world are those that neither children nor men can see. Did you ever see fairies dancing on the lawn? Of course not, but that's no proof that they are not there. Nobody can conceive or imagine all the wonders there are unseen and unseeable in the world.

Mostly Santa's supporters have made sure that he is firmly grounded in this world, though, and not relegated to the ethereal plane of, in Church's words, "faith, fancy, poetry, love, romance ... and ... the supernal beauty and glory beyond." That's actually Santa's saving grace – he has not been transformed, like poor old Yahweh, "into something ever paler and less substantial ... an 'ideal' ... a 'pure spirit'" (*The Anti-Christ* section 17). Santa Claus is a practical, this-worldly sort of demigod.

Consider how many movies have been made regarding Santa, exactly none of which cast aspersions on his fully material reality. It would be ridiculous, after all; we all know that Santa does not really exist, so what could be the point? Instead, we are treated to *Miracle on 34th Street* (1947), in which a department-store Santa Claus is declared the real McCoy by a judge of the New York Supreme Court. The animated films *Rudolph the Red-Nosed Reindeer* (1948) and *Santa Claus is Comin' to Town* (1970) embellish the Clausian legend with more of his back story; why he wears a red suit, why he goes down chimneys, why he lives at the North Pole, and so on. More on this theme is in the Supermanesque origins yarn found in *Santa Claus* (1985). The *Santa Clause* trilogy (1994, 2002, 2006) offers a twist on the classic tale, in which anyone who wears the magical Santa suit implicitly agrees to become Santa himself. In *Elf* (2003) a human baby is adopted by Santa's elves and then returns to the human world to find his father. *The Polar Express* (2004) features a doubting child whisked away on a train to the North Pole, where he meets Santa Claus and regains his faith.

Despite Santa's godlike powers, according to the movies Christmas is regularly imperiled by assorted forces of evil and frequently needs saving. Celluloid saviors of Christmas include Ernest, Elmo, Diego, Inspector Gadget, Mickey Mouse, Felix the Cat, and my personal favorites, the Bikini Bandits. But in all these movies Santa Claus is taken seriously – he is never treated satirically, skeptically, or lightly. Even the hideously misconceived cinematic abortus *Santa Claus Conquers the Martians* (1964) reaffirms the existence and virtue of Santa.

It's not merely Hollywood that props up (or gives props to) Santa Claus. The North American Aerospace Defense Command (NORAD),

STEVEN D. HALES

whose workaday mission is monitoring USA and Canadian airspace for hostile missiles and planes, has for 50 years also been in the business of tracking the movements of Santa's sleigh every Christmas Eve. In recent years NORAD has gone so far as to set up a website where the curious can see a CGI-rendered version of Santa's sleigh flying through the satellite imagery of Google Earth. The sleigh can be seen in numerous locations across the globe, with updates every five minutes.

Just as the myth of Santa Claus is the Christian myth writ small, there is a cultural parody of the atheist criticisms of Christianity in the form of tongue-in-cheek scientific debates over the existence of Santa. In a 1990 article in *Spy Magazine*, Richard Waller inveighs against Santa Claus by estimating how many children worldwide are due presents from Santa, how fast he would have to fly to deliver them all in one day, the average weight of a present, and how many flying reindeer would be needed to pull that mighty payload. He then calculates that upon liftoff so much energy would be generated that the reindeer would be vaporized and Santa would be flattened as if he were on a neutron star.

Of course, Santa's true believers step up to this challenge, and have suggested (1) that the sleigh travels close to light speed, causing a relativistic time dilation effect that gives Santa more time to distribute toys; (2) that there may be more than one Santa Claus, thus distributing the workload; (3) that frequent reloading trips to the North Pole reduce the mass of the sleigh and thus the energy needed to pull it; (4) that the non-uniform distribution of deserving children will allow more efficient routing and less required speed; (5) that Santa actually bulk drops toys from the sleigh, which shoot down multiple chimneys smart-bomb style and hence speed up delivery; (6) the flying reindeer have evolved skin like space shuttle tiles; and (7) Santa realizes all of his alternate quantum states at once, similar to the Wheeler-Everett interpretation of quantum mechanics. Then there are less plausible theories involving wormholes near the North Pole.

The Spirit of Giving and the True Meaning of Christmas

The faux debate about Santa's existence, his tracking by NORAD, and the inventive fables embroidering his story that pop up like apocryphal gospels, are all part of the considerable social commitment to keeping his myth a living part of our culture. Not that everyone loves the right jolly old elf. Jews and Muslims ignore him as best they can, and there are excessively pious Christians who, like their seventeenth-century Puritan forebears, frown upon all this secular merrymaking as a distraction from their cheerless worship.[7] Some philosophers too – fundamentalist followers of Immanuel Kant mostly – reject Santa because the moral law absolutely prohibits lying. In Nietzsche's apt phrase, Kant's "categorical imperative smells of cruelty" (*On the Genealogy of Morals*, II, 6).

Why do we invest so much in maintaining the myth of Santa Claus? It is adults that make Santa come alive, who don the red coat and white beard at the mall, who wrap the presents with a note that says "To Holly from Santa," who set out the milk and cookies (and carrots for the reindeer) whose consumption by Christmas morning serves as an existence proof of magic. Nietzsche writes:

> A people which still believes in itself still also has its own God. In him it venerates the conditions through which it has prospered, its virtues – it projects its joy in itself, its feeling of power on to a being whom one can thank for them. He who is rich wants to bestow; a proud people needs a God in order to sacrifice. (*The Anti-Christ* section 16)

Santa is just such a deity that we provide for our children.

What makes Santa the *de facto* Christmassian deity? God and Jesus – they want credit, they want praise, thanks, and worship. They have priests, sacraments, churches, law tablets, and covenants. Santa cares about none of these things; he doesn't even expect a thank-you note. God lays down heavy threats if you don't believe in him, and demands that you follow his moral code on penalty of death and torment. Santa asks only that children be nice, and his punishment for naughtiness (which he never follows through on) is merely a lump of coal. Christ promises life after death, an unprovably vague, otherworldly claim of no use in our ordinary lives. Santa, on the other hand, delivers real presents in the practical here-and-now. There is no issue of compulsory belief in Santa, since of course no grown-up seriously believes in such a being. With Christ, even adults are supposed to chuck their reason and believe in magic. Yet we keep the legend of Santa alive, like King Arthur or Robin Hood, a noble archetype of the virtues to which we aspire. Christ we are supposed to owe, but Santa we actually want.

Parents give to their children anonymously, assigning all credit to a fictional god with an endlessly capacious sleigh and flying reindeer. To give to our children in the name of Santa is to engage in the holy act of sacrificial offering. Santa is thus a symbol of the parents who not only do

STEVEN D. HALES

not expect gratitude, but actively avoid it by giving credit for the gifts to someone else. He is *our* ideal, the example of our strength and pride. Santa Claus is the modern god that Nietzsche was waiting for, the second coming in a red velvet suit.

Love is patient and kind, writes St. Paul in 1 Corinthians 13, it is not envious or boastful, or insist on its own way. Genuinely selfless love does not deal in threats and expectations, but in pure giving from the heart. In this manner it is Santa Claus who is the very embodiment of anonymous, selfless generosity – and that is the true spirit of Christmas.[8]

NOTES

1 *The Gay Science*, ed. and trans. Walter Kaufmann (New York: Vintage, 1974).
2 Friedrich Nietzsche, *The Anti-Christ*, ed. and trans. R. J. Hollingdale (New York: Viking Penguin, 1968).
3 Yes, Nietzsche scholars, I know he argues in *The Genealogy of Morals* that the Christians' conversion of dominance instincts into the bad conscience has made possible the highest forms of self-overcoming. But that's all beyond the present essay.
4 This is the argument of Bart D. Ehrman, *Lost Christianities* (Oxford: Oxford University Press, 2003), ch. 5.
5 For more on holly's connection to Christmas, see Christian Rätsch and Claudia Müller-Ebeling, *Pagan Christmas: The Plants, Spirits, and Rituals at the Origins of Yuletide* (Rochester: Inner Traditions, 2006), pp. 94–7, 156.
6 According to Rätsch and Müller-Ebeling, *Pagan Christmas*, pp. 90–2, mistletoe is still used as a fertility treatment in rural European folk medicine. See also Francis X. Weiser, *Handbook of Christian Feasts and Customs* (New York: Harcourt, Brace), pp. 84–5; and Susan Drury, "Customs and Beliefs Associated with Christmas Evergreens: A Preliminary Survey," Folklore 98, 2 (1987): 194–9.
7 On the Puritan view of Christmas, see Stephen Nissenbaum, *The Battle for Christmas: A Cultural History of America's Most Cherished Holiday* (New York: Vintage, 1996), ch. 1.
8 Thanks to Tim Johnson for his excellent and ruthless editing.

CHAPTER 15

SCROOGE LEARNS IT ALL IN ONE NIGHT

Happiness and the Virtues of Christmas

 "Marley was dead, to begin with." That is the familiar first sentence of Charles Dickens' classic ghost story, *A Christmas Carol*. It is a remarkably enduring story. Numerous editions are in print and there have been over a dozen film adaptations, and at least twice as many television versions. (One of my favorite film adaptations stars the Muppets, with Michael Caine as Scrooge, who was an excellent Scrooge. The seasoned actor demonstrated his brilliance by giving a serious dramatic performance while playing opposite Kermit the Frog and Miss Piggy.) Like the Christmas celebration, Dickens' story is about many things. But at its core, *A Christmas Carol* is about the moral and ethical aspects of the Christmas tradition. This sets it apart from many Christmas stories that focus on the religious aspects. Dickens explores the importance of developing the virtues of generosity and gratitude and the consequences of a life of greed and ungratefulness. In Scrooge's world, after death greedy and ungrateful businessmen are sentenced to wander the earth as phantoms filled with regret about past misdeeds, but impotent to right those wrongs.

A Christmas Carol shows us how the Christmas tradition can promote human flourishing by helping people to develop the virtues of generosity and gratitude. Without getting too technical, we will use the concepts and general framework of the virtue theory of ethics. However, don't be put off by the word "theory," as the concepts of this ethical tradition match up well with common sense. Virtue theory focuses on the qualities of a person's character through the contrasting notions of vices and virtues and how these qualities contribute to human flourishing, or happiness. This philosophical tradition provides a powerful way of thinking about some of life's most important questions: What kind of person should I strive to become? What constitutes a happy or flourishing life? How can a life fail? What character traits contribute to human flourishing? What character traits lead to a failed life? In sum, virtue theory provides useful ideas and concepts for answering life's important ethical questions. Of course, the proof is in the pudding. I hope the following philosophical interpretation of Dickens' tale will provide some useful insights into how the Christmas celebration can play a role in promoting an ethical life of human flourishing.

Happy as an Oyster

To begin, unlike Marley, Scrooge is alive, but just. He is a withered soul living a failed life. Dickens spends the first couple pages of his tale bringing this point home. The reader is greeted with an old misanthrope who is frigid inside and likes it cold outside. Of his many sour attributes, Scrooge's disdain for the company of others stands out. When Scrooge walks down the street, everyone is quick to avert his or her eyes; even the blind beggar's dog withdraws and looks away. This is exactly the way Scrooge wants it. Dickens tells us that, "It was the very thing he liked. To edge his way along the crowded path of life, warning all human sympathy to keep his distance." Scrooge is "self-contained and as solitary as an oyster." His desire to be left alone is one reason he detests the Christmas holiday. The Christmas celebration is a time that brings people together and ignites the spark of generosity.

To get the reader thinking about these aspects of Christmas, early in the story Dickens provides a conversation between Scrooge and his nephew, Fred. Fred is the opposite of Scrooge. He is as generous as Scrooge is greedy. Fred likes to laugh, loves the company of others and to celebrate Christmas; three things Scrooge detests. Fred stops by Scrooge's office to invite him, as he does every year, for Christmas dinner at his home.

However, Scrooge rudely dismisses the invitation, saying he will keep Christmas in his own way. Fred retorts that his uncle does not keep Christmas at all. The two then get into an argument over "keeping Christmas." Scrooge asserts that Christmas has never done him any good. In so many words, Fred points out that Scrooge is making a mistake by equating "good" with gold. He then offers a short monologue to demonstrate the error in his uncle's thinking. His speech concludes that Christmas is:

> The only time of the year, when men and women seem by one consent to open their shut-up hearts freely, and to think of people below them as if they really were fellow-passengers to the grave, and not another race of creatures bound on other journeys. And therefore, uncle, and though it has never put a scrap of gold or silver in my pocket, I believe that it *has* done me good, and *will* do me good; and I say, God bless it!

Christmas inspires a spirit of generosity in people, and this is part of the ethical core of the celebration. But Scrooge is blind to these kinds of goods; he has only one measure of value, profit.

How did Scrooge end up this way? Dickens does not provide a single narrative that explains the evolution of Scrooge's character. However, he leaves plenty of clues that the reader can use to piece together a reasonable story. One scene in particular provides an important clue. Scrooge was once engaged, but his fiancée broke it off. The Ghost of Christmas Past allows the old man to view this sad scene from his youth. The old Scrooge watches a fair young girl in a mourning dress, as she explains to the young Scrooge why their long engagement is now over. It is because Scrooge no longer loves her. She says that "another idol has displaced [her]." Scrooge questions, "What idol?" The young women answers, "A golden one." Scrooge seems aware of her point and attempts to justify himself, saying: "There is nothing on which it is so hard as poverty; and there is nothing it professes to condemn with such severity as the pursuit of wealth." His fiancée, who no doubt analyzed the failing relationship over and over, provides Scrooge with an insightful analysis of deep problems developing in his soul. "You fear the world too much," she tells him. "All your hopes have merged into the hope of being beyond chance and its sordid reproach. I have seen your nobler aspirations fall off one by one, until your master passion, gain, engrosses you." Scrooge fears that the contingencies of life might rob him of any possibility of security and happiness. His singular goal in life has become the acquisition of wealth to vouchsafe his security.

His Wealth is No Use to Him

In his 1941 book, *The Nature and Destiny of Man,* the theologian and social thinker Reinhold Niebuhr provides insights into the relationships between freedom, insecurity, power, and injustice. Niebuhr's book was first given as a series of lectures in Scotland under conditions of great anxiety and insecurity; Nazi bombs could be heard exploding in the distance as he spoke. Niebuhr observes that the condition of human freedom is chance that gives rise to insecurity. This creates anxiety, which is a permanent condition of the human position in the world. There is of course a sane desire to remove the dangers of chance from our lives. However, the quest for complete security is impossible. But, for Scrooge, this quest turns into an obsession, a distorted excess leading to vice and injustice.

Scrooge knows all too well that human life by its nature is insecure. Every day he witnesses the illness, misfortune, and the brutal poverty of Dickens' nineteenth-century London. On a deeper level, Scrooge learned about the unfortunate contingencies of life in two bitter and defining lessons. His mother died giving birth to him. Her untimely death led to an unhappy childhood for Scrooge. It appears that his grieving father rejected the little boy, isolating him from the family in a boarding school. Later, his beloved sister dies while giving birth to his nephew, Fred. Given these tragedies and his unhappy childhood, it is not surprising that Scrooge is anxious and fears life. He knows that some evil could be lurking around any corner waiting to rob him of his happiness. Driven by this fear, he does all he can to make his life more secure. He does this by pursuing wealth, but no amount of money can guarantee he will escape loss, illness, and death. Scrooge is raw with anxiety and obsessed with insecurity, so he grasps at wealth and pushes other people away.

But his quest for security through wealth is counterproductive. His nephew Fred observes, "His wealth is of no use to him. He doesn't do any good with it. He doesn't make himself comfortable with it." Scrooge's wealth is always in reserve to guarantee his security, and he always needs more because there is never enough. Many people with more fortunate childhoods than Scrooge also fail to realize that wealth can only buy so much security; it cannot buy happiness. Despite this being common knowledge, it remains a common error leading to ethical failings. One way to avoid this "happiness equals wealth" illusion is to get a better understanding of happiness.

The old saw about money not buying happiness needs to be qualified. If you are desperately poor, like the hordes of miserable and consumptive poor in Dickens' England, circumstances make it difficult to be happy. If you cannot feed yourself, if you cannot afford to go to the doctor when you are sick, then more money makes a huge difference. Bob Cratchit would be quick to let us know about that. Tragedy awaits him and his family if they cannot afford to take care of Tiny Tim's health. However, despite their poverty, the Cratchit home is a happy one. Dickens describes the family Christmas day: "They were not a handsome family, they were not well dressed, their shoes were far from being waterproof, their clothes were scanty.... But they were happy, grateful, pleased with one another, and contented with the time."

There is a relationship between happiness and wealth, but it is not one Scrooge would expect. Money contributes to happiness because it allows us to secure our basic needs. However, once people secure these needs, more money contributes very little to happiness. The reason being that money does not affect some of the most important things that make us happy and unhappy, day in and day out. The Cratchits are poor, but they are "pleased with one another." It seems that our real troubles and rewards come not from financial affairs, but from other people. These involve concerns about children, problems with close relations, and getting along with neighbors and co-workers. If you're difficult, irritable, unforgiving, intolerant, and unloving when you are making just enough money to get by, these same traits will undermine your happiness even when you are making more than you need.

A key feature of virtue theory is the idea that the end or purpose of life is happiness, or human flourishing, and there is a direct relationship between the quality of a person's character and happiness. However, it is easy to be misled by that statement. Happiness is not what it used to be; the concept has slipped on hard times. In today's popular culture, happiness is frequently understood, or misunderstood, in terms of warm feelings and emotional highs. That is why contemporary philosophers largely avoid the term, and it has been replaced by human flourishing. The ancient Greeks had an odd saying that captures a different conception of happiness: "Call no man happy until he is dead." By this, they didn't mean that life is so bad one could only be happy by escaping its miseries and woes through death. Rather, what they meant was that happiness is the judgment of a whole life lived virtuously. Happiness is based on what kind of person we become and what kind of life we live, not transient emotional states. For instance, the happy, or flourishing, person

DANE SCOTT

has acquired the virtues of generosity and tolerance; the unhappy one is greedy and irritable with others. Humans are fundamentally social animals, and to flourish we need quality relationships with co-workers, friends, and family. In order for these relationships to flourish, we must acquire the characteristics that allow them to flourish. We need to acquire the virtues.

To say that at the end of the story Scrooge is a happy person is to make a judgment of the quality of his character. It is not just to find out whether he is having pleasant feelings, although he is beside himself with joy at being alive. In the end, Scrooge is a happy man, not just because he is filled with "happy" feeling; drinking would do that, and after his experiences with ghosts he lived by the Total Abstinence Principle. Rather, we know he remains a happy man into the future because his character has been miraculously transformed. Dickens tells us that "he became a good friend, a good master, and a good man." This fits with the general conception of happiness and human flourishing found in virtue theory. Scrooge became happy by changing the quality of his character; he became a good friend and a good man. One cannot be happy when one is solitary as an oyster, or a clam for that matter.

All In One Night

Scrooge learns the lessons of a lifetime of missed Christmases all in one night. This was only possible because the Spirits helped him; Dickens conjured a miracle. Developing virtuous characteristics requires a process of cultivating habits of excellence. For example, most people are not naturally courageous. When children are exposed to threatening or uncomfortable situations they tend to react with either too much fear or too little fear. If these tendencies are not moderated, they become extreme and result in the vices of cowardice or foolhardiness. Fortunately, over time and with guided practice most children develop their capacity for courage. They learn to moderate their fear by successfully managing repeated exposures to fearful circumstances. This point can be easily seen with a mundane example. Fear of public speaking is a common dread, but most people are able to learn to manage their fear through practice and become courageous. For this to happen it is important that people have occasions for safe guided practice. The situation is similar with other virtues like generosity and gratitude. The Christmas celebration is an important opportunity for children and adults to practice these virtues. In a certain sense, the ethical core of Christmas is formed by the virtues of generosity and gratitude. In this section we will first look at generosity and then gratitude.

Like the Ghost of Christmas Present, generosity is the disposition of people with large and giving spirits. Conversely, a distorted excess of generosity is the vice of prodigality: lavish, excessive, and wasteful giving. Of course, that was never Scrooge's vice; his was greed. At the beginning of the story, Dickens offers this description of Scrooge: "But he was a tight-fisted hand at the grindstone, Scourge! A squeezing, wrenching, grasping, scraping, covetous old sinner! Hard and sharp as flint, from which no steel had ever stuck out generous fire." Dickens' phrase "generous fire" is a poetic insight into the virtue of generosity; generosity requires both good judgment and emotional fire. The fearful and severe night's lessons ignite in Scrooge the fire of generosity. At the end of the story he takes joy in a generous donation to the poor, in giving Bob Cratchit a raise, and in taking care of the Cratchit family.

One contemporary philosopher, Alasdair MacInytre, who has spent his career studying virtue theory, combines justice and generosity into a single virtue: just generosity. MacIntyre argues that a mixture of justice and generosity are among the most basic qualities, or dispositions, needed to sustain rich relationships and human flourishing.[1] I think Dickens would have approved of this insight; his conception of generosity is clearly mixed with a strong sense of social justice. For humans to flourish and be happy we must know how to give others what they are owed (justice), and we must be able to give without expecting something in return (generosity). This is difficult as it involves both good judgment and appropriate affections.

It seems that for most children their affections do not tend toward generosity; instead, they must be trained in this direction. Children must be taught to have the habit of "affectionate regard for others."[2] Directed practice and education are required to develop the disposition of uncalculated giving and graceful receiving.[3] Every Christmas season there is an opportunity for such training, for it is at these times that children can learn the satisfaction of generosity, while steering clear of the deficiency of greed and the excess of prodigality.

Sadly, as a boy, Scrooge was denied such opportunities. In fact, he received the opposite education. As was mentioned earlier, Scrooge's father left the boy to spend many Christmases alone at boarding school, while his classmates left to celebrate with their families. Dickens paints the scene: "'The school is not quite deserted,' said the Ghost. 'A solitary child, neglected by his friends, is left there still.'" At a formative time in his life, Scrooge was left out of the annual practice of uncalculated giving and graceful receiving. Scrooge missed many Christmases. As a consequence, he turned inward, and over the years his disposition hardened into a solitary miser. It is little wonder he came to hate the holiday season.

However, the night's three lessons miraculously transform Scrooge. His difficult and concentrated education frees him from the chains of greed and self-centeredness. The Ghost of Jacob Marley forecasts this lesson at the beginning of the night. His old partner sits in front of Scrooge, a phantom bound by chains. Marley explains his condition: "'I wear the chains I forged in life,' replied the Ghost, 'I made it link by link, and yard by yard; I girded it on by my own free will, and of my own free will I wore it.'" Marley then informs Scrooge that if he could see them, he would find that even longer chains bind Scrooge. How did these greedy, uncaring business partners lose their freedom?

Greed is the singular pursuit of one's self-interest. It leads to the hoarding of possessions, which cannot be given away. In contrast, one way of thinking about generosity is in terms of free will, where one resolves to make good use of one's freedom.[4] An act of generosity is born of freedom because a person doesn't have to give their time or money to others. They give it freely, expecting nothing in return. The greedy person is ruled by self-interest. Conversely, as one philosopher writes, "To be generous is to be free of self, of one's petty little deeds and possessions, one's little resentments and jealousies."[5] In an important sense, Scrooge's generosity is born out of gratitude. He is grateful that he is free to change the course of his life.

The Ghost of Christmas Future teaches Scrooge about gratitude by showing him the terrible consequences of his misspent life. The Ghost allows Scrooge to eavesdrop on the conversations of people talking about his death. From this he learns that his was a failed and wasted life. But Scrooge awakes Christmas morning grateful that his fate is not sealed. He is grateful for his life and the chance to change.

Gratitude is an important virtue. One mark of a person of moral excellence is a consistent sense of gratitude. Like generosity, gratitude requires the appropriate feelings, and feelings cannot be forced. In fact gratitude is having and expressing just the right emotions in response to something for which one should be thankful. Gratitude is not a duty, even though in some sense we are sometimes morally required to be grateful. Moral duties do not require right emotions, but right actions. Duties sometimes must be done despite one's feelings; they spring from obligation and commitments. Gratitude is as a thankful disposition toward life. Scrooge does not become thankful to be alive until he sees himself in the grave. There are two important aspects of gratitude that Scrooge learns from this experience. One is thankfulness for the past, the present, and the future. The other is thankfulness for a gift that cannot be repaid.

In the final section of Dickens' story, Scrooge resolves to become a better person, and exclaims: "I will live my life in the past, the present, and the future." In an important sense, gratitude requires a certain kind of relationship with time. As we have seen, Scrooge views the future with fear. On seeing the third Ghost, Scrooge exclaimed: "Ghost of the Future! I fear you more than any specter I have seen." Scrooge is fearful of the future because he never fully lives in the present, a consequence of his tragic past. That is one reason he never enjoys his wealth. One ancient philosopher remarked: "The fool's life is empty of gratitude and full of fears; its course lies wholly toward the future." Scrooge is obsessed and anxious about the future; he lives in fear. However, his newfound gratitude in being alive and free to change his fate allows him to incorporate his past into the present as he looks toward the future with hope. In a sense, he is freed from the past by developing a new positive perspective on freedom and chance. The future is an opportunity to change things for the better. He is no longer obsessed with defending himself against the insecurities of life; chance and freedom provide the opportunities for positive action.

The other aspect of gratitude is to be thankful for a gift that cannot be repaid. This is perhaps the religious or spiritual core of Christmas. For believers, every Christmas is a time to express gratitude for the gift of the Christ child. The heart of the Christian faith is to gratefully accept this unfathomable and undeserved gift that cannot be repaid. One purpose of Christmas is for Christians to pause and cooperatively express thanks for the gift of God's grace. But this does not mean that unbelievers cannot be grateful at Christmas time, even though they do not share the object of their thankfulness with Christians. For instance, using religious sounding language, one secular philosopher attempts to explain this feeling. He writes: "Life is not a debt: life is a state of grace, and being is a state of grace, therein lies gratitude's highest lesson." This describes Scrooge on Christmas morning. He is simply grateful for the gift of life. To an important degree, things like our health, the beauty of the world, and much more should be seen as gifts. In this way, a general sense of gratitude is a virtuous way to approach life, each other, and the world.

Keeping Christmas

One of the main themes of *A Christmas Carol* is learning to keep Christmas. At the end of the story Scrooge is transformed from a miserable miser into a good and happy man by learning to "keep Christmas better than any man alive." He learned the ethical lessons of Christmas, generosity and gratitude. These lessons are still available in the Christmas celebration, but it would be a mistake to conclude this essay without mentioning the cultural forces that may cause us to miss them. Keeping Christmas is in part to express our gratitude by creating the opportunity to nurture just generosity, while starving the vices of greed and prodigality. However, as is all too well known, Christmas can teach ungratefulness, greed, and prodigality.

There are clear moral dangers associated with the expressions of consumerism in the Christmas celebration. A distinction made by contemporary Canadian philosopher Charles Taylor is helpful in explaining these dangers. Taylor is interested in understanding what is involved in a person exercising their freedom as a responsible human agent.[6] Toward that end he uses the concepts of *weak evaluations* and *strong evaluations*. These concepts allow him to discuss the quality of our motives. Weak evaluations are measures of our preferences and desires. Strong evaluations are measures of moral worth. For example, my preferring a berry muffin to a cinnamon roll for breakfast of course does not make me a better person. This morning I may prefer one to the other, but tomorrow my preferences may change. Such choices are superficial. In contrast, strong evaluations determine our moral worth as human beings. That is, when we evaluate our actions and motives as generous or stingy, gracious or bitter, we are making strong evaluations. Weak evaluations concern preferences, while strong evaluations concern moral character.

The problem with consumerism is that it creates a culture dominated by weak evaluations. If we are not careful to keep Christmas it is easy to let it slide into a celebration of mere consumption. We spend our time concerned with mere preferences, while discussions of deeper moral judgments of character fade into the background. In a consumerist culture there is a tendency to let the products we buy define our worth as human beings, rather than traits like generosity and gratitude. Carried to the extreme, this makes us nothing more than the sum of our preferences as represented by the products we buy. This tendency in our culture is certainly a threat to keeping Christmas.

Fortunately, Dickens' enduring story can serve as a powerful antidote against the vices of greed and ingratitude that can slip into Christmas. Scrooge's nephew's words about the value of keeping Christmas are worth hearing every year: "It is the only time of the year, when men and women seem by one consent to open their shut-up hearts freely, and to think of people below them as if they really were fellow-passengers to the grave, and not another race of creatures bound on other journeys." So whether one sits down with some hot chocolate and a book, or a plate of Christmas cookies to watch classic films starring George C. Scott or Albert Finney as Scrooge, the many versions of Scrooge's story are excellent reminders of how to keep Christmas. It is good to consider the last lines of Dickens' story, even if they are spoken by a Muppet: "It was always said of [Scrooge] that he knew how to keep Christmas well, if any man alive possessed the knowledge."

NOTES

1 Alasdair MacIntyre, *Dependent Rational Animals* (Chicago: Open Court, 2001), p. 120.
2 Ibid., p. 121.
3 Ibid.
4 Andre Comte-Sponville, *A Small Treatise on the Great Virtues* (New York: Metropolitan, 2001), p. 94.
5 Ibid., p. 95.
6 Charles Taylor, *Human Agency and Language* (Cambridge: Cambridge University Press, 1985).

PART V

CHRISTMAS THROUGH OTHERS' EYES

CHAPTER 16

HOLLY JOLLY ATHEISTS

A Naturalistic Justification for Christmas

Christmas is awesome. A break from school and work, nestled conveniently in the middle of the most depressing season, special during-this-time-only music, movies and foods, visits to and from your favorite people, everyone bearing gifts – who wouldn't want a piece of this holiday? You get a bunch of people together, make an obscene amount of food, and then spend the next week in a delicious state of lethargy induced by the consumption of nothing but rich, yummy garbage. You spend too much money and acquire a mountain of new possessions that you don't need. This holiday is a wonderful occasion for engaging in a delightful assortment of classical sins – gluttony, greed, sloth – with none of the classical guilt. Sinning in the service of the celebration of the birth of the Lord Savior Jesus Christ doesn't really count, right? It's what any devout Christian would do.

But wait. Do you have to be a Christian to celebrate this holiday?[1] Is Christmas the yearly indulgence Christians get for dragging out of bed early on Sunday mornings, for believing the impossible without evidence, for self-denial of pleasures all year long? There are two main arguments supporting the celebration of Christmas by non-Christians. First, given Christmas and its trappings and rituals were not originally Christian, there's no reason to think the Christians have an exclusive right to it. Second, using the concept of *religious naturalism*, we can understand what atheists are doing when they celebrate Christmas in the same way that we understand both naturalistic religious practices and participating in various rituals by those who do not accept the metaphysical underpinnings of the practice.

The First Noel: Christmas's Pre-Christian Origins

It's no secret that Christians do not now have, nor have they ever had, a monopoly on Christmas. The Bible doesn't tell us when Jesus was born. Two of the four gospel accounts don't mention his birth at all, beginning their stories in his adulthood. The two gospels that do refer to Jesus's birth are Matthew and Luke, both of which agree that he was born in Bethlehem, with only Luke mentioning the famous detail about him being born in a manger.[2] Although presumably the people who began the Christian church – you know, Jesus's *friends* – knew when his birthday was, there is no evidence that the date of his birth was celebrated within the earliest years of the church. The biblical accounts of the early church only take us up to around the end of the first century CE, and after that the best information we have comes from the records of the early Church Fathers. The earliest extant record of Jesus's birthday is documented at May 20, by Clement of Alexandria in 200 CE. Twenty years later, Tertullian offered a list of church feast days. No Christmas yet. In fact, in 245, we have an interesting record of Origen of Alexandria condemning the celebration of birthdays by Christians. Why? In a religion heavily focused on the afterlife, it is the day of one's death – the beginning of one's heavenly life – that ought to be celebrated. This tradition is maintained in the modern celebration of saint days, which correspond to the dates of the saints' deaths, rather than their birthdays.

The first written record we have of the celebration of Christmas – the birth of Jesus on December 25 – within the Christian church was in 354 CE. The holiday's celebration and prominence spread slowly, not emerging as one of the two key dates on the church calendar (along with Easter) until well into the Middle Ages – more than a thousand years after Jesus's birth. However, the winter solstice was set at December 25 in 45 BCE. If you're having trouble doing the math, what this means is that December 25 was a popular festival day throughout the area which would eventually come to be known as the Holy Roman Empire a thousand years before those identifying themselves as Christians began to assign significance to

RUTH TALLMAN

that date as the birth of their savior. In other words, before Jesus was even born, everyone was already partying on and around December 25. As Christians evolved from a rag-tag group of commune-living, counter-cultural hippies into the Establishment, it makes sense that the Church Fathers would have thought it was a good idea to give its increasingly far-flung members a church-approved reason to do the partying they were already doing anyway.

The manner of celebrating Christmas, both at its origins and today, borrows heavily from non-Christian traditions. There is disagreement about the exact origins of the Christmas tree. This is because rituals and celebrations centering around trees were prominent parts of many ancient winter festivals. In darkest, coldest winter, when agricultural communities with no electricity and dwindling food supplies despaired of spring ever returning, evergreens stood as powerful symbols of hope. These trees were often decorated or glorified in some way, and clippings were brought into homes, formed into wreaths, and used as decoration during winter festivals.[3] Despite its ancient roots, this common trope was not adopted by Christians and incorporated into Christmas rituals until the sixteenth century, long after Christmas was established as a Christian holiday.

Kindly, gift-bearing father figures are another common element in many cultures. The most striking parallel with the Santa Claus myth is the pre-Christian Germanic god Odin, who rode an eight legged horse through the sky. Children who placed goodies for the horse in their shoes at night found their offerings replaced with gifts the following morning. Although Christians can trace Santa Claus's roots to the fourth century saint Nicholas of Myra, the figure did not become associated with Christmas gift-giving until the seventeenth century. Winter festivals have also long been occasions for singing, feasting, and exchanging gifts.

Okay, so the modern festival of Christmas isn't particularly original. The date and many of its rituals predate Christianity. Does this mean Christians aren't actually celebrating the birth of their savior when they observe the holiday? Of course not. The same practices can have different meanings at different times. What matters is the intent of those who engage in the practices, and the celebration of Christmas is a high holy day for many devout Christians. But that's not all it is. The same day and the same rituals can mean all sorts of things, and given that we know that the tropes surrounding this holiday are not original with or unique to a rigidly Christian definition of Christmas, it is impossible to suppose that non-Christians today might not find non-Christian meaning and value in the rituals, just as non-Christians in pre-Christian cultures did.

"Do they know it's Christmastime at all?" What Should Naturalists Do At Christmas?

Clearly, some of the meaning atheists might derive from Christmas will differ from the meaning derived by Christians. One place of divergence will be regarding the metaphysical underpinnings of the beliefs of Christians and atheists. One way to understand an atheistic mindset is in terms of naturalism. Naturalism is contrasted with supernaturalism. Naturalists reject the existence of God or gods[4] (as well as elfs and flying reindeer). If you can't see it, smell it, touch it, taste it, it's not real, for a naturalist. Yet, naturalists find meaning and truth in the vast complexity and beauty of the natural world. Naturalists come in many stripes; some embrace a high level of spiritualism while others tend more to the ways of hard-nosed science. What unifies naturalists is the belief that all that there is to life, all hope, value, and order we might possibly glean, will have to be found in the here and now – there is nothing else.

Most people think that if you don't believe in a god, the only other option is to reject all religious practices. Although some atheists do reject all forms of religion, many still think that religion is an important element of a life well lived. Before you reject this idea out of hand, you should be aware that some forms of Hinduism, Buddhism, Jainism, Confucianism, and Taoism are atheistic. There are atheistic Jews and cultural Catholics. These institutions are regularly identified as religions while lacking all belief in a supernatural god. So what is a religion with no supernatural elements? What is left if you take away God and heaven? George Santayana (1863–1952), a Spanish-American philosopher, defines natural religion as "that religion which naturally expresses the imaginative life of a nation according to the conceptions there current about the natural world and to the interest then uppermost in men's hearts."[5] As Santayana understands it, religion is a way of understanding and focusing on what is important in our lives. He understands religion as a cultural phenomenon, something that is done with others. So being religious, for Santayana, involves group worship and the sharing of values in settings such as churches, prayer groups, and family devotions.

RUTH TALLMAN

Religion is a way of connecting with those who share your values and concerns. For some people, those values and concerns center around supernatural elements, but they need not. Religious practices are ways of focusing on the things that are important to us. Atheists do not place importance on deities or heaven, but there are still many things they find important, and Santayana understands the practices that focus on those concerns as religious.

Why Deck the Halls? The Importance of Ritual

The philosopher Steven Cahn has written on the type of religious naturalism endorsed by Santayana. Cahn makes explicit many of the ideas that are in the background of Santayana's writings. Cahn writes extensively about ritual. Rituals are an important part of human life. They are a way to honor, remember, mark milestones, rejoice, and grieve. They instill in us a sense of place, belonging, heritage, and purpose. All cultures, regardless of the metaphysical belief structure they embrace, place a high value on rituals. Although some rituals have special theistic significance, such as the partaking of the Eucharist in the Catholic church, many of the rituals which we embrace are entirely secular. Handshakes demonstrate feelings of warmth and respect for those we meet. Graduations, birthdays, Fourth of July celebrations – these rituals are meaning-making without involving supernatural beliefs. Even very simple daily activities can become ritualized in a way that is helpful and comforting for those who engage in them. Coffee and NPR to begin the day. A kiss as you head out the door. Sharing a crossword each evening. Reading before bed.

Many rituals are entirely secular, but Santayana argues that naturalists might sometimes want to engage in an overtly religious ritual, even though they do not accept the supernatural explanation that theists place on the ritual. Many atheistic Jews keep kosher as an expression of their heritage. Cultural Catholics baptize their kids as a way of marking their entrance to a community they still find meaningful, even though they have rejected the metaphysical basis of the community. Why? If you've rejected the basis of the group, why still cling to the group and its practices? Santayana explains that the religious and the secular can be jumbled up in our heads as children.[6] We write letters to Santa and ask Jesus to forgive our sins. We decorate the Christmas tree and set up the nativity scene (which is really an awful lot like a doll house). Stories of bogeymen under the bed slosh together in our scared, confused minds with spooky poems about dying in our sleep and the possible loss of our souls. As comedian Bill Maher puts it, "If you switched the stories in the Bible with the ones that you had in your fairy tale books as a kid would you know the difference? ... Delilah, Rapunzel, a talking wolf, a talking snake.... There's a poison apple in the garden of Eden and there's one in *Snow White*, does it matter, who cares?"[7]

Adult atheists who were raised in Christian homes grew up thinking of Jesus as just another mythic figure, right there with Santa and the Easter bunny. But you know, Santa and the Easter bunny are pretty cool mythic figures, and shucks, so is Jesus. Adults enjoy Santa talk and rituals with no belief in his actual existence, and no one finds this particularly weird. We attend Halloween parties without accepting the metaphysical beliefs of its Celtic origins. We embrace myths because they help express our values and because they're fun.

Participating in rituals from our childhoods can be meaningful for us not because of some external power or purpose that the ritual is believed to have, but through the soothing or meditative power of the ritual in and of itself. Santayana gives an example: "A candle wasting itself before an image will prevent no misfortune, but it may bear witness to some silent hope or relieve some sorrow by expressing it; it may soften a little the bitter sense of impotence which would consume a mind aware of physical dependence but not of spiritual dominion."[8] The rhythmic recitation of a rosary, combined with the tactile experience of fingers creeping from bead to bead, might still serve as an act of meditation to those who do not believe that it will bring about any changes in the world outside of personal comfort.

In addition to ritual, humans find meaning through joining together as a moral community. A moral community is a group which you belong to because you share the values of others in the group. Churches have long been the prime example of moral communities. They are groups that form and are maintained based on the values of its members. Church congregations are collections of like-minded people who unite to share, celebrate, and promote their values. As it turns out, a moral community is a really useful thing to have. It is a support network, a place to develop friendships, a place to learn and grow, and an organization that can get things done better than unorganized individuals can. But there is nothing about a moral community that requires supernatural belief. Political parties are an example of naturalistic moral communities. Naturalistic religious moral communities unite based not on the basis of

RUTH TALLMAN

their non-belief in God, as some might suppose, but instead on the basis of the beliefs that they do share, such as devotion to the poor and disadvantaged, the promotion of education and freedom, and belief in the need for various sorts of social change. Sometimes a religious moral community will have theistic and atheistic members. Despite the disagreement on the level of metaphysical belief, these groups form and endure due to the commonalities they share, which the group members think override their metaphysical differences.

Despite the rejection of supernatural reality, many atheists acknowledge the importance of religion in contemporary culture. Renowned atheist Richard Dawkins has said:

> I'm not one of those who wants to stop Christian traditions. This is historically a Christian country. I'm a cultural Christian in the same way many of my friends call themselves cultural Jews or cultural Muslims. So, yes, I like singing carols along with everybody else. I'm not one of those who wants to purge our society of our Christian history. If there's any threat to these sorts of things, I think you will find it comes from rival religions and not from atheists.[9]

Writer and activist Dan Savage describes himself as an atheist and a cultural Catholic. He says, "I'm Catholic – in a cultural sense, not an eat-the-wafer, say-the-rosary, burn-down-the-women's-health-center sense."[10] In what sense is Dan Savage Catholic, then? He embraces Catholicism as a part of his mythic heritage. He reported in an episode of *This American Life* that he felt himself drawn back to his Catholic roots as he mourned his mother's death. Though Savage has stood in vocal opposition to the church's stance on homosexuality and abstinence-only education, among other things, he finds meaning and power in the ritual and community of the church of his youth.[11]

When I Was Small I Believed in Santa Claus, Though I Knew it Was Dad: Why Belief is Not Important

Bringing these ideas back to the specific subject of the celebration of Christmas by atheists, there are two ways we can understand what is going on. Probably the majority of atheists who celebrate Christmas do so because they were raised in a religious tradition which celebrated

Christmas. Out of that group, some engage in overtly religious acts. They display nativity scenes, sing "Silent Night," and attend midnight Mass. Santayana helps us understand these individuals' behavior. They are engaging in behavior which they find meaningful in and of itself, because of its connection in their primal memories of warm childhood feelings. They may also be motivated by a desire to share in experiences with their still-believing family members. Just like we play along with kids about the tooth fairy because we think they find value in their harmless false beliefs, so many atheists play along with their aging parents about their religious beliefs, if they think they are harmless.

Isn't this objectionably disingenuous? Isn't it wrong to engage in activities which send a message that you believe in something that you don't? Santayana doesn't think so. He says, "Do we marshal arguments against the miraculous birth of Buddha, or the story of Cronos devouring his children? We seek rather to honor the piety and to understand the poetry embodied in those fables."[12] It goes without saying that we don't believe Buddha was really walking around spouting poetry on the day he was born, and no self-respecting naturalist, regardless of how they behave on Christmas Eve, really thinks a man-god was born of a virgin in a barn, thus (somehow) causing a brand new star to show up in the sky. Provided the ritual is engaged in for honest reasons – the practitioner does not seek to ridicule the belief system, but rather finds an alternative meaning in the activity – the metaphysical beliefs of the practitioner are not important.

Santayana thinks atheists engaging in Christmas rituals, even those which are overtly religious, is not disingenuous because it is understood, provided the atheist is not closeted, that he does not believe in the metaphysical assumptions behind the rituals. This is similar to Westerners who practice yoga with a Hindu instructor. Yoga is a ritual which carries with it a host of metaphysical assumptions that are embraced by the Hindu, but not by his Western students. The Westerners are not lying about their beliefs when they practice yoga; they find meaning in the ritual, but the meaning they find is not identical to the meaning derived by the Hindu. Everyone knows the score, everyone is finding something of value in the experience, so, provided the Hindu instructor does not object, there is no problem with Hindus and non-Hindus engaging in a yogic ritual together.[13]

Other examples abound of Christians engaging in this type of inter-belief sampling. Consider the Western fascination with feng shui when it suits our decorating sensibilities, with no consideration of the complexities of the belief system of which it is a part. Think of the after-church crowd at the Chinese restaurant on Sunday afternoon, happily discovering their zodiac signs, exclaiming over what their sign spells for their love relationships. No one supposes that these good Christians are dabbling in the worship of foreign gods, nor do we worry that they are deceiving their Chinese waiters regarding their metaphysical beliefs. Just so, when atheists choose to engage in overtly religious Christmas rituals, there is generally no deception or other moral problem with this behavior.

Chestnuts Roasting on an Open Fire: What Christmas is All About

Some Christmas rituals are overtly religious, and Santayana has given us reason to suppose that there are good reasons for atheists to want to participate in these rituals, despite their rejection of the metaphysical beliefs which underlay the rituals. He has also explained why Christians should not find this particularly troubling – no more troubling than their own decision to engage in particular rituals which have metaphysical under-pinning in other religious traditions, such as yoga. It turns out, however, that most atheists have no desire to engage in overtly religious Christmas rituals. And, thank goodness for them, there is no shortage of Christmas rituals that have no necessary tie to Christianity.

Naturalistic Christmas celebrations involve Christmas trees, carols, cookies, and presents. Such celebrations can be extremely meaningful for those who engage in them. They are a time to join together with family and other loved ones and participate in yearly activities which have been passed down for generations. Grandmothers teach grandchildren how to roll out the cookie dough just so, while older cousins show younger cousins how to apply sprinkles while surreptitiously sneaking a bite of dough. Fifty years from now, those grandchildren will have become grandmothers, and the cycle will continue.

Christmas makes us slow down, shrug off some of our self-absorption, and take some time to savor the things we've been living and working for. It's a reason to get out the good dishes and to really throw your energy into a home-cooked feast. Christmas cards are the yearly nag which reminds us to touch base with old friends we would have no prompt to contact otherwise. Maintaining such longtime connections with those who were once key players in our lives, though they have now moved on, gives us a sense of place and continuity, reminding us who we are, from whence we came, and where we want to go. Christmas is a time to remember those in need, to reach into our pocketbooks and give what we have to others. It is a time to teach our children to do the same. Christmas is a totally fun way to teach others and to remind ourselves to be selfless, other-regarding people.

Let's not forget, however, that modernity is also about commercialism. Like it or not, it's part of the package. The experience of normal shopping, as opposed to Christmas shopping, is like the difference between watching a movie at home and watching it in the theatre. When you hit the stores in the weeks before Christmas, your senses are overloaded with the cultural markers you have been experiencing since youth. The mall glitters with decorations, the carols are unending – even your sense of smell is overloaded with a combination of spiced nuts and summer sausages being pedaled from kiosks. Moving through the crowds, you are a part of a vast cultural phenomenon which supercedes sect and creed. At no time as much as Christmas does our society become a melting pot of shared values and traditions.

That Spirit of Christmas: Christmas's Secular Humanism

Atheists share a great many values with their believing fellow Americans. One might argue that there is a secular spirit of Christmas which unites theists and atheists. When people today celebrate a naturalistic Christmas, they are celebrating a specifically modern phenomenon. As such, it is only natural that this spirit would be transmitted through modern media – movies and radio songs. It has often been argued that this spirit was born during the World War II years of the 1940s, when soldiers and families felt the pang of separation most strongly during the holiday season. This feeling was given shape and voice by a string of popular Christmas movies starring Bing Crosby and others, and with songs such as "White Christmas" and "I'll be Home for Christmas," all of which focus on particular secular elements of Christmas celebration, which stand as markers of the value of love, family, and togetherness during this time.

Perhaps the most famous example of the secular spirit of Christmas comes from the 1946 Frank Capra film, *It's a Wonderful Life*. Though not technically naturalistic (the film features angels), the themes emphasized in this movie embody modern secular values. The story's protagonist, George Bailey, is persuaded not to commit suicide not for fear of

RUTH TALLMAN

divine retribution, but because he is reminded that his life on earth is important. He, not God, was there to save his brother's life in a sledding accident when they were children. He, not God, prevented the pharmacist he worked for from accidentally poisoning a child. The message? George Bailey is important because he, not God, made the world a better place. The film has a clear moral message, but it is not a religious one. George learns (and we learn along with him) that personal ambitions are not how we ought to measure our lives. George failed to meet many of his life goals – he did not travel the world or become a successful architect. In fact, George is a pretty bad businessman. In the end, however, George realizes that he has succeeded where it matters – he loves and is loved, right here, right now, on earth. In fact, it is George's friends, clients, and neighbors who save him from the financial crisis which is the reason he decided to commit suicide at the beginning of the movie. Other human beings – not God – get George out of trouble. The climax of the movie is about people giving of themselves, out of love, to help others in need. The spirit of Christmas cannot be condensed down to a more pure essence than that!

Festivus for the Rest of Us

Certainly, there is a thing called "Christmas" which is a Christian celebration of the birth of a god. Yet there is also a thing called "Christmas" which is a secular celebration of love and humanity. Some have suggested that, if we really understand the tradition as having reached a point where it has diverged into two separate holidays, the naturalists ought to get their own damn name for their Christ-less Christmas. Frank Costanza's "Festivus: a holiday for the rest of us" from *Seinfeld* comes to mind.[14] But are there really two holidays? Or is there just one, celebrated in many ways? Perhaps the best way to understand Christmas as it stands today is in terms of a Venn diagram. The left circle is the Christian Christmas, which has elements of metaphysical belief not shared by atheists. The right circle is the naturalistic Christmas, which might have elements not shared by Christians. The portion of the diagram where the two circles intersect indicates the great deal of overlap between the values and practices surrounding the two holidays.

Christmas is about giving, sharing, and loving. It's a time when everyone celebrates the crazy fun impossibility of a fat man who can manage to slide down everyone's chimney in one night, even though most of us don't even have chimneys anymore. It's about faith in the power of the human spirit, about working toward a better tomorrow, where fewer people are sad, alone, hungry, or sick. This year, let's hope for a real Christmas miracle – Christians and non-Christians together, sharing the roast beast.[15]

NOTES

1 I would like to thank Jason Benjamin Oakes for inspiring this essay.
2 Luke 2:7. All biblical quotes are taken from the *Oxford Study Bible: Revised English Bible with the Apocrypha*, ed. M. Jack Suggs (New York: Oxford University Press, 1992).
3 This practice is referred to and condemned in the Old Testament (Jeremiah 10:2–4).
4 Most of them. Some, such as Baruch Spinoza, equate God with the natural world, believing that God is immanent – dwelling within all things – rather than transcendent. Naturalism is compatible with this kind of pantheist religion, but not with belief in a transcendent God (as embraced by mainstream Christians, for example), because naturalists believe there is no "other" realm in which God might dwell.
5 George Santayana, *The Life of Reason: Reason in Religion* (Amherst: Prometheus Books, 1998), p. 210.
6 Ibid., p. 230.
7 Bill Maher, "Be More Cynical," Kid Love Productions, 2000.
8 Santayana, *The Life of Reason*, p. 201.
9 BBC News, "Dawkins: I'm a Cultural Christian," December 10, 2007.
10 Dan Savage,. "R.I.P. J.P. II," *Savage Love*, April 14, 2005.
11 *This American Life*, episode 379, May 1, 2009.
12 Santayana, *The Life of Reason*, p. 226.
13 For more information about yoga as a Hindu religious practice, see Jean Varenne, *Yoga and the Hindu Tradition*, trans. Derek Coltman (Chicago: University of Chicago Press, 1977).
14 *Seinfeld*, episode 10, season 9, December 18, 1997.
15 I would like to thank Jason Southworth for his helpful comments on this essay.

CHAPTER 17

HEAVEN, HECATE, AND HALLMARK

Christmas in Hindsight

It is fitting that this essay appears in the section exploring Christmas through "other eyes." The perspective I bring is psychological in its formal view, rather than expressly philosophical. In addition, I'm writing about Christmas as a Pagan who views the holiday primarily as a secular, cultural event. I know there are others who have a similar view, but I think it's safe to say we are a small minority in the grand scheme of things.

Each decade of my adult life has brought with it a different religious perspective and a new look at Christmas. As a developmental psychologist I can see, in hindsight, the interplay of stages of maturity and faith at work throughout my journey. I choose to use my personal story not to trivialize or evangelize, but because religion can be a touchy thing, and I don't mind making fun of myself! My only goal here is to share a psychologist's view of human development and my personal journey through Christmases past in the hope that it sparks some personal reflection. If it brings a few chuckles along the way, even better!

My understanding of Christmas began as a child growing up in an urban neighborhood in Houston, Texas. It seems from the beginning I was destined to question the real meaning of Christmas. The words of many traditional carols, for example, caused me much confusion. Explain to a five-year-old on Christmas Eve, when it's 65 degrees outside in southern Texas, how we might go "dashing through the snow," or even why we might want to. If it snowed I couldn't ride that new bike I'm hoping to find on Christmas day. The holiday also brought me some concern, particularly regarding this stranger and his arrival down the chimney. In my Houston neighborhood I didn't know anyone whose house had a chimney. Furthermore, mine was a rough neighborhood, so all the outside doors had several locks and the windows had bars on them. The thought that someone could get into our house undetected in the middle of the night, even to deliver presents, was quite unsettling. Sure, the presents were nice, but if that old man could get in then others who were not so nice could get in too. I was relieved when my mother made up the story that she would wait up, make sure it was Santa, let him in, and make sure the door was locked when he left. Yes, I found Christmas puzzling from the very beginning.

Childhood and Christmas

During my childhood Christmas was celebrated primarily as a secular activity. My family somehow ignored most things religious, which is quite a feat in southern Texas. While in high school I realized that most of my peers claimed some religion, so I decided that I, too, should have membership in some religious group. Once I made my interest public it didn't take long for a fundamentalist Christian group to find me. And so began my spiraling journey through stages of faith and many new interpretations of Christmas.

Before we continue I need to provide some background in developmental psychology. As an area of academic study, for many years developmental psychology was really the study of childhood. Sigmund Freud, Jean Piaget, and other prominent psychologists believed that the most interesting time in human development was childhood. They are not alone – how many times have you heard or even said yourself that Christmas is really about the children?

Certainly, the changes occurring year to year during childhood are more dramatic than in adulthood, but just as certain is the fact that people do change between their twenties and eighties! It has been in just the last twenty-five years or so that developmental psychologists have studied adulthood, thus the theory is still catching up with the research. The theory most useful for my hindsight reflections on Christmas is the Stages of Faith model developed by James Fowler in the 1980s. While his work has been justifiably challenged for its limited roots in American

Christianity and Judaism, its emphasis on a linear, progressively more advanced scheme, and heavy reliance on cognitive and moral development, I find that the stages provide a useful lens through which I can better understand my own development and ponder my future path. Also, Fowler's theory of faith development is one of the few models of religiosity across the life span, offering insight into adult religious development.[1] Both recent research and my personal journey lead me to believe that, rather than a straight line of development progressing to an ultimate stage, adults may move forward, backward, and repeatedly spiral through the stages numerous times.

The first two stages in Fowler's theory of faith development are generally considered childhood and adolescent stages. Coming to my first serious interaction with organized religion as a high school student it's likely that I moved through the first two stages rather quickly. The first stage, *Intuitive-Projective Faith*, is a childhood stage in which the ability to imagine or pretend allows us to enter into dramatic religious feelings and emotions. Often, deities are characterized as superheroes. *Mythic-Literal Faith*, stage 2, is the point in which older children take to heart the stories, beliefs, and observances of their religious culture. Their focus is on facts, data, and fixed, literal interpretations of abstract information.

I can't recall wondering if Jesus or Santa could scale tall buildings or stop bullets with their bare hands, as I hear some superheroes can do, but I do recall equating religion with memorization of key facts. For example, do you know which books in the Bible relate the Christmas story?

One of the best examples I've witnessed to these early stages of faith came as I was assisting a Sunday school teacher in a presentation to preschoolers about Christmas. The teacher held up a poster illustrating the Christmas angel visiting the earth. Perhaps in an effort to bring scripture into the gender-neutral, politically correct age, the angel was depicted as simply a white human silhouette. One little boy suddenly became agitated and announced in a rather smarty-pants way, "That's a ghost and my momma says there's no such thing as ghosts!" He spoke with such authority that the teacher soon realized she couldn't convince the class otherwise. Being a wise, seasoned teacher, she calmly said, "Apparently the person who made this poster made a mistake. Let's make this the Christmas angel." She put the poster on the floor, gave the children crayons and markers, and asked them to correct any errors. When they were done the silhouette had been properly clothed in a long dress and boots, given long flowing hair and wings, and provided feminine facial features and make-up. Only then could the lesson continue.

Heaven is at Stake

After several years of research Fowler concluded that the primary stages displayed by most adults in most American churches and synagogues are stages three and four. In stage 3, *Synthetic-Conventional Faith*, we begin to appreciate personal relationships in our religious community, respect the authority of religious leaders, and value our religious heritage. This pride may show itself as a desire to be full participants in religious activities, as well as through displays of group membership, such as wearing t-shirts and hats with the group's name.

Of all my years in fundamentalist Christianity, these were the best for celebrating Christmas! I participated fully in the many activities in my religious community. We put together musical presentations, went caroling to nursing homes, and collected gifts for needy children. In hindsight I can see that Christmas for me at that point wasn't about gifts or theology as much as it was about being active with a group of like-minded people. Of course, Jesus was the reason for the season, but I must say my joy came from involvement in the seasonal activities.

Things changed when my life became busier than it had ever been. As a young adult trying to manage the demands of college, employment, and love relationships, I started to consider what I *had* to do at Christmas to be true to my faith. How had Christmas become such a burden, reduced to spending too much money, and that sometimes on people I marginally cared about, and enduring what felt like endless social obligations? What was the real meaning of Christmas? Is it hypocritical to honor the birth of this poor baby with glitz, glam, and expensive gifts? Would Jesus be happy with bling? In my search for answers I found that Puritans in England banned Christmas celebrations from 1647 to 1660, and New Englanders banned them in Boston from 1659 to 1681. In a bold move, I decided to live my faith. Take charge. Eliminate this evil secular influence:

- Christmas trees are Pagan – gone!
- Santa Claus, Elfs, and Rudolph are not biblical – gone!
- Gifts for family and friends when others are starving – gone!
- Christmas carols with no reference to the Christ child – gone!
- Become a crusader in the war against Christmas – done!

With enough self-righteousness to dampen even the slightest bit of fun, I shared my sobering message with all who needed to hear it. For heaven's sake, how can these practices continue!

MARION G. MASON

As I recall, my message wasn't well received. The resulting tension and confusing served as a catalyst, launching me into the next stage. The transition from stage 3 to 4 can be a difficult one. Whereas religious teachings and traditions are accepted in stage 3 as already proven information we should accept and internalize, the onset of stage 4 brings questions, doubts, and concerns about those one-accepted teachings. Stage 4, *Individuative-Reflective Faith*, involves the critical analysis of tensions between evolving personal beliefs and those defined by group membership. Fowler cautioned that we may experience "cosmic homelessness" during which we start to question where we belong in the religious world. I became overwhelmed by paradoxes in my thinking and hypocrisies in my behaviors. Yes, I love my neighbor as myself, but no, I'm not going to buy Christmas presents for all my neighbors. Yes, I want to spread the Christmas message, but no, I'm too tired to go caroling this evening. Developmental psychologists find that such tensions can catapult us to the next stage or into the abyss of cynicism. There were other issues in addition to thoughts about Christmas that sent me over the edge ... but down in the abyss I went.

Moving around the Spiral

Even though I couldn't seem to sort out my own mental confusion when it came to religion, I still felt the desire for a religious community. In my thirties I discovered Unitarian Universalism, and started yet another spiral through the stages of faith. As before, I don't recall ever thinking that Thomas Jefferson, Ralph Waldo Emerson, or P. T. Barnum were superheroes (stage 1), but I do recall learning the history and culture (stage 2) and quickly accepting official roles in congregational activities (stage 3). My attitude toward Christmas changed dramatically, and finally it was fun again! No need to worry that only strict thinking leads to heaven and hedonism leads to hell ... we don't believe in those places:

- Have a Christmas tree or don't.
- Give material gifts or donate something in someone's name.
- At Christmas celebrate your ethnic heritage, someone else's, or be unique.
- Jesus, Zeus, or Pan.
- Mary, Isis, or Hecate.
- It's all good.

Celebrating the Christmas season became a treasure hunt of its own. How can you go wrong when you decorate with a Scandinavian Yule goat and a Christian Advent calendar, and honor Sinterklaas (Dutch) by serving traditional kransekake (cake)?

As time passed I found myself venturing into stage 4 reasoning again. This time around was different, primarily because I was in a group that valued not only my questions but even the very process of questioning. Whereas in my fundamentalist days stage 4 brought the seriousness of honoring the "true" meaning of Christmas, in my Unitarian Universalist days it brought the seriousness of political correctness. For example, we would sing the popular carol "Joy to the World" with the modification that "the *word* has come." No *Lord* here. Suddenly, it became difficult to borrow Christmas traditions from others without falling into cultural appropriation. Heavy sigh. It was getting difficult again.

Hecate at the Crossroads

One day in my late thirties, while reflecting on my religious journey, I thought of how I used to study the Bible and wondered what would happen if I tried to study Nature in the same way? It didn't take long using the Internet to find there was a whole world of nature-religion practices under the label of *Paganism*. I quickly found websites, groups, and even academic resources, such as a Pagan seminary and the Contemporary Pagan Studies division of the American Academy of Religion. My journey through the spirals of faith was about to get very interesting.

My initial venture into Paganism quickly challenged my template of what defined a religion. Compared to what I knew of Christianity and even Unitarian Universalism, here was a group with basically no scripture, no organized or widely accepted theological doctrine, a relatively short history (or at least a sizeable gap between the earliest forms of religion and current ones), and only a loose network of organizations rather than a prescribed hierarchy. This group placed less emphasis on deity, allowing for many options. Here was a rapidly growing religious movement, full of energy and creative ritual. With my curiosity aroused and my inner child awakened from a long nap, I decided it was time to play. For once in my tightly wound, career-driven adult life I decided to just have fun with my religion.

MARION G. MASON

In hindsight I can see that breaking the religious template I had held for so long provided a different experience as I moved through the stages of faith. As I entered the first stage, *Intuitive-Projective Faith*, that childhood ability to imagine and pretend returned. Everywhere I looked in my natural environment entities were animated and meaningful. And, much like childhood thought, all such entities were good spirits, and of course, it all revolved around me! In stage 1, deities are practically superheroes, and few religions can boast in that regard the way we Pagans can! I'm sure Zeus the Greek God of Thunder or Sekhmet the Egyptian Warrior Goddess could take down Spiderman or Batman with no problem. But, as an adult, it's fair to ask whether I *really* believed the many pantheons of goddesses and gods existed in some current or literal form. Not *really*, but I enjoyed pretending and took my imagination as close to the line of sanity as I dared to go.

While enjoying my free-flowing imagination I did realize that I needed some grounding. Prompted to move into stage 2, *Mythic-Literal Faith*, I was filled with a seemingly insatiable thirst for facts, data, beliefs, and observances that create the culture of modern Paganism. The largest group within Paganism is the Wiccans, who practice various kinds of group and solitary witchcraft. While there is no consensus on approaches to deity, most Pagans I came across had one or several deities they "worked with." So, in my effort to fit in, I chose Hecate. In the earliest literature she was a highly praised Titan in the Greek pantheon. Over the years she lost status in classic literature, and later emerged as a Goddess of the Crossroads. I felt like I was at a crossroads, and perhaps her story had lessons for me.

This desire to gather as much information as possible also led to some discoveries about the origins of Christmas. Among the things most Wiccans hold dear are the cycles of the moon and sun, corresponding to holidays or the Wheel of the Year, with one of those special moments being the winter solstice. Early Christians, when arriving in a new land, would move their holy days to the times of Pagan gatherings to merge the events, so the Pagan side of the story goes, with the goal of later dominating the event. In some cases old traditions probably did die out or evolved into something new, but examples such as the involvement of Easter eggs at the celebration of Christ's resurrection and mistletoe at the time of Christ's birth demonstrate that the merging continues. Decorated trees, holly, mistletoe, and Yule logs have Pagan roots. Part of the tradition of wassailing was to sing to the trees in apple orchards to encourage a good cider harvest, as well as going from door to door singing. The Christmas season began to take on new meaning for me, and it was fun again. I was connecting with my ancestors. (Who, I might add, I romanced in my imagination to be all good people that I would like to connect with!)

Stage 3, Fowler's *Synthetic-Conventional Faith*, came quickly in my Pagan journey. It took several seasons of living the Pagan Wheel of the Year before I felt the anticipation of the various holy days. That stage 3 enthusiasm and pride for one's religious heritage soon set in. Give me the true "old time religion" (think Stonehenge) and don't mess with my Yule celebration! I found myself getting annoyed in stores and shopping malls with the constant stream of Christmas carols. It was as if I was feeling the inundating waves of Christmas culture for the first time. What about all the people who aren't celebrating Christmas? Much like when you're in a second marriage it feels good on occasion to criticize the first loser you somehow fell in love with and married, in a second religion it can on occasion feel good to get a little critical as well.

Hecate had brought me to a crossroads and I was determined that the whole world would know it! So, once again a crusader for the season, I sent out "Happy Solstice" cards rather than Christmas cards. In my home we had a "Solstice tree" decorated with fake wooden apples, cinnamon, and birds – natural objects rather than flashy glass ornaments. When someone said "Merry Christmas" I would respond with "Happy Holidays." That is, unless I was feeling particularly bold. On those days I might respond to "Merry Christmas" with something like "Thanks. I don't do Christmas but I appreciate the good wishes. Have a great holiday!" Just to make a statement we would give gifts on the solstice and take down the tree on Christmas Eve. By December 24 the party was over. My goal was not to evangelize or swing people over to my point of view, but rather to remind people around me of their homogeneous assumptions. Not everyone here sees the world the way you do.

It's Not about Me?

Just as in my Christian days, the transition from stage 3 to 4, moving into that evaluative *Individuative-Reflective Faith*, was a bit bumpy. After several cycles of the Wheel of the Year I found that my personal need for recognition as a Pagan lessened in intensity. Oh, I still have a desire to champion diversity, reminding people to watch their assumptions, particularly about middle-aged women. In hindsight, though, I now realize that stage 3 in faith development is really about identity. I didn't need to try to fit the definition of Pagan – I am Pagan and what I do becomes what Paganism is.

I also realized that, try as I might, I still had a lot of that Christian template overlaying my view of religion. I wasn't in error sending Solstice cards or educating others on the history of Christmas holly or mistletoe, but just as Chanukkah isn't the major holiday for Jews that Christmas is for Christians, Yule isn't a major holiday for Pagans either. As my Pagan cultural worldview became my normal routine, I found I had greater anticipation for the more important holidays occurring around the first of November and the first of May.

My enlightenment prompted memories of an exchange I had with a colleague of mine who is Jewish. During the time of my greatest involvement in Unitarian Universalism (UU) I was telling her about some UU event, and she remarked that UUs are basically Christian. I found her observation genuinely perplexing. As UUs we didn't pray "in Jesus' name" – in fact, we didn't pray at all. The words to any hymns with a Christian foundation, like the Christmas carols, had all been changed. No self-respecting fundamentalist Christian of the ilk I used to be would agree that UUs were Christian. She pointed out that the UUs met on Sundays, followed a program of hymns, readings, and a sermon similar to Protestant Christian services, and celebrated Christmas along with other Christian holidays. She has always been one to challenge my thinking, and although I couldn't see it from her perspective, the conversation stayed with me. Now, years later, I understood what she meant. Not that there's anything wrong with the Christian or UU religious services, I have to agree with her that they are much more similar to each other than they are to a Pagan experience. And, based on what she said, perhaps a Jewish experience as well. A significant part of my new understanding of religion in general, my own journey, and the celebration of Christmas, was the awareness of cultural and personal evolution. Most people and religious organizations change and adapt over time. They are not stagnant, but rather growing and developing just as I was.

It's Not Me or You: It's Hallmark

In my fifth decade of life my fundamentalist Christian days seemed far away. Christianity was another world religion, much like Buddhism or Hinduism, worthy of respect but rather foreign to me. The emotions had faded, the personal pet-peeves wilted, and finally I didn't feel the need to be a crusader for anything. I may be displaying little more than my own hubris to think I'm transitioning into stage 5, *Conjunctive Faith*, as Fowler's stages 5 and 6 are rare. Stage 5 involves the reworking of our past beliefs and ideology, a clarified sense of self (both positive and negative characteristics), and an honest acceptance of whatever we call *faith*, including the paradoxes and unanswered questions. Fowler describes the breakthrough of stage 5 as the recognition of meaning in traditions, symbols, and rituals, while simultaneously recognizing the limitations and distortions of those very resources. These days I often describe my personal spiritual mythology as something similar to artistic expression that, though symbolic, I believe helps me cope with difficulties and challenges me to be a better person. Also in Conjunctive Faith we begin to appreciate the influences of social class, religious tradition, ethnicity, geographic location, and cultural myths on our personal formulations of faith and belief. In American culture Christmas is not mine or yours, but rather a movement that has a life of its own.

Once I was able to put down my emotional lens I found that one of the driving forces behind Christmas celebrations, and perhaps the most powerful of all, is the industry that has grown worldwide around the holiday. We buy Christmas trees, lights, decorations, special foods, music, and Advent calendars. We have Black Friday, the day after Thanksgiving which often puts an entire year's worth of profit into store coffers. (So, how early in the year have you seen Christmas items in retail stores?) We also have Cyber Monday, directly following Thanksgiving, on which people order online all the items they didn't get on Black Friday at local retailers. Not stopping with home décor and gifts, we buy wrapping paper, bows, and tags, and make many trips in the car to deliver all these goods. We may even need to travel by train or plane to deliver gifts. Meanwhile, media outlets respond with the release of blockbuster movies, the postal service releases new stamps, and many cities and towns plan parades and local festivals. Yes, the truth is often revealed if you follow the money and the market trends.

Spiraling Around the Christmas Tree

Through my religious journey the Christmas season has become symbolic of many things, much like a parable. Every time I get fascinated with the holiday I learn something new about myself and move further along in my own spiraling journey. I learn more about my religious and

MARION G. MASON

societal culture and my small place in it. Much like a parable that has different meanings to different listeners, I can now happily say "Merry Christmas" to anyone. For me, the phrase is cultural, said in recognition of a seasonal and economic marker that brings a shared conversation, much like the weather, major sports, or current movies. I realize the holiday doesn't have that same meaning to many who celebrate around the world, and that's fine. My desire to *own* Christmas has faded, as well as my assumption that such sense of ownership is even desirable!

Where to now? Who knows. Each decade in my life has brought a new religious outlook, and as I am quickly coming upon yet another decade of life, I am excited to see what's around the next turn of the spiral. To complete Fowler's journey, the final stage is called *Universalizing Faith*. It is a rare and abstract stage that is, by its very nature, difficult to describe. Stage 6 is embodied in those few people who have dedicated their lives to their highest religious principles. These individuals have lost their need to preserve their own sense of self or personal desires and have taken on an attitude of reckless abandon in living out their religious purpose. I doubt I'll evolve into Gandhi or Mother Teresa, so for now I'm content to be who I am – a happy Pagan taking a sentimental look at Christmas in hindsight.

NOTE

1   J. W. Fowler, *Stages of Faith: The Psychology of Human Development and the Quest for Meaning* (San Francisco: Harper and Row, 1981).

CHAPTER 18

FESTIVUS AND THE NEED FOR SEASONAL ABSURDITY

If I have to sit through one more Christmas dinner I'm going to break the space-time continuum and have the whole thing sucked into a vortex of non-existence. I say *a* vortex because I ponder if there can be *the* vortex. The indefinite article of *a* seems to coincide with the indefinite nature of non-existence. (A colleague of mine, though, questions if this does not make "multiple vortexes of non-existence," which makes the whole issue moot.) This is my usual attitude as the happy holidays harp around. *Happy*? When are they happy? What's happy about spending hundreds of dollars from an already beleaguered paycheck? What's happy about putting even more charges on my credit card, a card that already shares an allegorical connection to Roanoke? The same colleague mentions that my stepdaughter's eyes will sparkle. I fail to see how sparkling eyes restructures the reality of the Christmas season.

And that reality is consumerism.

America may be a city on a hill but that hill swarms with department stores, strip malls, and overpriced coffee houses. Consumerism is one of the three pillars of our democracy. The other two are an ill-informed media and a longer-lasting light bulb. From consumerism, we set the tone for the year and every year upcoming. Life in America is not based on family values or republican ideals. Life is based on monstrous mega-stores catering to a shopping compulsion.

This is acceptable. I prefer it over living in a country striving to actually have a light bulb. As I am a consumer I am a direct contributor to the gelatinous mass that is the GDP (or was). I can get a burger that tastes the same at roughly the same price in each of our fifty states, Puerto Rico, Guam and the District of Columbia. I take pride in that. Where I draw the line, though, is when I'm a told that I, who already spend more in a day than most people in the rest of the world spend in a month, need to spend even more to make the Christmas season "successful." Really? That's the goal? To make the season successful? What is successful? A better quarter for American corporations this year than last? So many presents under the tree that when unwrapped my living room looks like a paper mill? What about all that "good will towards men?" What about baby Jesus in the manger and the Three Wise Men and Santa Claus and doing well to others? The questions we ask each other at Christmas raise certain objections. "What did you get me?" Not, "Hey, I'm glad you didn't get hit by a car today and are able to spend the 25th with me." But, "What did you get me?"

There is madness in a holiday manufactured around both a corporate quarter and the Christian religion. Christmas, in its very wording, carries a religious connotation. One cannot escape the name of Christ in Christmas. One may not want to. This is not the issue. The issue is the encroachment and entrenchment of consumerism driven by corporate demand into the holiday of Christmas. Companies plan for the Christmas season months to years in advance. They plan not for the outpouring of kindness and generosity, but for the outpouring of product, of merchandise. They create a need in mockery of the needs Christmas was originally intended to highlight: generosity, good will, love, and compassion. We no longer seek to help the less fortunate. We seek to fill our houses with guilt-laden loot.

If the life of Christ and the habits of our Christmas shopping coincide, I am blind to it. Other people are equally blind. People, despite the dialogue from the thrones of brokers and other agents of darkness, do not wish to stay so blind. All people want to see and all people want release. When society as a whole is unwilling to break loose from destructive habits, people of average means will break free independently.

This brings us to Festivus, a television holiday.

"In the beginning" … there was Festivus

Festivus do what now? This is asked by people, like my mother, who have never watched *Seinfeld*. Festivus is perhaps the first secular American holiday (though there are arguments in favor of the Super Bowl). Billed as an anti-holiday, Festivus is an occasion where family and friends gather around a dining room table or in a living room, as location is secondary, and practice *not* having good will towards men, *not* exchanging gifts, and *not* remembering that they are supposed to be kind and generous to each other. It is often observed on December 23, though this specific date is arbitrary.

Festivus is an occasion to tell the people in the room what you *actually* think of them, engage in wrestling matches, and show your pagan ancestry by worshiping around a single unadorned aluminum pole. Tinsel is forbidden. There are also Festivus Miracles which have nothing to do with actual miracles. The holiday does not end until the head of the household is pinned to the floor. If your father is Chuck Norris, that would be the Festivus Miracle.

In short, Festivus is a great knock against consumerism and needless spending. There are actually two origins to the phenomenon that is Festivus. There is the popular origin whereby Festivus was featured in a subplot on the *Seinfeld* episode, "The Strike."[1] Frank Costanza, played by the incorrigible Jerry Stiller, created the holiday after suffering an existential crisis brought on by a futile tug-of-war match with a rival father for a toy. Then there is the obscure origin. Dan O'Keefe, one of the writers on *Seinfeld*, had a very strange and satirical father named Daniel O'Keefe. Daniel O'Keefe invented Festivus in 1966 as a way of celebrating his and his wife's first date and then subsequently subjected his children to it and its odd mutations for the next several decades.[2]

Despite O'Keefe's admonitions that the actual Festivus is different than that portrayed by the television series, it is exactly the TV version of Festivus which has captured American enthusiasm, albeit a minority of enthusiasm. As Jason Alexander, a.k.a. George Costanza, notes in the introduction to Dan O'Keefe's book on Festivus (one of only two books actually written on this subject), *Seinfeld* was a great contributor to popular culture.[3] Alexander then goes on to declare his freedom from the holiday in impassioned language, thanks to O'Keefe's writing. It is moving.

The elements of Festivus are legendary, an unadorned metal pole devoid of tinsel, the airing of grievances, and the wrestling and pining of the head of the household to the floor. We will discuss these elements more at length, but there is a relevant question gnawing the mind. What does any of this have to do with philosophy? It's a given that Festivus is a lark and a most excellent way to annoy Southern Baptists (something to do with Festivus and the unraveling of our moral fabric, or something like that). However, what possible philosophical underpinnings can Festivus lay claim to? If the proletariat want to celebrate the anti-Christmas with zero gifts and barbaric practices of familial violence that's their business, but in the serious realm of intellectual discourse we need something better than a lack of tinsel (on a side note, Stoicism was developed on this very lack of tinsel).

Festivus and Pragmatism

If there is any coherent philosophy from which the American holiday of Festivus takes its cue, it is the American philosophy of pragmatism. Pragmatism is best defined as the philosophy of "whatever works," whatever contributes to human flourishing, helps us organize human lives and accomplish whatever it is we need to accomplish. If a people hold onto a belief and it works for them and gets things done because of it, that's good. That's pragmatism. It's like when your grandfather puts chips inside his sandwich. There is no real reason for it. Lettuce provides much the same crunch. But your grandfather wants it that way. So you leave him alone. Pure pragmatism.

As the prestigious *Internet Encyclopedia of Philosophy*[4] teaches us, "pragmatism is a philosophical movement that includes those who claim that an ideology or proposition is true if it works satisfactorily."[5] The word "satisfaction" sums up pragmatism. If an idea works for us, say "time is money," and we design our entire outlook on that idea and find success (whatever it is that we define as success), then we consider that idea, based on pragmatism, philosophically sound and philosophically satisfying. In this regard, though, the philosophy of pragmatism is a philosophy in only the most surface of ways. It is more movement than philosophy. It has no codified system or strict analytical sequence. One cannot deconstruct pragmatism in the abstract. One can only test it in relation to its results. And its results are dependent upon the intention of its user. Its truth is related to the specific situation and has no relevance to an overarching philosophy or system of thought. It is true in the moment and thus, for us, a truth.

So if we discover later that "time is *not* money" then we discard this truth which we may have vehemently defended previously in favor of what we have discovered is "actually" true, currently. Truth, then, is a malleable concept for us based upon how it impacts our lives. We dictate the terms of truth rather than truth dictating the terms to us (and if ever there was an American attitude towards truth and reality, this is it). We should have no problem with declaring a proposition true and then turning our backs on it later. Experience directs us and we have no qualms. Thus, ultimately, pragmatism is more a way of viewing philosophy than an actual philosophical system. We hold true whatever it is that works. There are no tenets or creeds. There is not a pragmatist litany. There is only experience. Pragmatism, then, is the philosophy that holds that we should do what we want to do, if we find that it's what works for us when we do it.

We can see this thinking in Festivus. Festivus, as we have it from *Seinfeld*, was forged in the very spirit of pragmatism. Frank Costanza's struggle in a toy store brought his holiday experiences into focus. Consumerism had corrupted Christmas. As Mr. Costanza refused to contribute to a hollow holiday, he was forced to abandon it. It no longer worked for him. What is interesting is that Frank Costanza had issue with buying gifts by social coercion but did not have issue with observing a holiday. The idea of a holiday still worked for him but Christmas, as practiced, did not. Rather than consign himself to defeat, he developed a holiday more in his line of thinking. This is also in keeping with the pragmatic method: "the utility of a theory is a matter of its problem-solving power."[6] Or rather, Costanza's problem was that he felt the need to celebrate a holiday in December. Yet his need was a spiritual one, or at least an intellectual one. Christmas did not work for him because Christmas had become commercial. It demanded of him an attitude which was philosophically inconsistent with his mentality. In searching for an answer he realized that stripping away the commercial, as well as the expected altruism, from the holidays would provide a better framework for what he needed. As can be expected in a holiday opposed to consumerism, the needs are few.

Elements of Festivus

The Festivus pole

Every holiday needs a focal point. For Festivus, it is a basic aluminum pole of undetermined height. "This unadorned length of lusterless metal or something that looks like metal is the one item of Festivus that nearly everyone agrees is essential."[7] Humans, by nature, are abstract animals and need objects and symbols to represent their meaning. The Festivus pole captures the very essence of the holiday because it is without decoration and lacks a collection of presents at its base. It is as if it says, "I'm only here to remind you that I shouldn't be here."

This basic pole relieves observers of a number of common Christmas chores and arguments. It requires zero maintenance. Should it break, one can drive down to the hardware store and pick up another. Aluminum poles are always in season. The Festivus pole is popular then because of both its utility and simplicity. It makes sense. We look at it and say, "Yeah, I get that." It best serves its function as a symbol and does not as yet have attached to it a complicated history like the Christmas tree, where the original intention is lost. (What exactly was this original intention? A "back to nature" movement of the pagans? Or was it like most mysteries in history, the result of a dare? "I bet you four pieces of flint I can fit a tree in my house." "Make it five and you're on.") Regardless, the Festivus pole works on both a mental and practical level, thus it is consistent with pragmatism and explains its popularity. (There may also be a subconscious connection here to a child playing with a cardboard box rather than the gift the box was storing. There is not space, sadly, to explore this connection.)

Airing of grievances

By far the most famous of all Festivus traditions, the airing of grievances is perhaps the only real reason to celebrate. It's the first thing people remember and the last thing they enjoy. It is a simple process. Stand up and tell everyone in the room what you really think of them and tell them the ways they have disappointed you over the last year.

On the surface this is not the best of ideas. It makes no sense to air a grievance to a room full of loved ones. And yet it does, if everyone gets a turn. It is fairness and catharsis merging together in the weirdest of ways and seemingly at the most inappropriate of times. This is in stark contrast to the traditional approach. During the Christmas season we often bury our frustrations and try our best to get through. It takes on all of the planning and approach of a military campaign. "Don't say anything about my brother being out of work." "Remember to thank grandmother for her gift. I don't care if you don't like it." "Look, I spent Thanksgiving with your hippy parents. You're spending Christmas with my normal ones." (One wonders what a hippy Christmas is like.) Festivus eliminates this stress by embracing rather than suppressing the issues family members have with each other. On the surface the Festivus practice of the airing of grievances is horrid. And then we remember last March, then June, and that particular day in September. The airing of grievances is something of a reverse confessional. I'm not confessing my sins. I'm confessing yours.

There is a need for this. Everyone knows it. Despite the example of "normal people" on television and in family friendly movies, modern life for nearly everyone is one of restraint. We are not able to express an honest opinion. We are not able to say what we think. We must weigh our words in light of our company's mission statement or by the bumper sticker on our neighbor's car. Men and women go around all day long holding in their own opinions, their own thoughts, their own declarations. They keep them and restrain them in an effort to get along. This may be why there are more fights during the holidays than at any other time. Stress compounds under duress. At the end of the year we need release over reform. In reality, the Christmas admonition to be good to each other is not working well. Or rather our current social constructions do not properly provide for such altruism. We cannot combine selflessness and consumerism at such intense levels. As it is not working well it is not pragmatic, and by a pragmatist's standards (and if there ever was one it was Frank Costanza), if it is not working, it is not true. Add to both the philosophical inconsistency and the emotional stress of the occasion the pressure of gift-giving and relative-hopping on Christmas day, and it is easy to see why airing grievances is so much more attractive than giving gifts. It pulls at us and we yearn to it.

And it works. It works because it is by choice and by group choice. In contrast to George's father forcing Festivus on his family, people who celebrate it in real life do so with excitement. "Festivus is celebrated because people want to celebrate it, not because they have to."[8] Thus Festivus, and the airing of grievances in particular, fills a need that the current expression of Christmas does not fill. Festivus satisfies. It is practical and therefore pragmatic.

This observance, though, should not be confused with abusing people for the sake of abusing people, a common complaint. It is not the speaker's intention to hurt those around him, but rather a need to purge a frustration. Once it is purged it is purged. There is no harping in an airing. Add to this the equality of the practice, that everyone participates, and the airing of grievances is both healthy and pragmatic.

What makes this even more acceptable is the final element of Festivus: wrestling.

Wrestling

It is no surprise that Festivus ends on the high note of combat. It is a natural progression from the airing of grievances. While wrestling is not limited to the head of the household, the holiday does not end until the head of the household is pinned to the floor. There is something very Greek about this practice. As it is, this practice further reinforces the iconoclasm of Festivus. The Christmas season traditionally emphasizes good will and charity. There is nothing charitable about wrestling. There is something fulfilling about it though. It is both tragic and satisfying to best your father strength for strength, triumphing for a brief moment over the symbol of both your frustration and your future. And further, the son defeating the father sets the framework for the next Festivus. For the father, by being beaten, develops a grievance against his son. Festivus perpetuates itself. Whatever perpetuates itself naturally (as does Festivus) rather than an occasion maintained by intentional grinding effort (such as the consumerist version of Christmas) is far more practical and, if practical, true. Festivus has then a construction which is both methodical and spontaneous.

Festivus Declining

Sadly, the genius that is Festivus is showing signs of breaking from its original purpose. A holiday against consumerism can not long handle public exposure. What sets Festivus apart from every other holiday in America is its lack of purchases (well, that and the pole). Festivus is intended as a purge rather than an accumulation. It works in its streamlined practicality. It is a Greek tragedy played out in the living room. Once the show is over the audience has experienced catharsis and may resume the ordinary business of living.

The difficulty here is that more and more businesses are beginning to offer Festivus merchandise. There are now Festivus t-shirts, mugs, and posters. There are recipes for Festivus dishes which mean trips to the grocery store during the busiest shopping season of the year, further undermining the Spartan holiday and strengthening the traditional Christmas consumerist approach. There are even websites advertising Festivus poles for sale. As previously mentioned, there are two books written on Festivus, still in print and ready to ship. In reality there should be none, nor should this essay exist (but let's not split hairs).

The more products there are to buy the greater the exposure to consumerism. Much like those who celebrate Christmas, observers of Festivus will move from choosing to spend money to feeling expected to spend. "God, it's Festivus again. I have to run to the store to buy for the dinner. Why are we celebrating this again? I thought it was supposed to make things easier." The greater Festivus grows in popularity the less it will maintain its original purpose, that of gathering together to purge disappointments. The more it spreads the less it will be as expected to be, much like Christmas. At such time when the made-up holiday which makes sense to a surprisingly large number of people ceases to be practical it will cease to be pragmatic.

Pragmatists will have no issue with dumping the holiday in favor of something else. For it is in the vary nature of pragmatism to keep the motor running until it busts and then look for a new motor. God willing, the pragmatists will have a new holiday to celebrate before we begin seeing "put the Fest back in Festivus" bumper stickers on a legion of soccer mom minivans.

Festivus Enduring

Despite the signs that Festivus is moving away from its stated purpose, the holiday itself is unsuspectingly important. The strength of the holiday lies in its permission, in its break from good behavior, at least for an evening. We all have moments when we need to "get something off our chests." Since we lack a suitable avenue to do so, we end up exploding at loved ones at inappropriate moments. This creates arguments which beget bad experiences and resentments. Christmas often appeals to our better natures by ignoring our worse. It is imbalanced. We have no release during Christmas, no escape. Festivus has better balance. We air our grievances and wrestle each other. We get it out. Festivus accepts that we have frustrations and need a better avenue to deal with them than taking the higher ground. There is no oxygen in those high places. It is hard to breath. That is where Festivus differs. For many, it is a breath of fresh air.

As it continues to provide that cleansing breath Festivus will be celebrated and the world's true pragmatists will expand their lungs. When Festivus drops its central purpose and becomes but one more broken holiday filled with spending and getting, the pragmatists will abstain.

CALEB HOLT

A Philosophical Airing of Grievances

In an effort to truly capture the essence of Festivus it is incumbent upon us, under the demands of pragmatism, to consider a real world example. To that end I have provided the following list of grievances against famous philosophers (deceased) and/or philosophies (mostly deceased with vestibules of lingering vitality thanks to philosophy departments in various universities scattered across America and the world). Philosophy has, at some time or another, let all of us down. Either we were inadequate to its demands, or it was inadequate to ours. For that reason, we air our grievances. The wrestling match, however, is postponed indefinitely. Festivus will not, as a result, end this year.

- Plato: The only one in the cave is you sir. But on a side note, what exactly does this ideal cave look like?
- *Aristotle*: Reason (and the demands to publish or perish) urge that for a teacher to truly be respected he must write his own papers and not have his students following him around all morning taking notes. And while it is unfair to berate you centuries later for scientific discoveries you could not possibly have made, those scientific discoveries prove that you never wrote anything down, subjecting your thoughts to the unending fear that your students paraphrased you incorrectly.
- *Socrates*: Please see Aristotle.
- *Bertrand Russell*: The table is there sir and it has a Christmas goose on it.
- *Existentialism*: That crisis isn't just a way to sell more books is it?
- *Pragmatism*: Having no method as method only works in Eastern philosophy and you were created in America by an American so ... grievance.

And finally:

- *Isms in general*: It just keeps breeding new terms. I cite *consumerism* as an example. Does this concept really deserve an ism? The ism of buying things as a philosophical attitude towards life and fulfillment? This grievance may not be justified.

Happy Festivus.

NOTES

1 Allen Salkin, *Festivus, the Holiday for the Rest of Us* (New York: Grand Central Publishing, 2008), p. 8.
2 Ibid., p. 7.
3 Dan O'Keefe, *The Real Festivus* (New York: Penguin, 2005), p. v.
4 *Internet Encyclopedia of Philosophy*, online at www.iep.utm.edu/. Special thanks to Dr. David Kyle Johnson, also of *Christmas – Philosophy for Everyone*, for telling me about this website. It sure beat reading the actual books written by William James.
5 Douglas McDermid, "Pragmatism," *Internet Encyclopedia of Philosophy*, 2006; at www.iep.edu/p/pragmati.htm (accessed June 22, 2009).
6 McDermid, "Pragmatism."
7 Salkin, *Festivus*, p. 19.
8 Ibid., p. 58.

CHAPTER 19

COMMON CLAUS
Santa as Cross-Cultural Connection

The broad smile is the same, as is the twinkle in his eye, but there is something decidedly different about this larger-than-life Santa. For starters, his warm red suit is unbuttoned to display the celebrated "bowl full of jelly" physique and his feet are bare. Surrounded by palm trees and flowers, the Santa figure in downtown Honolulu greets all with a friendly shaka wave.[1] A second difference is the composition of the crowd receiving the greeting. In a state with no racial or ethnic majority, religious views also demonstrate a variety uncommon on the mainland US. The secular Santa is able to bridge religious differences at the time of year when they seem most acute. While some communities battle over religious displays on civic property, the Hawaii Santa allows a focus on common concerns, such as the love of children and the often-futile attempt to keep them in line.

Character of Claus

Santa has taken his lumps for representing commercialism at what many religions consider to be a holy time of year. He has surely strayed from whatever religious roots predated his reinvention as Coca-Cola icon. It is also true that he is most often associated with shopping malls these days;

and surely the wish most often whispered into his ear by anxious children is not for world peace but rather something featured at one of the retail stores sponsoring his visit. Yet he also continues to represent a common wish for something more than material gifts – a call to our better selves as individuals and communities.

The story of Santa includes a touch of magic that invites our participation. Movies such as *Miracle on 34th Street* commemorate the combination of Santa's special ability both to deliver gifts himself in a manner that defies laws of nature, and to inspire ordinary humans to acts of kindness and generosity in the course of their daily lives. As parents, we lend Santa a hand in providing gifts and in perpetuating the story of how they arrived under the tree. It is a different sort of belief than that inspired by, say, Tinkerbell, who must have our belief in order to survive. Santa survives our disbelief, we just miss out on the fun. The same sort of "secret act of goodness" dynamic is involved in anonymous donations of gifts to those less fortunate at Christmas time. Even more mundane duties such as delivering the mail take on the character of a mission when the letter carrier wears a red Santa hat and considers herself to be helping deliver Christmas gifts rather than forced to work with a holiday on the doorstep.

The view of Santa as representative of our collective good will is celebrated in the famous newspaper editorial reassuring eight-year-old Virginia of his existence: "He exists as certainly as love and generosity and devotion exist."[2] It equates Santa with universal ideals such as "faith, fancy, poetry, love, romance" that are real but unseen. Santa does, however, have a physical representation in the sense that mere universal ideals do not. The name "Santa Claus" produces this now standard physical appearance as well as the associated myth in anyone over the age of two in much of the Western world. The ubiquity of the reference makes "Santa Claus" useful in philosophy when discussing fictional characters, as a representative of the category of things that don't exist in this world, or of "universals." We may have different concepts of "beauty" or we may not recognize a character from *War and Peace*, but we share a common conception of Santa.

Increasingly, Santa is being recognized as a symbol of Christmas in other countries, as well. In this global perspective, Santa has a somewhat different role with regard to Christmas than in US history. For some in the US, Santa is seen as a competitor to Christ in usurping the religious meaning of the holiday. A traditional exhortation to "keep Christ in Christmas" takes aim at a secular Santa and the materialism he is seen to

CINDY SCHEOPNER

represent. However, in countries without large Christian populations, or in which Christmas is not traditionally celebrated, Santa just represents a fun, new holiday with interesting customs regarding food and decoration. For example, in Japan Christmas is a celebration with many familiar trappings: buildings and homes decorated with Christmas lights, elaborate displays in stores that feature Christmas trees and Santa figures, exchanges of gifts and cards. There are local touches. It is customary to eat a special Christmas cake on Christmas Eve and it is a special night for lovers to celebrate with romantic dinners. But there is no directly competing religious connotation.

While many religions have sacred winter celebrations, they are unlike December 25 as a combined religious observance and secular holiday. The proximity of Hanukkah to Christmas causes a dilemma for some: whether to increase its importance to serve as an alternative to Christmas celebrations, or to maintain its status as a minor Jewish holiday and avoid the characterization of a "Jewish Christmas." The date of the Islamic New Year varies according to the lunar calendar, but often falls in December. It is celebrated quietly, with prayers and readings of scripture. A more significant holiday, Eid al-Adha, falls in late November or early December of the Gregorian calendar during recent years. It involves feasting and family and community gatherings. The lunar month of Ramadan is generally earlier in the autumn, as is the Hindu observance of Divali (the Celebration of Lights). They escape the close association with Christmas, as does the Buddhist celebration of the New Year. Especially for children, the ubiquitous nature of Christmas in the United States calls for some sort of response by non-Christian families. In this sense, Santa's secularism can make the celebration of Christmas an event apart from religious observances. Nothing about the Santa myth connects directly with Christianity if it is encountered as a current social event rather than historical development.

Christmas Crowd

The crowds sharing a shaka with Santa in Honolulu certainly represent this diversity of religious background. As with the mainland, Hawaii's religious majority is evangelical and mainline Protestant with a combined 44 percent, according to a recent survey.[3] However, the state's Buddhist population is counted at 6 percent compared with only 1 percent on the mainland and, although small, the categories of Hindu and "other religions" are double that of the mainland. The number of "unaffiliated" at 17 percent is the fourth largest category (after evangelical Protestants, mainline Protestants, and Catholics). However, there is a type of religious affiliation not counted in the survey, probably because it does not exist on the mainland. That is the quasi-religious cultural practice of invoking traditional Hawaiian customs.

Traditional Hawaiian blessings are common at civic events where "religious" invocations would be suspect on the mainland. The traditional blessings honor the host culture in the same way that leis serve as greeting, honor, and celebration. As examples, before beginning official meetings, a prayer is often sung in Hawaiian. A Hawaiian blessing is part of most groundbreakings, including recently those for a new Disney development, the Waikiki Beach Walk, and new military barracks on an Army base. The governor's website shows many photos of her with a shovel at groundbreakings begun after a ground blessing. No church-state conflict is seen in these observances. They are considered to be a mark of respect shown by civic, business, and educational leaders to the Hawaiian host culture. The cultural and spiritual aspects of these actions are not teased apart into what might be considered secular and what is religious – they remain joined as they were in practice back when one culture inhabited these islands before contact with the Western world. These customs also are not seen to conflict with the many religions now practiced in Hawaii. The same individual may take part in a Hawaiian ground blessing and a Catholic Mass without difficulty.

Hawaii's racial and ethnic composition is much more colorful than in any of the other 49 states. The United States as a whole is 66 percent white (not including Hispanic), according to the US Census, while whites are just 24 percent of the population in Hawaii.[4] The number of Asians is almost 40 percent in Hawaii, compared to just over 4 percent for the entire US. The next largest racial group is "persons reporting two or more races": almost 19 percent in Hawaii, less than 2 percent for the US as a whole. It is important to note that "Hawaiian" is a specific racial and ethnic group now about 9 percent of the state's population, but less than 1 percent of the entire country. Unlike other states, people who live in Hawaii are not called "Hawaiians"; the usual term is "islander." So people can be Hawaiian and live in any state, if they are members of that ethnic group. In contrast, no matter how long I live in Hawaii, I will never be Hawaiian, and neither would any of my children just by virtue of being born here. With such a diversity of ethnic and racial groups, Hawaii is certainly not free from racial difference or tension, but the lack of a single majority race is significant. Some sort of cross-racial dialogue is part of everyday conversation in Hawaii. (It is probably also true that people uncomfortable with difference do not stay long on the islands.) It is difficult to imagine that any child in Hawaii goes through the day without encountering someone of a different race or ethnicity.

How does this religious and racial diversity relate to Santa? In two ways. First, nothing strips away difference like a list of who's naughty and who's nice. The tendency of children to misbehave and the utility of a mythical character willing and able to administer punishment and reward is not lost on parents of any persuasion. While children may be dazzled by the prospect of gifts, parents are free to use Santa's darker side to the extent they wish as a tool for household harmony. There may or may not be religious connections – again, that is up to the particular parent. It is entirely possible to participate in the Santa story along with any religious viewpoint or in stark opposition to them all.

The second impact of diversity is Santa's ability to maintain a distinct identity while allowing for customization. As noted earlier, the name "Santa Claus" produces a fairly consistent image and set of attributes in the mind of anyone acquainted with the term. However, differences in versions of Santa do not seem troubling. A "signing" Santa who reads the wishes of deaf children from the movements of their fingers does not seem to be a contradiction. If Santa in his essential self had signing as one of his magical powers, all individual department store Santas would also have that power. That is not the case. But if one community produces a signing Santa who is available at specific times for children who are hearing-impaired, no one feels moved to claim that he is not Santa. The Santa image seems large enough to allow for differences among individual versions.

The question of Santa's racial malleability is more intriguing. An African-American Santa in a community where children share that racial identity seems to be inclusive – the Santa story is available to all. Young children who sit on the lap of a Santa who looks like they do may feel more acceptance. However, the impact of an ethnically identifiable Santa in a diverse community is less predictable. One department store Santa or another of varying ethnicities seems representative of the community. But a Santa that is part of a civic display representing the entire community is another matter. Making him any particular ethnicity seems to call attention to racial difference rather than inclusion. In this case, relying on his traditional appearance seems safest – most of us are introduced to the Santa story with the image of him with a red coat, round belly, white beard, and white skin.

Civic Claus

The appearance of the Santa figure in the municipal display in Honolulu captures the spirit of the state. In customizing the figure to include casual (un)dress and a shaka, Santa takes on an island attitude – something that unifies amid difference. Whether Christian, Jew, Muslim, Buddhist, or Other, we are each different from our fellows in faith on the mainland just because we share this rock in the middle of the Pacific Ocean. The Santa at Honolulu Hale ("hale" is Hawaiian for "house," Honolulu Hale is the name for city hall) identifies with us as islanders, as parents, as children – universal descriptors across racial or religious differences. The essential elements of the Santa story appeal to themes we share as human beings. This image of Santa keeps the identifying characteristics of both image and myth while customizing it to our locale, serving as a symbol of inclusion.

The choice of the Santa figure, rather than a religious symbol, to be the municipal display contrasts with Christmas controversies in other cities and towns. Many communities in the US have battled over nativity displays on government property. Specifically religious displays produce a conflict between the two provisions for religious liberty in the First Amendment of the US Constitution: the right to the free exercise of religion and the prohibition against laws establishing an official religion. When a Christian nativity scene is placed inside a courthouse, the US Supreme Court has been concerned that it looks like the government is favoring that religion over others. Some communities have wanted to retain the Christian nativity scene that is so central to Christmas and so have added a Jewish menorah or other religious or secular symbols to try to address the Court's concern. Many have done so grudgingly – after all, Christmas *is* a Christian holiday, not Jewish or Muslim or Other. Some court cases have addressed where the displays are placed, who puts them up and cares for them, or who pays for the display. The central issues in each case are the same: groups within communities want to celebrate the religious nature of Christmas and feel their government should be able to accommodate this desire, while the Supreme Court feels compelled to guard against the appearance that Christianity is either the official religion of the United States or is somehow favored over other religions (or no religion).

A pivotal Supreme Court decision in this regard is *Lynch v. Donnelly* (465 US 668, 1984). The question before the Court was whether the City of Pawtucket, Rhode Island could include a crèche in its annual Christmas display. The display in the heart of the shopping district included many decorations associated with Christmas, including, according to the Court, "a Santa Claus house, reindeer pulling Santa's sleigh, candy-striped poles, a Christmas tree, carolers, cutout figures representing such characters as a clown, an elephant, and a teddy bear, hundreds of colored lights, a large banner that reads 'SEASONS GREETINGS' and the crèche at issue here." In that context, the Supreme Court held that the inclusion of the crèche was no more of an endorsement of religion by the government than the printing of "In God We Trust" on coins. (It should be noted that, although the Court has said the coin phrase is not unconstitutional, it is far from uncontroversial.)

Five years later, the Court again considered Christmas displays with religious implications in *County of Allegheny v. ACLU* (492 US 53, 1989). This case involved two holiday displays on public property in downtown Pittsburgh. The first was a crèche placed on the Grand Staircase of the Allegheny County Courthouse by a local Roman Catholic group. The second display was an 18-foot Hanukkah menorah installed just outside the City-County Building next to the 45-foot Christmas tree. The Court issued a highly fragmented decision finding the first display in violation of the Establishment clause but not the second. The setting of the crèche all by itself inside the courthouse was seen as government support and promotion of the religious view expressed. However, the same endorsement was not implied by the menorah because it was part of a display that included the Christmas tree and a sign declaring the city's "salute to liberty." The majority opinion said the predominate element in the display was the Christmas tree, which is not now a religious symbol although it once was. The combination of the tree, sign, and menorah does not represent either endorsement or disapproval of any one specific religious view. Three of the justices on the Court would have held both displays to be unconstitutional, four would have upheld both displays.

The guidance to be drawn from these two opinions is far from clear. A Pew Research Report notes that lower courts have since reached very different results based on very similar facts.[5] At least one observer notes that they seem to indicate religious displays are legally acceptable if they are accompanied by plastic animals that dilute their religious nature enough to make it innocuous and asks: "If the government is going to display religious symbols, why shouldn't it treat them with respect?"[6]

Another observer notes that the only way for religious groups to argue in favor of displays on public property is to say the displays don't mean anything important – surely not the point the groups wish to make.[7]

Concerns voiced by some Christians include the idea that the United States has historically been a Christian nation and that forcing the removal of religious displays from government property denies both that legacy and the current free expression of religion in a manner that had become customary. Many are untroubled at the idea that such displays indicate government establishment of religion because they feel Christianity *should* be given a privileged place in the United States. Two surveys conducted by the Pew Research Center in 2005 found that 83 percent of Americans said displays of Christmas symbols should be allowed on government property and 74 percent believe it is proper to display the Ten Commandments in government buildings. A year ago, two Christian groups set up a nativity scene in front of the US Supreme Court as part of an effort to encourage Americans to put up similar displays in front of public buildings across the United States.[8] The groups were concerned with an erosion of the public expression of faith, especially during the Christmas season.

Ironically, the earliest Christian settlers on both the mainland and the islands of Hawaii forbade the celebration of Christmas as extra-biblical. The first American missionaries to Hawaii shunned Christmas and any other celebration or custom not specifically mentioned in the Bible. On the mainland, seventeeth-century Puritan New England had laws forbidding the observance of Christmas.[9] The Christian groups who broke with the Catholic Church and the Church of England deemphasized Christmas in the early colonial period. These included Quakers, Baptists, Presbyterians, and Methodists, along with Puritans (Congregationalists). Those who still celebrated Christmas, such as Lutherans, Catholics, Dutch Reformed, and Anglicans, did so in a low-key manner, focusing on church or home. Well into the 1800s the celebration of Christmas was a local matter. The first state to make Christmas a legal holiday was Alabama in 1836.

The first missionaries in Hawaii were Puritan and carried with them their distaste for Christmas celebrations. Captain Cook first sighted the islands of Oahu and Kauai just after Christmas in 1777 and missionaries arrived aboard the *Thaddeus* in 1820, but the first official Christmas celebration was not until 1862.[10] That year, the government of Hawaii publicly celebrated Christmas. King Kamehameha IV and Queen Emma had arranged for a branch of the Church of England to be established in

Hawaii. Bishop Stanley and his mission arrived in October of 1862 and quickly went to work, according to the bishop's diary:

> Until this year, Christmas had never been outwardly observed here at all. Business had always been transacted as usual, and even the schools used to reopen after recess about the 20th, as if on purpose to ignore that day. We resolved to inaugurate a different state of things, and no longer to suffer the birthday of our blessed Lord to pass without due honour. The king, who is heartily with us in all our proceedings, proclaimed a general holiday for that day.

That first celebration was a grand one! The temporary cathedral was decorated with cypress boughs and beautiful flowers. The king lent all his silver candelabra to make the church ablaze with light for midnight services. The church litany was first chanted in Hawaiian (translated by the king) then in English. The services included a procession around the church and at its conclusion the real spectacular began. At the same time as a salute from the battery, the face of Punchbowl[11] was "lit up by flaming tar barrels which were sent cascading down from the crater's rim." Outside the cathedral doors, a procession formed. The king had provided twenty 8-foot long torches made of kukui wood and coconut fibers dipped in tar. The king, clergy, choir, and congregation marched through the streets of Honolulu singing Christmas carols, surrounded by a torch-bearing guard of honor. When the procession reached the palace, fireworks were set off. Along with the Anglican extravaganza, the Roman Catholic Cathedral of Our Lady of Peace was illuminated with wreaths of light. When its doors were opened at midnight, the magnificent main altar and side altars in the wings of the building were beautifully decorated. Religious services celebrated Christmas at Catholic and Episcopal churches and the church at Kawaiahao. They were the only churches to officially celebrate Christmas until 1895, when the Central Union Church added a service when Christmas did not fall on a Sunday.

Rather than a Christian holiday in contrast with other religions, Christmas was a holiday celebrated by some Christians and not by others in the early days of this country. The United States Congress met regularly on Christmas until 1855. Public schools in Massachusetts met on Christmas Day until at least 1870. The association of Christmas with Christians, generally, is relatively recent. Our Puritan forefathers would likely frown upon religious displays along with their contemporary secular cousins and tell us all to get back to work.

Symbol of Supremacy?

Even those willing to accommodate religious difference seem not to appreciate the significance of being the majority religion. On the mainland, Christian displays in the courthouse went unchallenged for many years because Christians were the majority in those towns or cities. Allowing other religions to *also* place displays or symbols on government property at times of special significance does not minimize the appearance of Christian dominance, rather it calls attention to difference. When Christian displays were paid for and sponsored by local governments, it made being non-Christian seem less American. When one is a member of a minority, racial or religious, it is easier to appreciate the Supreme Court's concern that the government must represent all citizens while religions are free to make their own private distinctions.

Now that private groups sponsor many displays, the implication has changed, but still can carry unpalatable connotations. The whole process of displaying symbols with religious significance identifies members of the civic community according to their religious distinctions. If I challenge a crèche in the courthouse, I am challenging the chosen expression of (at least part of) my community. If I am privately offended but do not challenge it, I feel not part of that community. Either way, choosing a display that excludes some members of a civic community based upon their religious (or irreligious) beliefs creates a division where none need exist. Surely we are still fellow citizens in all the relevant ways: we vote on taxes, send our children to the same schools, elect public officials based on their opinions of taxations or mass transit. How we choose to worship (or not) is a freedom guaranteed by the Constitution. Allowing a holiday decoration to identify me as different from my neighbor seems to have no positive effect.

Common Claus

Santa as secular symbol side-steps the controversy. He is clearly not representing any religious viewpoint, despite his vaguely Christian, pre-Coca-Cola roots. Secular Santa is free to represent the secular aspects of Christmas. He can not only record who is naughty and nice, but also nudge children toward nice behavior through rewards (or the lack of

CINDY SCHEOPNER

them). The magical properties of Santa allow people to participate in the "Christmas spirit" of generosity without appealing to any particular religious tradition. Santa as Christmas symbol is able to embrace both gift giving and altruism without conflict. Further, his image is universal enough to prompt inclusion, yet capable of customization to reflect each community's uniqueness.

While Hawaii offers an interesting illustration, the model can be universalized across physical locations and cultural difference. It is not difficult to imagine a Cowboy Santa Claus kicking up his heels in Kansas, or a Climbing Claus scaling peaks in Colorado. Each physical location gives its community a common ground to celebrate, and what better time than Christmas to look for what unites us? To return to the Supreme Court case: what if Pawtucket, Rhode Island traded in its parade of religious, imaginary, and fanciful representations to focus on Santa? What does a Rhode Island Santa look like? That sort of quest leads to questions of the characteristics that unite us as a community. Similarly, Pittsburgh could rally around a common Santa configuration in the same way it rallies around sporting mascots. In a particularly successful year, Steeler Santa could lead the parade. With Santa at city hall providing a visual representation of community, individual differences can be added by neighborhood, church, and shopping center. They then serve as amplifications of the many associations that link most individuals to multiple allegiances rather than as markers of division and distinction. I can be happily a member of the political community (city and state), a particular neighborhood, a religious denomination, and various civic groups without conflict – my primary identity, and that of Secular Santa, reflects the richness of my community rather than "Christian" or "Not." To quote the elf himself (via Clement C. Moore), "Merry Christmas to all, and to all a good night!"[12]

NOTES

1 Julie Mehta, *Mele Kalikimaka* (Honolulu: Mutual Publishing, 1991), p. 15. A shaka is a greeting in Hawaii, formed by extending the thumb and little finger and shaking the hand from side to side.
2 "Yes Virginia, there is a Santa Claus," online at www.newseum.org/yesvirginia/.
3 Mary Adamski, "View from the Pew: Hawaii's Religious Landscape," *Honolulu Star-Bulletin*, March 7, 2009; online at www.starbulletin.com/features/view fromthepew/20090307_view_from_the_pew.html.
4 Hawaii, State and County Quick Facts, US Census Bureau; online at http://quickfacts.census.gov/qfd/states/15000.html.

5   "Religious Displays and the Courts," *Religion and the Courts: Pillars of Church-State Law* (Washington, DC: Pew Forum on Religion and Public Life, 2007).

6   Michael W. McConnell, John H. Garvey, and Thomas C. Berg, *Religion and the Constitution* (New York: Aspen Publishers, 2006).

7   "The Christmas Wars: Religion in the Public Square," transcript December 12, 2006, Pew Forum on Religion and Public Life.

8   "Nativity Scene Goes to US Supreme Court," *Christian Broadcasting News*; online at www.cbn.com/cbnnews/486017.aspx?Print=true.

9   Bruce David Forbes, *Christmas: A Candid History* (Los Angeles: University of California Press, 2007).

10 Meiric K. Dutton, *Christmas in Hawaii* (Honolulu: Advertiser Publishing, 1950).

11 Punchbowl is a volcanic crater now in the center of Honolulu and home to the National Memorial Cemetery of the Pacific since 1948.

12 Clement Clarke Moore and Jesse Willcox Smith, *'Twas the Night Before Christmas: A Visit from St. Nicholas* (Boston: Houghton Mifflin Harcourt, 2002).

AFTERWORD

The existence of this book surprises me. Of course, *my* existence might surprise you. I wish it didn't. Oh! for the good ol' Middle Ages, when my positive existential status was just assumed. But before I open that package of complaints, I have to be honest. I never intended for this *Christmas thing* to catch on. I thought I'd just be nice one December and throw some chocolates at good kids and lumps of coal at bad kids. (I'd been drinking.) But the very next year all the parents expected me to do it again. ("Little Sebastian has grown accustomed to certain traditions.") Before I knew it, I was locked in year after year. I even died and people still expected me to deliver. (Explain that one, O wise philosophers.) I had simply been the patron saint of sailors – a good gig, what with the fried fish and all. Now, hundreds of years later, everyone's virtually forgotten about the sailing part and I'm still delivering presents. Do something nice one time....

All sorts of pretenders have sprung up since I've been driving the sleigh. Some guys even copied me before I showed up. I refer you to those "wish they were still popular" Norse gods Odin and Thor. I assure you I am the *original*. During the Middle Ages (man were those crazy days) I had on staff a demonic goat-man called Krampus to help out with the scaring of the bad kids. My bishop's hat just wasn't pulling it off. However, contrary to what some in this book claim, Krampus isn't me (well, maybe a little, but I swear it was only that one time). I don't even look like a goat (although I still wear fur). But what I never understood was the moniker "Hold Nickar" the Germans gave me for a while – that and fruitcake. I don't get fruitcake.

Somewhere along the way, I gained a bunch of weight, lost my bishop's hat, my flying horse turned into flying reindeer, and I moved from Heaven to the North Pole (not exactly a promotion). In the twentieth century someone finally gave me a wife (because I sure didn't pick her), and now kids write letters telling me what they want. (I'm not sure why. I guess omnipotence precludes generosity.) I am also the subject of numerous poems and movies (from which I have yet to receive a single cent in royalties) and Christmas is a worldwide phenomenon. Again, none of this was expected. At best I thought the holiday would be slightly more popular than St. Patrick's Day. (Oh, how I hated him with his four leaf clovers and his green beer.) That there is now a book exploring the philosophical implications of Christmas and my role in it is astounding.

But, overall, I liked this book. (I wish someone else was Santa Claus so *I* could get it for Christmas.) It was good to see so many on my side of the "War on Christmas." People lying to their kids to convince them I exist is, and always will be, a good idea. I was especially fond of Steven Hales who apparently thinks I'm better at this whole Christmas thing than Jesus (but let's not get all "Beatles" with this). And, given that I was guilt-tripped into this job in the first place, I can certainly understand those who are critical of the entire holiday. Yes, it now represents consumerism and hollowness, and sure maybe the way I have to treat my elfs to meet production quotas makes me guilty of "labor exploitation." (These twentieth-century terms. How quaint!) But what I couldn't abide was this assumption that everyone seemed to make throughout the book – the assumption that I don't exist.

I'm okay with not being paid by corporations (though I'm certainly due). I'm okay with Little Sebastian asking me yet again for a real live pony because he was a good boy and didn't hit his sister with a baseball bat. (Sorry Sebastian. A live pony is not happening. You know how much manure my gift bag can hold? It's bad enough flying around all night with eight reindeer. Don't be so selfish. Next time ask for a yo-yo.) I'm even okay with bad movies about me starring Dudley Moore. But doubting my existence?

Look, we all know that man is gifted with rationality. We all know he is a logical creature trying to make sense of himself and trying to discover the exact nature of reality and his relation to it. Okay, I get it. I get that if something cannot be verified by empirical data then that is usually a good indication it does not exist. No dispute. But I don't ever remember labeling a gift "To: Kyle. From: Santa, hoping you're a real boy and not a figment of my imagination." I just assume the kid exists. I just do. I mean,

I do have other reasons. Introducing an existential crisis to a six-year-old would make me a cruel immortal indeed. (I leave that to the Great Pumpkin.) But seriously, readers, is a little blind faith too much to ask?

Because I have a code I will not deny presents to any good children who belong to the philosophers contained herein. (See that? I'm not denying something. Look how easy it is, philosophers.) But I will put all the contributors themselves (and anyone else who questions me) on the Naughty List. You, the glorious proletariat who are not philosophers but citizens with real jobs, don't have to worry. Your reading this book will incur nothing in the manner of a Santa-Smackdown. In fact, I encourage you to buy it for a friend and give it as a gift for Christmas. That way I don't have to force an elf to retype the whole thing just so I can deliver it on time. (See. I don't *really* want to exploit my workers. I have to, due to variable costs. Back off Marx!)

At any rate, I hope you enjoyed your book.

NOTES ON CONTRIBUTORS

Santa's Elves

SCOTT F. AIKIN is a Lecturer in Philosophy at Vanderbilt University. He specializes in informal logic, epistemology, and philosophy of religion. He has authored articles appearing in *Philosophical Studies, Argumentation, Informal Logic,* and *Philosophical Forum.* His *Pragmatism: A Guide for the Perplexed* (co-written with Robert B. Talisse) was published in 2008. He has been trying out the holiday greeting, "Bah, Humbug!"

GUY BENNETT-HUNTER is Gosden Scholar at Selwyn College, University of Cambridge. He has done undergraduate and postgraduate work in philosophy at the University of Durham and has published articles on existentialism and aesthetics. He is currently working on the philosophy of religion, writing about the concept of ineffability.

MATTHEW BROPHY is a Scrooge who teaches business ethics as a Visiting Instructor at Minnesota State University, Mankato. He resides with his beautiful wife and above-average child in Minneapolis. Matthew, who received his PhD in philosophy from the University of Minnesota, still believes in Santa.

WILLIAM E. DEAL is Severance Professor of the History of Religion in the Department of Religious Studies and Professor of Cognitive Science in the Department of Cognitive Science at Case Western Reserve University. His teaching and scholarship focus on theory and interpretation in the academic study of religion, religion and cognitive science, comparative religious ethics, and Japanese religious and ethical traditions. He is co-author of *Theory for Religious Studies* and author of *Handbook to Life in Medieval and Early Modern Japan*. He admits to serenading his cats with "Here Comes Santa Claus" while working on this project in the midst of the summer heat. They seemed little amused.

ERA GAVRIELIDES is a teaching fellow at King's College London. Prior to obtaining her PhD from King's College London she studied for an MPhil and completed undergraduate studies in philosophy, politics and economics at Oxford University. Her research interests include ethics and Greek philosophy. Era lives in London where she hosts an annual Xmas tree cookie decoration party.

ERIN HAIRE is a graduate student at the University of Tennessee with an undergraduate degree in philosophy from Clemson University. Erin's research focuses on the relationship between political philosophy and environmental ethics, with an emphasis on environmental policy. Her Christmas wish list includes a new Lego set, first edition poetry collections, and world peace.

STEVEN D. HALES is Professor of Philosophy at Bloomsburg University. He was recently Visiting Professorial Fellow at the Institute of Philosophy, School of Advanced Study, University of London. His work in popular philosophy includes *Beer and Philosophy* (2007), *What Philosophy Can Tell You About Your Dog* (2008), and *What Philosophy Can Tell You About Your Cat* (2008). His serious boring work is in epistemology and metaphysics, like *Relativism and the Foundations of Philosophy* (2006).

RICHARD HANCUFF teaches English and works in the Center for Excellence in Teaching and Learning at Misericordia University. His research primarily deals with cultural approaches to twentieth-century American literature and issues of national identity. His most recent article analyzes African-American journalist George Schuyler's 1926 working tour of the southern United States. He fondly remembers Christmases past, thoroughly enjoys Christmas present, and looks forward to Christmases future, although he wonders if Santa's disciplinary mechanisms are more stringent for the adults than the children.

CALEB HOLT is the Learning Resource Coordinator at Heald College. He finally completed his bachelor's degree majoring in English after listening to the advice of his American Literature professor that English was the world's most versatile degree. He has since moved to California and proven the inaccuracy of that statement. Among his greater accomplishments are creating and editing a student journal at Heald College in Stockton, CA (America's number one "do-not-move-there" city) and taking four months to print out the last twenty years of an actual Cambridge man's writings, stored on only one single flash drive. He does not personally celebrate Festivus and lists this failure in his daily airing of grievances.

DAVID KYLE JOHNSON is Assistant Professor of Philosophy at King's College in Wilkes-Barre, Pennsylvania. His philosophical specializations include philosophy of religion, logic, and metaphysics. He has also written chapters on *South Park, Family Guy, The Office, Battlestar Galactica, Quentin Tarantino, Johnny Cash, Batman, The Colbert Report,* and *The Onion.* He edited a book on the NBC show *Heroes* and is now co-editing *Introducing Philosophy through Pop Culture* with William Irwin. Every fall, he teaches a liberal arts seminar on Christmas where his students learn the history of Christmas and Santa Claus. And, every Christmas, Krampus shows up at his door threatening retaliation if he doesn't stop it.

ZACHARY JURGENSEN is a PhD candidate at the University of Oklahoma, concentrating in aesthetics. His current research interest focuses on the aesthetic value of video gaming, as well as the ontology of video games. As a child, he managed to successfully use a Red Ryder BB gun several times without ever shooting his eye out.

SCOTT C. LOWE is Professor of Philosophy and Chair of the Department of Philosophy at Bloomsburg University of Pennsylvania. His main area of research and teaching is in social and political philosophy. He has published articles on the principle of fair play and on the justification of terrorism. His current interest is in the political philosophy of Richard Rorty. He is the editor, along with Steven Hales, of *Delight in Thinking: An Introduction to Philosophy Reader.* His article, "Ebenezer Scrooge – Man of Principle," recently appeared in *Think* magazine.

VICTOR LYONS is Academic Dean and Professor of New Testament at Foothills Christian College, Wilkesboro, North Carolina. He is the author of *Comentario Bíblico Mundo Hispano, IX, Proverbios-Cantares* (3rd edition, 2003). He has been a pastor and missionary as well as adjunct faculty member at Brewton-Parker College, New Orleans Baptist Theological Seminary, Seminario Nacional Bautista de Chile, and Moscow Theological Seminary of Evangelical Christians-Baptists, Seminario Bautista Internacional de Cali, Colombia. He is a member of the Society of Biblical Literature and the Evangelical Theological Society.

MARION G. MASON received her PhD in developmental psychology from Ohio State University. Now a Professor of Psychology at Bloomsburg University of Pennsylvania, she spends most of her time teaching and mentoring undergraduates. She is also an instructor in the Pastoral Counseling Department of Cherry Hill Seminary, an online institution training Pagan clergy and leaders. Whether online or bricks-and-mortar, it's like opening a Christmas surprise for Marion each time she receives some new software or technological gadget for her classroom.

MARK MERCER is an Associate Professor and Chair of the Philosophy Department at Saint Mary's University, Halifax, Nova Scotia. He works mainly in philosophy of mind and epistemology. He frequently contributes articles on popular themes to daily newspapers and he writes a weekly column for his campus paper under the name "The Cranky Professor." One of his recent outrages against Christmas was a column in the Ottawa *Citizen* in which he argued that parents ought not lie to their children about Santa.

DUSTIN NELSON is a graduate student at the University of Tennessee pursuing his PhD in philosophy. His current research focuses on environmental virtue ethics and his broad philosophical interests lie in environmental ethics, epistemology, and philosophy of science. Dustin's best Christmas present of all time was a pair of hybrid glove-mittens that he affectionately called glo-mits.

STEPHEN NISSENBAUM is Professor Emeritus of History at the University of Massachusetts, specializing in American cultural history. Professor Nissenbaum's major publications include *Sex, Diet, and Debility in Jacksonian America: Sylvester Graham and Health Reform* and, with co-author Paul Boyer, *Salem Possessed: The Social Origins of Witchcraft*. Santa wishes to thank Professor Nissenbaum for setting the record straight about what a good fellow he has become in his very fine book, *The Battle for Christmas*, which was a Pulitzer Prize finalist in History in 1997.

NOREEN O'CONNOR teaches literature and professional writing as an assistant professor in English at King's College, Pennsylvania. Her research focuses on twentieth-century women authors, narrative theory, and the idea of cultural trauma. Her most recent article, "'Thinking Peace into Existence': Narrating Trauma and Mourning in Freud, Woolf, and Morrison," is forthcoming in a collection entitled *Woolf, Women, and War*. She has lived in 14 states, but no matter where she moves, Santa's surveillance system always finds her. It is extremely powerful.

TODD PRESTON is Assistant Professor of English at Lycoming College, a small liberal arts college in northeastern Pennsylvania. His research interests are wide ranging, having written on authors as disparate as Melville and Chaucer, but he most often focuses on the literature, language, and culture of Anglo-Saxon England. While typically prone to enjoying all things Christmas in moderation, he has admitted to an immoderate fondness for eggnog.

CINDY SCHEOPNER recently completed her MA in philosophy at the University of Colorado, Boulder, where she focused on philosophy of religion. She also holds a (somewhat older) JD from Baylor University and is now fusing them into study of the philosophical interaction of law and religion as a doctoral student at the University of Hawai'i, Mānoa. She still sets cookies out for Santa, but is pretty sure he prefers them with a good single-barrel bourbon.

DANE SCOTT is the Director of the Center for Ethics at the University of Montana and Associate Professor in the Department of Society and Conservation. He holds a doctorate in philosophy from Vanderbilt University, an MA in philosophical theology from the Graduate Theological Union, and a BS from the University of California, Riverside. Prior to moving to Montana, Dr. Scott was Associate Dean of the Honors College at Western Carolina University, as well as director of the Humanities program. Dr. Scott specializes in bioethics, environmental ethics, and agricultural and food ethics, and is also interested in the philosophy of technology, American pragmatism, and the philosophy of religion.

JASON SOUTHWORTH is a graduate student in philosophy at the University of Oklahoma and is Adjunct Instructor of Philosophy at Fort Hays State University. He has contributed chapters to many pop culture and philosophy volumes, including *Batman and Philosophy, Heroes and*

Philosophy, *X-Men and Philosophy*, and *Steven Colbert and Philosophy*. Rather than be funny here, Jason would prefer to be a little sappy and thank his father, Patrick, for exposing him to good Christmas music like "Christmas in Hollis" by Run DMC, "Father Christmas" by the Kinks, and Springsteen's version of "Santa Claus is Coming to Town" with the rambling intro. Now if everyone would play these songs instead of Nat King Cole, Trans-Siberian Orchestra, and (God help us) Kenny G, he wouldn't have to do all his holiday shopping online. Okay, so he threw in a joke anyway. It's a season of forgiveness; let it go.

RUTH TALLMAN is a graduate student in philosophy at the University of Oklahoma and Adjunct Instructor of Philosophy at Fort Hays State University, Kansas. She has written chapters for other pop culture and philosophy volumes, including *Heroes* and *Arrested Development*. She wants to know if Clarence, you been, you been rehearsin' real hard now so Santa'll bring you a new saxophone, right?

S. WALLER is Associate Professor of Philosophy at Montana State University, Bozeman. She is currently working on the philosophy of animal minds (especially dolphin and wolf minds), focusing on understanding their possible belief states and inferences. She would like to know what it is like to be a wolf for Christmas, but since Santa doesn't have a mind, he doesn't believe her. And since dolphins do seem to have the capacity for understanding metaphor, she will be asking them instead.

WILL WILLIAMS is a graduate student in the Department of Religion at Baylor University. Having received a graduate degree in religion from Duke Divinity School, he went on to be ordained at First Baptist Church of Augusta, Georgia in 2005. His paper on Kierkegaard and Ecclesiastes was recently published in the multivolume series *Kierkegaard Research: Sources, Reception, and Resources*. If the price of fossil fuels continues to rise, Will plans to enact his strategy of intentionally getting onto Santa's Naughty List in order to make a killing in the underground commodities exchange through this free and ample supply of coal and switches.